SET THE
NIGHT
ON FIRE

SET THE NIGHT ON FIRE

LIVING, DYING, AND
PLAYING GUITAR WITH THE DOORS

ROBBY KRIEGER
WITH JEFF ALULIS

Little, Brown and Company
New York Boston London

Little, Brown and Company
Hachette Book Group
1290 Avenue of the Americas, New York, NY 10104
littlebrown.com

First Edition: October 2021

Little, Brown and Company is a division of Hachette Book Group, Inc. The Little, Brown name and logo are trademarks of Hachette Book Group, Inc.

The publisher is not responsible for websites (or their content) that are not owned by the publisher.

The Hachette Speakers Bureau provides a wide range of authors for speaking events. To find out more, go to hachettespeakersbureau.com or call (866) 376-6591.

ISBN 9780316243346
Library of Congress Control Number: 2021941971

Printing 1, 2021

LSC-C

Printed in the United States of America

CONTENTS

CONTENTS

This book is dedicated to Lynn Ann Veres, my wife of fifty years (so far). She's the only person I've ever met who lets me be me. And that's why I'll always love her.

SET THE NIGHT ON FIRE

THE HENRY HUDSON HOTEL

"Robby! This is God speaking! And we're gonna throw you right out of this universe!"

It wasn't God on the phone. It was Jim Morrison. I hung up.

The call came in at some ungodly hour in the fall of 1966. The Doors had recently arrived in New York City to play a monthlong residency at the Ondine Discotheque, to finish the mixing of our debut album, and to make a promotional film for our first single. We were playing five half-hour sets each night, finishing just shy of sunrise. I valued the little sleep I was able to get.

Our lawyer had arranged for us to stay at the Henry Hudson Hotel in midtown Manhattan. On the floor above us the Chambers Brothers had a series of suites, so we often ended up getting stoned with them after coming home from our respective gigs. On our nights off, drummer John Densmore and I explored jazz clubs in the Village. During the daylight hours, keyboardist Ray Manzarek and his girlfriend, Dorothy, ventured out to the museums. Even though the New York crowd hadn't heard our songs before, they seemed to dig us, and the local groupies seemed fascinated by these mysterious aliens from California. I had brief flings with several of them, including Rory Flynn, a six-foot-tall model I knew from back in L.A., who also happened to be Errol Flynn's daughter. I found out later that the groupies at Ondine's compared notes with one another and bestowed ratings on their conquests. I didn't get much attention from anyone after Rory, so I must not have rated too highly.

We were a young band on our way up. There was plenty of cause for celebration. But as usual, Jim celebrated harder than the rest of us.

The night after my phone call from God, we went to Thanksgiving dinner at our producer Paul Rothchild's house in New Jersey, and Jim celebrated so hard that he was hitting on Paul's wife right at the table. Paul took it in stride, but when he gave us a ride back to the Henry Hudson Hotel, Jim kept grabbing Paul by the hair, causing him to swerve and nearly crash. It took the whole band to drag Jim back to his hotel room. We hoped if we could just get him into bed he'd wind down and pass out. Instead, he stripped naked and jumped out the window.

Jim had a particular technique for jumping out of windows. I'd seen him do it a few times before. Back then, John and I were sharing a house in Laurel Canyon, and one night, Jim stopped by when we had some girls over. He decided to freak the girls out by breaking into a run and leaping off our balcony. His jump included a well-timed twist that allowed him to grab hold of the ledge, where he would dangle for a while until he got the attention he needed. Then he would pull himself up, to the gasping relief and accelerated heartbeats of any females who had witnessed it.

Our Laurel Canyon house was only two stories tall, though. This time Jim was dangling a dozen floors above the unforgiving concrete and honking traffic of Fifty-Eighth Street. And judging from the gratuitous nudity, he was even drunker than usual, so I didn't have much confidence in his grip.

We raced across the room to pull him back in. If we hadn't been there, he probably wouldn't have been able to rescue himself. Then again, if we hadn't been there, he probably wouldn't have jumped for the shock value in the first place. Once we pulled him back inside, Jim tackled me onto the bed. While John and Ray secured the window, Jim kept me pinned down as he jokingly writhed around, pretending to put the moves on me. Sure, it was the sixties, but I didn't swing quite that far. I shoved him off the bed and watched him cackle with laughter on the floor.

Looking back, I think Jim subconsciously knew that John or Ray would never have put up with his impromptu Greco-Roman seduction act. Jim was always driven to test his limits, and even at his most intoxicated, he was still instinctively aware of exactly what those limits were. That night, he saw me as the band member with the best sense of humor. So I was the limit he decided to test.

It's funny to me now, but it wasn't funny to me at the time. I was twenty years old, the youngest member of the band. I didn't have any authority over these guys, and I didn't have any understanding of how to cope with this level of chaos. I was constantly being placed at the crossroads between rock 'n' roll stardom and scooping our lead singer's brains off the pavement.

We stayed in Jim's room for another hour or so as he calmed down and passed out. The next day he greeted me as if nothing ever happened. Jim rarely remembered his drunken fits, leaving the rest of us to pick up the pieces. I told him what he'd done, and it was like he was hearing a story about someone else. His reply, as usual, was something like "Wow, that's terrible" or "Oh, I'm sorry. I didn't realize."

His apologies were so simple, and yet so hypnotic. I still don't know how he got us to forgive him for half the stuff he did. There was something about his sober nature that made you feel bad about holding a grudge. Hanging from a window ledge, wrestling me naked on his hotel bed, all of it after embarrassing us in front of our producer and waking me up in the middle of the night with prank calls—why was I putting up with it? How can a simple apology cover it? Why was I sticking with this band when one of its crucial elements seemed bent on destroying everything?

All I knew was that I could never walk away. We were still playing small clubs, and we were still unknown to most of the world, but I could already see the future. I knew that Jim could be as big a rock star as anyone who had come before him, and I knew the Doors had the potential to become the biggest group in America. Regardless of whatever else might happen along the way, I was all in.

Two months later, we released a debut album that would prove my instincts right and that would forever alter the trajectory of our lives. But in the ensuing years I would repeatedly be reminded of the lesson I learned at the Henry Hudson Hotel: Jim Morrison may not have been God, but he most certainly had the power to throw me right out of this universe.

THE WORST HAIR IN ROCK 'N' ROLL

A critic once said I had "the worst hair in rock 'n' roll." It stung pretty bad, but I can't say they were wrong. I always battled with my naturally frizzy, kinky Jewfro, so one day my friend Bill Wolff and I experimented with Ultra Sheen, a hair relaxer marketed mainly to Black consumers. The results were remarkable. Wolff, as we all called him, said, "You're starting to look like that jerk Bryan MacLean," which was the closest he ever came to giving me a compliment. MacLean was the guitarist for Love, and his lustrous mop top resembled that of Rolling Stones guitarist Brian Jones. I don't know if I looked as good as MacLean or Jones did, but it was a marked improvement over my usual bird's nest.

Our hair relaxer experiment happened to occur about a week before Wolff and I auditioned for the Doors. Wolff tried out a few days before I did and I was surprised he didn't get picked. He was a much more experienced and technical player than I was. We had taken flamenco guitar classes together, we had formed a jug band together, we had played as part of a folk trio together, and we had jammed in an acid rock band with Doors drummer John Densmore together. Wolff was the Doors' first choice. I was their second. But my hair looked better, and my bottleneck made all the difference.

If you walk into a music store today, you can pick up a professional guitar bottleneck made of chromed steel, glazed ceramic, lightweight titanium, borosilicate glass, or even high-tech carbon fiber. When Wolff and I were learning guitar, we just smashed bottles. My favorites were the cheap California champagne bottles because they had the perfect shape, and the glass was slightly thicker than most wine bottles. Sometimes we'd put in the effort to tape up the jagged edges or melt them over a flame, but usually I just left them sharp. I figured if I ever got into a bar fight somewhere it might come in handy.

Wolff and I loved listening to records by Blind Willie Johnson, Blind Lemon Jefferson, Blind Willie McTell, the Five Blind Boys of Alabama...their lack of sight apparently left them with a heightened sense of slide guitar. We didn't have a teacher who could instruct us on bottleneck technique, so we did our best to figure it out on our own. Originally I was a purist and exclusively played acoustic, but just before my audition for the Doors I had become enamored with the sound of a bottleneck slide on an electric guitar.

So one day in the fall of 1965 I drove my electric guitar, my amplifier, and my weaponized California champagne bottleneck to a parking lot behind an office building in Santa Monica. At the edge of the lot was an alley, and in that alley was a little dilapidated house. Inside the house lived a guy named Hank, who graciously allowed the Doors to use his Yamaha piano and rehearse in his cramped living room. No neighbors meant no noise complaints.

I had previously met everyone in the band, so there was no need for introductions, and John had already given me a copy of their six-song demo, so I came prepared. The first song we ever played together was my favorite of their six tracks: "Moonlight Drive." The demo version was much more bouncy and bluesy than the one we'd later record together, and Jim sang in a fluttering high register that Doors fans would hardly recognize today. The guitar part plodded predictably in time with the piano. I played along faithfully.

Then I asked if I could try something. I slipped on my bottleneck and we ran through the song again as I wove in a warbling, spaced-out slide riff. Between my flamenco fingerpicking and my Muddy Waters bottlenecking I guess I stood out from the other candidates. Jim went crazy for the sound of the bottleneck and said the Doors should use it on every song. And that's why I ended up getting the gig over Wolff. All it took was one song to know it felt right.

The hair relaxer wore off after a few months and my sexy mop top went back to looking like a frayed Brillo pad. But thankfully by then I had proven myself indispensable, and the Doors couldn't get rid of me any more than I could get rid of the worst hair in rock 'n' roll.

I rehearsed once more with the Doors at Hank's house, during which one of Jim's friends dropped by. Jim dragged him into a back room, slammed the door, and started shouting at the top of his lungs. As their muffled screams bled through the walls, I stitched together the context: this guy had fucked Jim over on some sort of drug deal. I don't know what type of drug, or whether there was too little of it, or whether the money wasn't right, but either way, it sounded like someone was going to get killed back there.

Ray, John, and I exchanged awkward glances and a few comments but otherwise pretended not to notice. It was our first shared act of burying our heads in the sand when it came to the erratic behavior of Jim Morrison, and it was my first disturbing taste of Jim's dark side. In the moment I didn't see it as any sort of red flag; for all I knew, Jim had a perfectly good reason to scream at that guy.

But up until that point he had been so reserved, so the sudden turn was startling, to say the least.

As we ran through some more songs to try and drown out the noise, I stood there, unnerved, thinking to myself, *This guy is our lead singer?*

Eventually Jim and his friend reemerged. No explanation was ever given. Jim was visibly pissed off. Rehearsal was over.

BEWARE THE STARE THAT THREATENS ALL MANKIND

I wonder if I identified with all those famous blind blues artists due to the fact that the universe has never been kind to my eyes. If you look at old promo photos of the Doors, I'm often squinting due to my sensitivity to all the bright flashbulbs. I still have to force myself not to squint in photos today. I had LASIK surgery in the nineties, twice, but it wore off after a few years, and then I developed cataracts and had to have surgery on them, and then I had to have radial keratotomy surgery in my left eye, where they had to physically cut into my cornea to correct the farsightedness from the cataract surgery, and meanwhile the iris in my right eye doesn't close properly because it got whacked with a tennis ball (by an eye doctor, ironically).

As a young kid growing up in perpetually sunny Southern California, I was always athletic and confident. My twin brother, Ronny, and I excelled at golf at an early age, we were both on the gymnastics team at school, and we were always picked first for kick-ball teams. I had a passion for baseball and I'm sure it's something I would've pursued more seriously if my eyes hadn't gone bad at the height of my Little League career. I just had a harder and harder time seeing the fucking ball. I was eventually banished to right field, hoping the ball wouldn't come my way so I could avoid embarrassment. My grades plummeted as well—since I couldn't see the chalkboard—and one day when I pointed out a plane in the sky that wasn't there my parents finally put the pieces together and took me to get glasses.

But only nerds wore glasses. I was a cool kid. A popular kid! Wearing glasses would bring all of that crashing down. So when I left the house in the morning the glasses went into my pocket until I came home again. My parents noticed that my grades weren't improving and again put the pieces together. Contact lenses were relatively new at the time. They were hard plastic shells that didn't let in enough oxygen, so you could wear them for only short periods of time, but anything was better than being uncool.

I took to the hassle and discomfort of wearing contacts so well that I ended up as a guinea pig for Hollywood. The 1960 sci-fi hor-ror movie *Village of the Damned* features a bunch of creepy children with hypnotic powers and glowing eyes. Before production began, I went in for a screen test to demonstrate how the eye effect would look on film. I assume my ophthalmologist recommended me; Dr. Roberts said I was his youngest patient ever to wear contacts. The lenses they had made for the film were hard, gold-painted corneal shells with a tiny pinhole in the center to see through. They were even less forgiving than my usual lenses, so one of the crew mem-bers had to put numbing drops in my eyes to deaden the pain. It was exciting at first to be on a real soundstage with all the big lights and cameras, but after a few hours, when the drops wore off, my eyes were screaming for relief. I put on a brave face but I'm sure it became clear that they couldn't possibly expect a full cast of kids to comfortably act in those things. I loved the movie when it came out, but likely due to my excruciating screen test, they scrapped the corneal shells and created the glowing eyes in postproduction.

My non-sci-fi contacts helped me see somewhat better, but my grades hardly rebounded, my athletic confidence never fully returned, and when I hit junior high my face exploded with zits and I gained a bunch of weight. All but a few of my friends from grade school turned on me. I went from being one of the most popular kids at school to being a total outcast, and I was hazed mercilessly by upperclassmen. Whatever was left of my self-esteem was beaten out of me, and I transformed from a popular extrovert into the shy, quiet guy I am today.

Thankfully I wasn't the only kid going through an awkward phase. Bill Wolff always stuck by my side, and my twin brother, Ronny, was also a loyal companion. Keith Wallace lived next to an orange grove where we'd all engage in blood orange fights, and Steve Davidson let us spy on his older brother as he tried to bed his girlfriends. We spent every weekend of our junior high years on a perpetual search for a party, but even if we had found one I doubt we would've had the nerve to go in.

Destruction and vandalism were our other outlets. One night my friends and I snuck into a housing development under construction in Brentwood, broke some windows, plugged up all the sinks, and left the water running. We justified our actions under a banner of protesting overdevelopment, but in truth we were just bored. And sexually frustrated.

Somehow we always got away with our antics—until the time Bill Wolff and I decided to play chicken with a couple of tractors on the construction site of the new Palisades High School. They had left the keys in the ignition: how could we possibly resist that kind of temptation? It turns out tractors are pretty hard to drive, with all those levers and stuff. We got them moving but didn't know how to work them too well, so we eventually smashed into each other and beat it out of there. I don't know who saw us or how they recognized us, but later that day the police came to my parents' door. I'll never forget the disappointed look on my mom's face. I had broken her heart.

I shied away from abject destruction after that but I found new forms of mischief when I entered high school. My friend Roy Thompson had an older cousin named Steve Scott who had a driver's license, so he'd steal his mom's '57 Chevy station wagon and we'd cruise around looking for trouble. One night we stole a box of fifty wrenches from behind a hardware store just because it was there. On other nights we'd spot a car full of gang members, flip them off, and the chase was on. Steve knew the alleys of Santa Monica like the back of his hand. He didn't have much engine power at his disposal in that station wagon, but he could outmaneuver anyone. And if they got too close, Roy and I would hurl stolen wrenches at our pursuer's car.

Roy, Steve, and I would create our own meager little parties by driving up to beer outlets and stealing their half-empty kegs (to us they were half *full*). One of the local street gangs—either the Dukes or the Gents—once paid us to provide beer for a graduation party, since we always bragged about how easily we could procure kegs. We scavenged what we could from the nearby outlets, but on that particular night all the kegs we found were nearly empty. We dropped off our haul at a local park where the party was already in full swing. These were white guys straight out of *West Side Story*, with their gang names embroidered on varsity jackets, but they were still pretty tough compared to us. When they realized we had given them practically dry kegs, we peeled out in Steve's mom's Chevy while the gang chased after us with baseball bats.

My parents tried to keep my brother and me away from our troublemaker friends, because clearly none of this was our fault: we were precious little angels being corrupted by an evil influence! But I kept getting into trouble and my grades kept sinking, and when it turned out I would have to repeat my junior year of high school, reality finally set in. My parents enrolled me at a private prep school near Silicon Valley called the Menlo School. It was over 350 miles away from all the bad apples I was spending time with, like Bill Wolff.

Except a year earlier, Bill Wolff's parents had the exact same idea. Instead of putting 350 miles between us, they inadvertently put us in the same dorm.

Bill Wolff and me in our Menlo uniforms

+ + +

Every morning in elementary school, all the students would gather around the flagpole with our hands on our hearts, and a kid named Loring Hughes would play the bugle as the Stars and Stripes were raised. While everyone else focused on the flag, I focused on the bugle. I don't know if it was the sound of it or the fact that Loring was the center of attention for the whole school, but it was the birth of my desire to become a musician. I took some trumpet lessons but they stuck me in the third chair position in the school band, and eventually demoted me to steadily pounding on a bass drum.

Guitar was the next instrument that called to me. I first strummed one at my friend Bob Wire's house when I was twelve, and I kept finding excuses to hang out with him and strum it again. I was intrigued by the guitarists in my neighborhood, like Henry Vestine, who would later go on to play in Canned Heat. Whenever I walked by Henry's house, I would hear the liquid sound of his electric guitar, heavy with reverb and tremolo. Less famous but more influential to me was a guy named Hial King, who was a master of saxophone and drums as much as guitar. His playing impressed me for sure, but what really stuck with me was his look. At first glance, most people probably noticed his greasy pompadour hairdo and his polished penny loafers. But behind it all he was short and dumpy and not much better looking than me, the outcast nerd. Yet all the girls were interested in him. That set off a light bulb in my brain: the guitar could be the cure.

When I arrived at Menlo, there was a Hawaiian guy named Keoki King who lived across the hall from me and had an old Martin 000-21 acoustic. He had found it in a barn on his dad's ranch so it was in rough shape, but I hope he held on to it: it would be worth thousands today. He didn't play guitar much so he was always happy to loan it to me. After our classes we would be locked in our dorms, so the choice was either studying or twanging away on Keoki's guitar. To me, that wasn't a choice at all.

I played Keoki's guitar practically every night at Menlo until I finally got an instrument of my own: a traditional flamenco-style acoustic made of lightweight cedar with an ebony fretboard, sculpted by master Mexican luthier Juan Pimentel. Once I picked it up, I almost never put it down. And my theory about the guitar being the key to coolness was proven correct: everyone at school suddenly became my best friend so they could get their hands on my Juan Pimentel acoustic.

Aside from the extended rehearsal time, Menlo also bathed me in new music brought in by other students from all over the country. For the first time I heard Robert Johnson. And B. B. and Albert and Freddie King. The blues. The real deal blues. It was also the peak of the American folk revival, which fed me Joan Baez, Ramblin' Jack Elliott, Lead Belly, and—my personal all-time favorite—Bob Dylan.

Rounding out the mix was a healthy helping of flamenco. My dad had a record called *Dos Flamencos,* an entrancing ballet of classical guitar by Jaime Grifo and Niño Marvino. The intricacy and delicacy of it left me awestruck. Bill Wolff and I decided we would be the next Dos Flamencos. But we were still Dos Beginner Guitarristas.

Over the summer break, Wolff and I split the cost of guitar lessons with some notable flamenco instructors: Peter Evans and Arnold Lessing. They used to play regularly at a place called Casa Madrid on Pico Boulevard, accompanying traditional Spanish dancers who mesmerized Wolff and me with their expressive moves and swishing, swirling sevillana skirts. With regular lessons and diligent practice, we went from terrible to not bad pretty quickly. And when we returned to school, we continued to hone our skills every night after lockdown.

In addition to the gossamer, ethereal sound of flamenco, I was also drawn to the clunky, campy sound of jug band music. Well, not so much the sound as the image. The guys on the cover of the first Jim Kweskin and the Jug Band album looked like goofballs, but they also looked stoned, and being stoned was cool. Wolff, in fact, immediately ran out and bought round blue sunglasses just like the ones jug player Fritz Richmond was wearing on the album cover, predating John Lennon's trendsetting round sunglasses by several years. The music itself was so unapologetically corny that it felt almost defiant. My schoolmates and I snuck out to see Jim Kweskin and Dave Van Ronk live at clubs around the Bay Area. We also caught a show or two featuring Mother McCree's Uptown Jug Champions, with Jerry Garcia, Ron "Pigpen" McKernan, and a fellow Menlo student named Bob Weir, all three of whom would later go on to form the Grateful Dead. Everyone at school always talked about how cool Bob Weir and the Mother McCree's guys were, so my friends and I started thinking that if we formed our own jug band, we could be the cool guys everyone was talking about.

The beauty of jug band music was that it didn't require too many real instruments. I played guitar, Wolff pulled double duty on guitar and washboard, Scott played kazoo, Jerry played a washtub bass, and Phinizy sang and played the jug. We called ourselves the Back Bay Chamber Pot Terriers, which was Phinizy's idea. He was from the Back Bay area of Boston. The rest of us were California born and bred, so the name didn't make much sense. But we heard if you were from the Back Bay you were cool, and Phinizy used to have a band with the same name and wanted to use it again. Out of all the bands I've been in over the years, it's certainly not the worst name I've played under.

We performed only once, at a meeting of the school's Women's Auxiliary. I thought we'd be off in a corner somewhere providing background music while the ladies socialized, but when we arrived there was a stage and microphones and rows upon rows of well-dressed, middle-aged women sitting and staring at us expectantly.

We ran through a handful of jug band covers, mostly Jim Kweskin songs like "Washington at Valley Forge." With the *tchk-tchk-tchk* of the washboard and a chorus that went "Voe doe dee o doe," it was objectively silly music, and certainly not what a room full of moms would have preferred. The weight of self-consciousness was heavy on my shoulders as we played. But they loved us! They didn't jump out of their chairs and dance or anything, but it really seemed like their smiles and applause were genuine. Maybe they were humoring us, but it was my first time onstage, and the validation of a crowd — even just a crowd of politely clapping old ladies — was enough to ensure it wouldn't be my last.

The Back Bay Chamber Pot Terriers

✦   ✦   ✦

Keoki was a good friend not only for loaning me his guitar but also for introducing me to his sister, Jeanie. She attended an all-girls Catholic school half a mile down the road from Menlo. We met up at school dances and went surfing together, and she was one of the first girls I ever made out with. One night Jeanie and I were imagining the future, and talking about where we saw ourselves. I said I was going to become a professional guitar player. I wonder if she believed me.

WICKED GO THE DOORS

When I look back over my life I don't see everything in sequence. I recall moments. Sensations. My memories are rarely linked chronologically. Or even logically. Sometimes they're brought to the surface by the sight of an old photograph, the sound of an old song, or, as once was the case, the smell of tear gas.

It's actually tough to describe the smell of tear gas because by the time the odor hits you, you're more preoccupied with its effects. Ray and I were performing together in Bogotá, Colombia, in 2009 when the military tried to shut down the show by tossing tear gas canisters into the venue and barring the doors from the outside. I couldn't even see the cloud; I was just playing my guitar when suddenly I started gagging. Ray and I stopped midsong as our eyes watered up. The crowd panicked. We retreated backstage, where our manager stuffed wet towels under our dressing room door. Our crew passed out water to people in the audience and paramedics were running around treating people who were injured. The military guys kept threatening our crew, but after an hour or so they finally backed down, the cloud of tear gas dispersed, and we were able to finish the set to an appreciative and clear-eyed crowd. It wasn't the most pleasant experience, but it was one that transported me back in time, and helped me empathize more closely with what Jim must've gone through at the New Haven Arena.

The infamous New Haven concert is cited in every retelling of our band's history, so I suppose I should offer my account here. And maybe even take my share of the responsibility.

It was the end of an exhilarating year: our song "Light My Fire" had changed everything over the summer of '67, and by the fall, our second album, *Strange Days,* joined our debut album in the top five. Jim's drinking habit had grown in parallel with our success, so the members of our band and crew rotated the chore of attempting to keep him as sober as possible on show nights. On December 9, 1967, that chore had fallen on me. Jim and I were enjoying a quiet dinner with our respective dates before our show in New Haven, Connecticut. He wasn't drinking more than his usual amount, but his usual amount was more than usual to most people. I had yet to discover a successful strategy to lure Jim over to moderation. Arguing didn't work. Saying nothing didn't work. Encouraging him didn't work. That night I went with gentle nagging: "Are you sure you wanna order that?" and "Come on, man, we have a show in two hours."

It didn't work.

Later that night I was in our dressing room when I heard Jim screaming. We all went running out to see what happened and found Jim yelling at some cops and the cops yelling back. During the commotion we stitched together what had happened: Jim was making out with his date in a shower stall when a police officer confronted him, thinking he was a random member of the crowd who had snuck backstage. Jim allegedly mouthed off, and the cop allegedly sprayed him with Mace. I had no problem believing the story. Jim loved mouthing off to cops, and cops loved having an excuse.

When I inhaled tear gas in Bogotá it wasn't the same as being maced directly in the eyes, of course. But once Jim's eyes were washed out he seemed relatively fine. It turns out that one of the reasons the police switched from the chemical form of Mace they all used in the sixties to the pepper spray they use today is because Mace was often ineffective against people under the influence of alcohol. So maybe it was a good thing my nagging at dinner hadn't worked: Jim's drinking may have actually saved the day!

The show itself—or at least the portion of it we got to play— went pretty well. If anything, the Mace probably sobered Jim up a bit. As we started playing "Back Door Man," Jim launched into his now-famous rant about the little blue man in the little blue suit with the little blue cap who had temporarily blinded him backstage. The crowd cheered Jim on as we jammed behind him. Like at all the best Doors shows, we were creating a moment. A specific connection with a specific audience that would exist only on that specific night. I was completely oblivious to the dozens of police officers waiting in the shadows until the house lights came up and the shadows were removed.

Suddenly we were surrounded. A police lieutenant marched onto the stage and Jim offered him the microphone: "Say your thing, man." Even at that point I wasn't really nervous. What were they going to do, arrest him? Onstage? In the middle of a show? For telling a completely true story?

As it turned out, yes. The police grabbed Jim and the crowd went wild. Ray, John, and I stood there in shock.

The name Bill Siddons should be better known among Doors fans, as he is truly the unsung hero of our band's story. Bill was our tour manager at the time, and tour managing is always a thankless job. You work your ass off and rarely get credit for all the things you do right, but you get immediately excoriated for anything that goes wrong, even if it's something beyond your control. Almost every band out there has a tour manager they don't appreciate enough. But being the tour manager who had to mop up after the Doors was a special kind of headache.

Bill—only nineteen years old at the time—was the one who intervened when Jim first got maced backstage, and now he was the one throwing himself onto a cop's back and yelling, "Leave him alone!" By the time Ray, John, and I followed him offstage, Jim was already in the back of a squad car, and Bill had switched his focus to protecting our gear from the rambunctious crowd.

There was literally no precedent for this. In 1908, Italian opera singer Carlo Albani was arrested onstage in Boston during a performance of Verdi's *Il Trovatore* due to a pending lawsuit, but even then the constable let him finish the show. This was the first time in recorded history that a musical artist was arrested onstage in the middle of a set. Can't blame us for freezing up without any idea what to do.

Bill called our managers, our managers called our lawyer, our lawyer called the cops, and Jim was released on bail, which Bill paid out of our earnings for the night. None of this was Jim's fault, so for once none of his trademark apologies were necessary.

A few weeks later the entire incident was detailed in a feature story in *Life* magazine, with beautiful play-by-play photography. The cops, in their frenzy, had scooped up a *Life* reporter, a *Village Voice* jazz critic, and a photographer. This ensured that the press would be fully on our side, and it ensured that Jim's arrest—unlike Italian opera singer Carlo Albani's—would feature prominently in the historical record. We were thrilled with the article and the photos. Jim came across as a righteous rebel and the police came across as uptight buffoons. And you didn't have to be a defiant teenager to see it that way: even my parents were on our side when they read the story.

It was never our style to dwell on things, so after the dust settled we moved on and didn't really discuss it. But it turned out to be a moment of double-edged mythmaking that affected everything from then on. We became outlaw legends brimming with counter-culture credibility. But we had also created an expectation of chaos. Our audiences became less interested in creating their own unique moments with us and more interested in reproducing the moment in New Haven. The headline in *Life* summed up the road we were now on: "Wicked Go the Doors."

On December 9, 2012—exactly forty-five years to the day after Jim's arrest—I played New Haven with my jam band, Robby Krieger's Jam Kitchen. A man approached me backstage and introduced himself as the son of the cop who maced Jim. He was polite and friendly, and he had followed in his father's footsteps and become a police officer. He officially apologized for his dad's behavior. On behalf of the band that his dad helped make famous, I accepted.

SEND MY CREDENTIALS TO THE HOUSE OF DETENTION

They took Romilar cough syrup off the shelves in the seventies because too many teenagers were abusing it to get high. In 1964, I was one of those teenagers.

One night when I was on break from Menlo I happened to be buzzing on Romilar with Bill Wolff; my brother, Ronny; and some other friends when the cops kicked in the door. They didn't care about us or our cough syrup; we just happened to be in the wrong place at the wrong time. The wrong place being a random drug dealer's house. The wrong time being the night the dealer tried to sell two kilos of pot to a couple of undercover narcs.

I had two bags of weed in my underwear, but even after two separate searches the cops missed them. Later that night while killing time in a Hollywood holding cell, I asked my cellmate Wally — who was in for murder — what I should do with the weed. He said we might as well smoke it since it would probably be his last chance to get high for a long time. The obvious odor somehow didn't alert the guards, but it did make our other cellmates insist that we share. All in all, not a bad night.

But my parents were not pleased. This was exactly the type of stuff that made them send me to Menlo in the first place. My dad was furious when my name and my brother's name—or, more to the point, our family name—popped up in an article about the bust in Santa Monica's *Evening Outlook*. As angry as my dad was, he still helped my brother and me out. He hired a big-time lawyer named Grant Cooper, who would later go on to defend Sirhan Sirhan, the guy who assassinated Bobby Kennedy. It was major overkill for our meager little bust, but it worked: even though we had just turned eighteen, Grant Cooper convinced the court to try us as juveniles. We got probation.

We didn't know the dealer personally. We were taken to his house by a guitarist we had met on the Sunset Strip who offered to sell us a couple of ounces. When the drama was all over, Grant Cooper left us with some sage advice: "Stop hanging around with musicians."

My parents may have hated the trouble I got into while hanging around with musicians, but that didn't mean they hated music. My dad had an impressive record collection. Lots of boogie-woogie 78s by Black artists—records that probably wouldn't have been found as readily in the other houses in our upscale Pacific Palisades neighborhood. And lots of classical symphonies and John Philip Sousa marches. In fact, my love of music was born the first time my dad played me Prokofiev's orchestral *Peter and the Wolf* soundtrack when I was little.

Stuart Krieger was a serious man. Bald. Suits. Drove a Buick. Basically a living, breathing clip art image of a 1960s dad. He went to school for aeronautical engineering at UCLA and Caltech and worked with defense contractors to design airfoils for military aircraft. Quite a few Nazis met their end thanks to planes my dad helped build, like the Lockheed P-38 Lightning and the Northrop P-61 Black Widow. He also worked on early versions of Northrop's flying wing and was part of the team at the top secret Skunk Works facility. Later he started his own engineering firm, Planning Research, which was successful enough to be listed on the New York Stock Exchange — at which point he upgraded his Buick to a silver Maserati Ghibli. He worked long hours to give his family a comfortable life, but he also made time to coach my Little League baseball team. We got along well (when I wasn't being detained by the police), but he was the textbook definition of "square." I respected and loved him; I just never wanted to become him.

Marilyn Krieger was the yin to my father's yang. She dyed her hair blond and did everything she could to emulate the look of her idol, Marilyn Monroe. While my dad listened to Sousa, my mom listened to Sinatra. While my dad spent all his free time on the golf course, my mom painted and taught me how to work with oils. She also taught me what little she knew about piano. Her repertoire was limited to a single song called "My Dearest Dear," from a 1939 British musical, which she played and sang beautifully. She loved discovering new music on the radio, and most significantly for me, she discovered Elvis. His "Hound Dog" single, with "Don't Be Cruel" on the B side, was soon on very heavy rotation in our house.

I can't possibly complain about the environment I grew up in. It was a healthy balance of art and science, and it was a life of privilege and financial security. Living in Pacific Palisades—an affluent suburb just north of Santa Monica—meant safety and serenity and easy access to the beach. The doors in our neighborhood were never locked. My brother and I hitchhiked up and down the coast without fear of abduction or murder. We'd stay out skateboarding well after dark and our parents never worried. My family even had a regular cleaning lady and a part-time cook. We made Beaver Cleaver look like Sid Vicious. So, like any teenager with nothing to rebel against, I rebelled.

Menlo was supposed to straighten me out, but it was the first place I tried pot. My friend Scott—the kazooist from the Back Bay Chamber Pot Terriers—imported some stuff he called boo from his friends back in New York. We didn't know it was pot at the time. It had this enigmatic name and we smoked it out of these ornate opium pipes we picked up in Chinatown. When the high hit me I burst into a giggling fit because I imagined myself as a king, with everyone else in the room as my subjects. I don't know why that was so funny, but I couldn't stop laughing.

Boo was a perfect way to cause mischief without causing any property damage, but like all my other forms of adolescent rebellion, it caught up with me. After Bill Wolff and I graduated high school, we were driving around in his car when some cops tried to pull us over. Wolff had an ounce of weed on him and asked, "What do we do?"

Referencing an old joke about the Lone Ranger and Tonto, I said, "What do you mean 'we,' white man?"

I was stoned. It seemed funny at the time.

I told Wolff to stick it in his pants, having learned from my previous experience that they may not check his crotch, but in a panic he tossed the weed out the window instead. The cops saw it, of course. We ended up at the West L.A. police station, scared shitless as all the officers on duty messed with us:

"Get the scissors, guys, we got some longhairs here! We're gonna have some fun!"

We were transferred to the men's jail downtown, stripped naked, sprayed with a delousing agent, and stuffed into stiff, ill-fitting uniforms. We were told that since we had a previous record from our other bust, we'd get at least two years.

There was no laughing or smoking with cellmates this time. It was just me, lying on my rack in the dark, thinking about what it would really mean to be locked in a cell for two full years of my life. Fear kept me awake all night. The walls, the bars—this time it was all real.

And then the next morning they gave me breakfast and let me out.

It was a lucky break. They knew it was Bill's car and they saw him throw the weed, so they prosecuted him and didn't bother with me. Thankfully he avoided jail time, but it was a wake-up call about the potential consequences of petty rebellion. I drastically cut back on my weed use after that, and never carried it around for fear of getting busted. I still wanted to experiment with substances that could help me achieve new perspectives, but from then on I would find ways to do it legally. Like with LSD.

+ + +

About fifty years after Wolff and I got busted, two police officers approached me in the Austin airport when I was flying home after a gig with my group, the Robby Krieger Band. The airport cops sternly informed me that their dogs had sniffed out a small amount of pot in the golf bag that was among my checked luggage. It had probably been in there for months, stuffed in the corner of some pocket, long forgotten about. I showed the cops my medical marijuana card. They thanked me and moved on. For the times, they are a-changin'.

THE LIVING ROOM

One day, soon after I entered ninth grade, my family and I were all playing golf together at the Riviera Country Club. I was standing by the ball washer at the forward tee of the fourth hole when my dad hit his drive from the back tee, thirty yards behind me. His ball whizzed through the air and, impressively, found my skull. It knocked me out cold.

I woke up and my mom rushed me to the hospital (while my dad and brother continued their game). My skull was fractured and as part of my treatment I had to take a course of special antibiotics, which gave me the shits. I spent weeks on an all-yogurt-and-ginger-ale diet, and as a result I dropped over forty pounds, which I never gained back. It's not a diet I would recommend, but I can't argue with the results. Girls still didn't want to talk to me, but at least I regained some of my social confidence and my ability to balance on a surfboard. I sincerely doubt the Doors would've let me join their band if I had remained overweight, so in the end I suppose I should thank my dad for fracturing my skull.

I should also thank my dad for recommending our band's attorney,

Max Fink, another unsung hero of the Doors' story. We would go on to become his most notorious clients, but before us he represented Lucille Ball and Desi Arnaz, among others. When Jim was arrested in New Haven, Max was the one who got him out and who ultimately got the whole thing reduced to a twenty-five-dollar fine. He helped us with contracts, paperwork, management personnel, trials, and every other legal swamp we waded into. He was even the one who arranged our stay at the Henry Hudson Hotel in New York. We thought he was getting us some sort of discount on the rooms, but I'm pretty sure we paid full price, and I'm pretty sure he got a kickback. He was a shark, but he was our shark.

My dad recommended Max at some point after the third time the Doors rehearsed. Or at least attempted to rehearse. We couldn't practice at Hank's anymore, so I offered up my parents' house. My dad worked all day, so we could make all the noise we wanted. Ray, John, and I set up our gear in the living room and chatted while waiting for Jim to arrive. But Jim never showed. After an hour, Ray started making calls.

Eventually we found out Jim was in jail in a dusty little town called Blythe, which is a little more than halfway between Los Angeles and Phoenix. From what I could gather, Jim and his friends Felix and Phil had driven out into the desert and stopped at a bar full of bikers. Somebody said something they shouldn't have and a brawl broke out. The cops came and scooped everybody up, and Jim spent the night in the drunk tank. I never got all the details. I'm not even sure how Jim got home. I think Ray may have had to drive out there to collect him. My dad took note of the incident, and other similar incidents that occurred as the band got off the ground. He put us in touch with Max Fink and said, "You're gonna need a good criminal attorney."

+ + +

I almost laugh when I think about it now, but Jim didn't make much of an impression on me when I first met him. A week or so before my audition, John Densmore brought him over to my parents' house to recruit me for their new band. Jim was quiet. He wore muted, drab clothes. There was nothing "rock star" about him. They told me their band's name was the Doors.

If I'm being perfectly honest...I thought it was stupid.

Jim explained that the name was inspired by Aldous Huxley's *The Doors of Perception,* which, coincidentally, I had read about a year earlier. I probably won some points with Jim for understanding the reference, but I still wasn't wild about the band name. To anyone unfamiliar with the Huxley book, it wouldn't make any sense. I remember thinking that if the band was called Perception instead, it would at least have a ring to it. "The Beatles" had a ring. "The Rolling Stones" had a ring. "The Doors" had a thud.

The music on their six-song demo was only okay, but the lyrics to "Moonlight Drive" and "End of the Night" rattled around in my head long after Jim and John left my house. They had something there. I still might not have bothered to audition, except for the fact that they already had a deal with Columbia Records. I was especially starry-eyed because the guy who signed them was Billy James, who had worked with Bob Dylan. The singer, the band name, and the music weren't all that impressive, but a deal with Columbia Records was. I figured it might be worth a shot.

A few months after I joined the Doors, Jim strolled into the Columbia offices one day on a heroic dose of acid. I have no idea what he said or did in there; all he told us was that he and Billy James had met with some of the higher-ups at the label. Jim seemed proud of himself. When he was on acid he thought he could control people's minds: "I had those guys eating out of my hand. I just told them where it was at. We're going to be the biggest band on Columbia." Soon after, we found out that we had been dropped.

It's possible we would've been dropped either way. "Signed" was a nebulous term. The Doors had a development deal, which was something labels handed out to dozens of artists at a time. Whichever bands became popular would be kept on the label; the others would be tossed. Billy James believed in the Doors, and had been working hard to get his bosses excited about us, but the demo was amateurish and we were struggling to get gigs. Jim's psychedelic meeting with the Columbia execs was obviously the last nail in the coffin. Billy James was sorry to see us go, but in a strange twist, he ended up working with us anyway when he later took a job with Elektra Records. Early on, he offered us some prophetic words about Jim Morrison:

"If he ever gets power, watch out."

Ray saw something in Jim when Jim first sang a song to him on the sands of Venice Beach, and Ray's confidence never wavered from then on. John saw something in Jim, enough to convince me to audition for the band. I didn't see it. Not at first. Not the way Ray and John did. I liked Jim personally. He had a gentle nature when he wasn't screaming at drug dealers or getting in bar fights or nuking record deals. Even my mom found him charming—she saw him as a soft-spoken southern gentleman. He wrote great lyrics, but he wasn't yet a crooning, leather-clad sex god. All I saw was a shaky-voiced, corduroy-clad introvert.

Jim rarely had a fixed address in those days. He was either living on his friend Dennis Jakob's rooftop, or staying with Ray, or finding different girls to take him in. You never knew where Jim was going to sleep on any given night, and neither did he. So when my parents went on vacation to Europe for a few weeks, I offered Jim shelter at our house. He brought over a bunch of dog-eared poetry notebooks. I brought out my guitar.

We had already worked on songs like "Break On Through" and "Light My Fire" with the band at our rehearsals, but this was the first chance Jim and I had to collaborate one-on-one. Jim had lyrics for songs like "Strange Days," "The Crystal Ship," and "Waiting for the Sun." I had words and music for "Love Me Two Times" and "You're Lost Little Girl." I showed Jim a Ravi Shankar–influenced raga I was working on, and he pulled out a couple of stanzas to a song he called "The End." We traded ideas for licks and lyrics and bonded over the thrill of creation as new music flowed out of us.

Finally, like Ray and John, I saw it.

Writing with Jim was a uniquely inspiring experience—one that I haven't been able to replicate since. And while Jim was staying with me, he was generally well-behaved. My grandfather was there to chaperone us, which was a little embarrassing for me. He was a quiet old man who barely registered as a presence in the house. I apologized for his having to be there, but Jim said, "No, man, he's cool. I like him." Just as Jim had surprised me with his violent side, he could also be shockingly polite. He didn't drink much while we were hanging out, so he was the sweet, friendly, funny Jim that was so easy to like. Maybe this band was going to work out after all.

But then one night while he was staying with us, Jim went out drinking with my brother, Ronny, and they were pulled over by the police. Jim launched into a tirade against the cops, using language I'm hesitant to repeat, especially in a modern context. Jim, in so many words, accused the officers of carrying guns only to compensate for their unusually small genitalia. He referred to them multiple times by a very harsh derogatory term for homosexuals, and further postulated that—due to their aforementioned homosexuality and modest-size genitalia—they lacked the bravery to use their guns.

Thankfully the cops didn't shoot them just to make a counterargument. But Jim and my brother both ended up in jail, and this time I was the one who had to post bail. It was a bit of a blemish on our otherwise productive and enjoyable time together, but it didn't spoil the creative energy we had generated, or the new bond Jim and I had forged. It was still clear to me that the Doors had a bright future.

We were just going to need a good criminal attorney.

New York Show Is a Riot

Police remove a young man from the stage of Singer Bowl in Queens, New York, after a wild melee that followed the appearence of a combo called "The Door." The group was singing when about 200 teenagers rushed the stage and began breaking up things. Three were injured and two arrested but the musicians fled to safety.

—Examiner Photo

THE RIOT CONCERT

People sometimes ask me about the infamous Riot Concert. I always have to ask them to be more specific. They're usually referring to a show at the Chicago Coliseum in May 1968. According to reports, Jim invited the audience onto the stage, a fan leapt off the balcony, and the crowd ended up tearing up the chairs and breaking down the barricades.

I have no memory of any of that.

It's not that I was too drunk or stoned. And sure, I'm getting older, but I don't think that's it either. It's just that Jim invited the crowd onto the stage all the time. And chairs are usually the first victims of any riot. As for the guy jumping off the balcony, maybe I was just looking at my fretboard at the time? But I don't recall anyone after the show saying, "Hey, did you see that guy jump off the balcony?!" You'd think that would've been a detail worth discussing in the dressing room.

I wish I could offer some insight or perspective on the Riot Concert in Chicago, but truthfully it was just another night on the road with the Doors. In Phoenix we played the state fair in front of thousands of people, Jim encouraged several hundred of them to climb onstage, the police shut down the show, we were permanently banned from Phoenix, and I have no distinct recollection of any of it.

I do remember playing the Singer Bowl in New York during the summer of '68. Jim crawled around on his belly and the crowd rushed the stage. We would've kept playing but the venue cut off the PA system and cops escorted us backstage. The crowd overwhelmed security and, as usual, busted up the seats.

And I clearly remember another night somewhere in the Midwest, where we had a chillingly quiet and bored crowd for the majority of the evening. There was no applause between songs. Jim did what he did at all those other headline-making concerts: he baited the crowd, he writhed around, he used coarse language. Nothing. We finished our set and left the stage to the same stony silence that had followed all our previous songs. Then, a few minutes later...an explosion of thunderous applause. The crowd fucking destroyed the place. We weren't scared; we were just amazed because it seemed to come out of nowhere. I don't know if it was pent-up energy, or if it just took a moment for Jim's incitements to sink in, or if the crowd just didn't know what to make of us at first. But yet again, hundreds of fans rushed the stage, and yet again, hundreds of innocent chairs met their untimely demise.

We enjoyed the idea of pushing limits, and it seemed like the crowds enjoyed it as much as we did. If the crowd didn't riot, we felt like we hadn't done our job. And if the crowd didn't get a taste of New Haven, they felt like they didn't get their money's worth.

Strangely, though, there was never Doorsmania in the same way there was Beatlemania. No matter how crazy our concerts got, we didn't have girls chasing us down the streets or fans mobbing us at airports. Every now and then we'd have fans surrounding our car, reaching through the windows, and trying to grab Jim's crotch, but it was the exception, not the rule. When we played the Spectrum in Philadelphia, the promoter hired several rather large bodyguards to escort us to the stage, but only because we had to march directly through the crowd to get there. We occasionally employed a bodyguard or two elsewhere, but we never needed a full security detail to hold back screaming teenage hordes. And we liked it that way. Every kid fantasizes at one point or another about Beatles-level mass adoration, but we realized quickly what a burden it could become. You can't turn off that kind of fame when it's inconvenient. Jim, naturally, was the most recognizable band member, but I never envied him for that—I considered my relatively low profile to be a luxury. I felt like a fly on the wall watching an amazing story unfold, and if things ever got too hot, I could run away without being chased. In general, we all felt lucky that we could live our lives and treat our fans like fellow human beings. Even at the Singer Bowl, the site of one of the most savage chair massacres in history, Jim spent some time before we went on walking among the crowd, politely chatting with people, and signing a few autographs. There was no screaming. No hysteria. Can you imagine a member of the Beatles or the Stones calmly walking around a concert venue without incident after their third album had come out?

It's actually crazier today than it ever was when the Doors were touring. No one jumps on my car or tries to grab my crotch, but I'm regularly approached by fans when I go to the grocery store, and if I'm spotted by the crowd before a show with the Robby Krieger Band, I'm quickly surrounded by people asking for autographs and selfies. I'm extremely flattered by the attention, and I'm always happy to make time for the fans who have supported me for so many years, but it's funny how different the vibe is now. Whenever I land at an airport or walk into a hotel lobby, there are inevitably several eBay sellers there with stacks of albums and memorabilia for me to sign. I usually don't mind accommodating them, but sometimes it's unsettlingly morbid: they're trying to get my autograph before I die.

I honestly haven't given much thought to why our crowds reacted so differently to us than to the other popular bands of the day. When it came to casual interactions, I assume it was just that we, or at least Jim, exuded a sense of being one of them. We never thought we were above anyone, and people reflected our mellow attitude back to us. When it came to the riots, it's still a mystery. Was it the lyrics? The music? I'm proud of what we created, but I don't think we accidentally unlocked any secret magic phrases or notes that put our fans under a mystical spell. Was it Jim's stage presence? Was it the era? Possibly, but the chaos extended long after Jim was gone, and well into the new millennium.

When I reunited with Ray in 2002 to play Doors songs, we toured around the world and found the same pandemonium we had experienced decades before. In Detroit they stormed the stage and made off with a snare drum, and someone even snatched the glasses right off Ray's face. In Houston a bunch of crowd members stripped naked. In Buenos Aires the rich members of the audience had a fancy seating area up front and the poorer audience members were relegated to standing room behind them, and it wasn't long before the standing room ticket holders took over the VIP seating area, smashed the chairs to splinters, and turned the scraps into a bonfire. The venue staff hosed down the flames while we played, and the rich people stood for the remainder of the show, just like everyone else.

If anyone could ever figure out a way to replicate and bottle the exact formula that has consistently driven Doors fans into a frenzy over the years, they would be gloriously wealthy and horrifically dangerous. Whether it was the combination of chords we used, or the lyrical imagery we brought to life, or Jim Morrison haunting them in person or in spirit, I'll never know. But whenever the lights are low and the music of the Doors starts to play, something always stirs.

The chairs at the Singer Bowl. In memoriam.

GUITARRAS RAMÍREZ

I try to make time every day to play at least one of my 1963 José Ramírez III acoustic guitars. Since 1882, the Ramírez family from Madrid has been making guitars known around the world for their craftsmanship, power, and tone. One of José's models can even be found in the collection of the Metropolitan Museum of Art. During my final year at Menlo my dad was heading to Spain on business, so I begged him to find the Ramírez shop and bring me back a souvenir. My dad came back with not one but three guitars from José's shop: two flamenco, one classical. I don't know how he managed to get them all back to the States while juggling the rest of his luggage, but my appreciation for the depth of that gesture was matched only by my love for how rich the guitars sounded. My dad paid a few hundred dollars for them. They're worth thousands today, but I could never sell them. Good guitars are meant to be played.

My dad didn't always embrace my musical hobby so thoughtfully. He originally agreed with the legal advice I was given after my first arrest: "Stop hanging around with musicians." When he saw me applying to colleges, he must've thought he had set me on the straight and narrow. But in truth, the only reason I wanted to go to college was so I could major in Not Joining The Army. By the summer of 1964, JFK was dead, LBJ was gradually sending more and more troops to Vietnam, and I was at a ripe age for the draft. Menlo was a preparatory school for Stanford University, but my grades weren't good enough to get in, so I got my first draft deferment by joining Bill Wolff at UC Santa Barbara instead. Wolff had actually been accepted to Stanford, but he chose UCSB because he thought his college days would be better spent surfing and chasing girls than working hard. I couldn't argue with his logic.

I took mathematics classes because, well, I had to take something, and I knew it would make my dad happy. Despite my resistance toward Menlo, I was glad I had ended up there because it exposed me to so much new music, and despite my apathy toward college, I was glad I ended up at UCSB because it exposed me to a community of musicians. By that point I was good enough to offer other students guitar lessons, and I took more flamenco classes from fellow student (and future famous playwright) Frank Chin. The student union building always had a guitarist or two jamming in one corner or another, so I'd occasionally join in. I met one of the DJs from the campus radio station and he invited me to perform in the studio a few times. And there were open mic nights at a dive called the Red Rutabaga in nearby Isla Vista where I could strap on a harmonica holder, don a work shirt and jeans, and do my best Bob Dylan impression, or where Bill Wolff and I could play blues covers on guitar with our friend Bob Cranson accompanying us on harmonica.

Other than Dylan, two of my biggest influences at the time were the Paul Butterfield Blues Band and Koerner, Ray & Glover, so their songs were the ones I covered the most. Paul Butterfield was an electric Chicago blues outfit, and their guitarist, Mike Bloomfield, had a way of making his guitar sing with a loud sustain that bordered on psychedelic. Koerner, Ray & Glover played a blend of folk and blues that was surprisingly soulful for a bunch of white boys, and John Koerner played a seven-string guitar with a distinctive jangly sound. Later on when I joined the Doors, I, ahem, "borrowed" Mike Bloomfield's riff from the song "Mellow Down Easy" for "Break On Through," and I even more shamelessly borrowed a riff from an obscure John Koerner song called "Southbound Train" for "Love Me Two Times." Years later I met John Koerner and pointed out the similarity between our riffs, but he said he hadn't noticed, so I guess I stole it the right way.

Folk. Blues. Flamenco. Jug bands. Never rock 'n' roll, though. It was too simple. Too easy. Sure, I loved Elvis as a kid. And before that I used to ride my bike to the Santa Monica Boys Club and plunk nickel after nickel into the jukebox to listen to "Rock Around the Clock." In junior high I was even the president of our school's Little Richard fan club. But by the time the early Beatles and Beach Boys stuff popped up, I had become a snob. My musical education at Menlo and UCSB had me turning up my nose at the electric guitar. That all changed on the night of February 26, 1965.

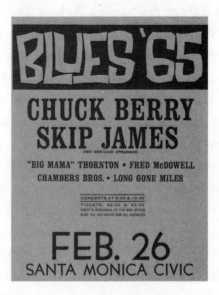

Chuck Berry was headlining a show called Blues '65 at the Santa Monica Civic Auditorium, and Wolff convinced me to go. I only agreed because Delta blues legend Skip James was on the bill, along with the Chambers Brothers and Big Mama Thornton. I had heard some of Chuck's songs and they were fine—they just didn't excite me. But when he took the stage, those songs took on a new dimension. Part of it was probably due to the Acapulco gold we were smoking. But part of it was the undeniable magic of 1965 Chuck Berry. This was before the days when he turned cynical and punched a clock onstage. This was the duck-walking, fast-talking Chuck Berry who inspired so many other rock guitarists before me. The energy he had, the excitement he generated in the crowd…it all seemed to stem from something most of my folk, blues, flamenco, and jug band heroes lacked: a Gibson ES-335 electric guitar.

The next day I took my first Mexican acoustic guitar down to the Ace Loans pawnshop in Santa Monica to trade it in for a cherry-red Gibson ES-335. That's what Chuck used, so that's what I would be using from then on. But it was way out of my price range. The pawnshop guy offered me the entry-level Gibson SG Special instead. I didn't want to leave empty-handed. At least it was a Gibson. And at least it was red.

The act of literally trading acoustic for electric was a major turning point in my life, but the months that followed held two more turning points that were equally significant. The first was trying psychedelics for the first time. The second was reconnecting with my old high school friend John Densmore.

John was a year ahead of me at University ("Uni") High School when I was a freshman, so I didn't know him all that well. Then I transferred to Palisades ("Pali") High School in my sophomore year, and Menlo after that. But John and I were connected through a mutual friend named Bob Brunner, who was in my class at Uni and in the school jazz band with John. Another mutual friend,

Grant Johnson (who would later go on to record with Gene Vincent and Jackson Browne), was a brilliant keyboard player who had been raised on music lessons from his mom, a professional cellist. Grant's mom's friends were all top-notch jazz players, and they would gather at Grant's house to jam. John and I got to know each other from hanging out at Grant's house and marveling at all the musical skill on display, but our one-year age gap kept us from growing too close, and he was way more into jazz than I was. I never envisioned us playing in a band together.

I don't remember how John and I ended up running into each other again when I was home from UCSB, but he and I and Bob and Grant and Wolff formed a small circle of friends who would get stoned and frequent jazz clubs around L.A. We spent quite a few nights at Donte's in North Hollywood, or Shelly's Manne-Hole, owned by drummer Shelly Manne, and we saw greats like Mingus, Wes Montgomery, and Rahsaan Roland Kirk, a blind multi-instrumentalist who played three saxophones at once.

It wasn't long before Grant suggested we start our own band: the Psychedelic Rangers. Bob played bass, Grant played piano, John obviously played drums, and Wolff and I played guitar. It's kind of a stretch to call it a band; it was really just an excuse to jam and drop acid. We never played any gigs and the only song we had was called "Paranoia," which was written by Grant and based on my fear of being busted for dope after my previous drug arrests:

> You walk out the door and you turn out the lights
> Your hands are twitching and your head feels light
> Oh, the lights on that car seem a little too bright
> Don't they?
> Your eyes are red and your skin is white
> And that black-and-white fever has got you uptight
> Paranoia!

In the summer of '65, Wolff and I decided we'd ditch UCSB and enroll at UCLA instead. I felt like I had already gotten everything I could out of the Santa Barbara music scene. So much more was happening in L.A. And math is math: did it really matter where I was taking those classes?

Wolff and I ended up playing guitar in another band, the Clouds, which was a return to our folk roots. The brains of the operation was singer-guitarist (and occasional *Leave It to Beaver* actor) David Kent, who wrote all our songs and copied Bob Dylan much more successfully than I did. David was older than me and Wolff, so he tended to boss us around, but he was actually a pretty talented songwriter. The only lyrics I remember, though, were from a song called "Praying Mantis Mother," which went something like, "Oh you praying mantis mother with your wings of silver silk / Trying to feed your babies but you used up all your milk." The Clouds recorded a few songs at Gold Star Studios in Hollywood, just like Ritchie Valens, the Ronettes, and the Righteous Brothers before us, and the Beach Boys, the Ramones, and Charles Manson after us. But our demo never attracted any interest from labels, and I don't think we ever even played a gig. Meanwhile, John had joined the Doors and was recruiting Wolff and me to audition for their vacant guitar slot. The Clouds — as clouds always do — slowly dissipated.

Once I joined the Doors it became harder and harder to pretend to care about college. I was taking psychology classes but had no intention of ever becoming a psychologist. I was taking calculus classes but had no intention of ever becoming a... person who gets paid to do calculus. The only thing I paid attention to was my Indian music class because I intended to be a musician. After I'd skipped out on almost an entire semester of calculus, the professor said he would have to fail me for lack of attendance. I pleaded and bargained with him and got him to agree that if I got at least an A minus on the final exam, he would give me a C for the semester. For two days straight I stayed up studying on Methedrine, a then-legal version of crank in the form of easy-to-swallow tablets. And I aced that fucking test.

Soon after, though, I got my second draft deferment, and UCLA never heard from me again. I never told my parents that I dropped out, but by the time they figured it out, the Doors had a gold record, so they didn't make much of a fuss.

As I navigated the path from aimless mathematics major to professional musician, the red Gibson SG Special I had bought at Ace Loans was always by my side. It's the guitar I used in my very first band, the guitar that got me into the Doors, the guitar I used at all our early live shows, the guitar that helped me write "Light My Fire," and the guitar I played on most of the songs on the first two Doors albums. It helped set me on the course my life was meant to take.

It was stolen from the Doors office a few years later.

There are no distinctive markings on it, so it would be impossible to track it down or even recognize it. And why would I ever write down the serial number from a cheap pawnshop guitar? If it's still out there somewhere, I'm sure the person who has it has no clue they're in possession of one of the most significant artifacts of my entire life. But I've honestly never really lamented its loss beyond the minor hassle of going out and buying another SG.

It served its purpose. The object doesn't matter. The music does. I just hope whoever has it still plays it from time to time.

THREE WORDS

A devout Buddhist once approached me, positive that he had deci-phered the secret meaning behind "Light My Fire":

"It's the fire that burns in your third eye."

I said, "You're right, man."

Jim always told me not to tell people the meaning behind my lyrics. "Let them interpret it. Sometimes they'll come up with a better idea than you had." The third eye concept wasn't what I intended, but it's my favorite interpretation so far.

When the Doors first started, we only had a few songs from the original demo and a few others we were working on. Our live set was mostly rounded out with covers: "Gloria" by Them, "Don't Fight It" by Wilson Pickett, and our own version of John Hammond Jr.'s version of Willie Dixon's "Back Door Man." Jim encour-aged the rest of us to bring in some lyrics because we didn't have enough original material, and he didn't want the sole responsibility for songwriting on his shoulders. This is a crucial detail about Jim Morrison that often gets lost in discussions about our band. Many people think of Jim as an auteur who came in with fully formed ideas and fearlessly captained the creative process. I don't want to take one shred of credit away from Jim's massive contributions; I want to give him additional credit for being a true collaborator. He never let his ego claim the territory of Main Songwriter. He was never so precious with his words that we couldn't offer lyrical input, and we enthusiastically welcomed his invaluable ideas for musical hooks and melodies. On the majority of our albums the songwriting is credited to "the Doors" rather than any of us as individuals. That was Jim's idea, long before any of our singles made a splash. Even though he likely stood to make more money by crediting himself as the main lyricist, he thought it was important that we remain united and not squabble over the genetic makeup of every single song. Even on later albums where songwriting credits are listed individually, we still split the money evenly among all four of us. Jim always wanted what was best for the Doors as a whole.

When Jim tasked us all with bringing in original material, though, I was the only one who gave it a shot. Jim always talked about using "universal" themes in his lyrics that would stand the test of time, and speak to people of the past, present, and future equally. It occurred to me that there was nothing more universal than the four elements: earth, air, water...

Fire.

There it was. The element that could warm you or burn you. The stuff of ancient Greek myths. A metaphor for love and lust, or a sly reference to lighting a joint. The Rolling Stones had previously cracked the Billboard top one hundred with a song I liked called "Play with Fire," so I figured I was on the right track. I sat in my room strumming my Gibson SG Special with the Stones song on in the background and tossed around phrases until finally it clicked.

Light My Fire.

I was still gathering my lyrical confidence, so I only managed to put together a verse and a chorus. Musically, though, I wanted to show off a little. Standard rock songs generally used only three chords. I decided I would try to use every chord I knew. I started off with G, D, F, B flat, E flat, A flat, and A, but I worried about going overboard, especially with the flat chords that were so rarely used in rock 'n' roll. I pared down the verse to something simpler: A sus 2 to F sharp minor, and back again. (Everyone who covers the song always plays some form of an A minor instead of that A sus 2 because Ray's organ part fills in the notes I'm not playing and creates an aural illusion. A small but perfect example of why the Doors worked best as an ensemble.) I kept the chorus simple, too, using a classic G, A, D progression. But I couldn't resist throwing in a B7 and an E7 to at least keep it interesting.

The next day I sang and played my new song for the band. Jim came up with the second verse about the funeral pyre. I poked fun at him for always wanting to write about death and funerals, but Ray loved it: "It's cool! It covers the whole spectrum of getting higher and going lower!" Jim's other stroke of genius was changing the last line of the chorus. Originally it was just the phrase "Come on baby, light my fire" three times in a row, but Jim suggested a simple but effective change: "Try to set the night on fire."

While I had originally written the tune with a folk sensibility, John gave the song much-needed dynamics, with a Latin-inspired rhythm that built a sultry mood during the verse and offered rock 'n' roll release during the chorus. Later he would put a rim shot crack at the beginning, starting the song on the four rather than the one, which was another simple but essential contribution.

As Ray and I struggled with a way to get from the solo back to the verse, I took the opportunity to throw in all the original chords I had been so worried about. Even those poor, overlooked flats. The whole composition ended up unintentionally walking a wobbly line between what's technically called a circle of fifths and a circle of fourths. It was a rarity at the time to construct a pop song that way.

The end result sounds deceptively simple, but when you include the A minor 7 and B minor 7 that form the bedrock of the solo section, it adds up to a total of thirteen unique chords. I'm glad I didn't know more about music theory at the time; otherwise I might not have had the guts to break the rules.

Ray's famous organ intro was the final piece of the puzzle, but originally it wasn't an intro at all. It was part of the transition from the solo to the verse. While Oliver Stone's movie *The Doors* shows Ray creating it in a matter of minutes, he actually spent months gradually perfecting the version you now hear on the record. And it was our producer, Paul Rothchild, who had the vision to suggest that we use that transitional part as both an intro and an outro. If you listen to our live recordings from the Matrix in San Francisco, you can hear the original arrangement and you can wonder, like I do sometimes, how different life would've been for the Doors if Paul hadn't made that formative suggestion, or if Ray's mom hadn't forced him to take all those classical piano lessons before going out to play basketball.

The solo section of the song evolved on its own as we played it live and engaged in free-form jazz experimentation to fill out our early sets. We all idolized John Coltrane as the ultimate musician. Whatever the chords were at the foundation of a song, Coltrane could play any note at any time at any speed over them and make it sound right. He wasn't bound by scales or modes. He found freedom between the staves. So we used his version of "My Favorite Things" as a jumping-off point and tried to see how far out we could go before getting lost. Since I could never hope to come close to Coltrane's abilities, I hedged my bets by taking influences from Indian music as well. Nearly every night I would fall asleep listening to Ravi Shankar's *In London* album. I burned his long ragas into my brain and infused our jazz solos with Indian scales and licks.

Some nights our experiments were more successful than others, but the solo section is what allowed the song to live beyond what you hear on the record. It's impossible to calculate how many times I've performed "Light My Fire" both during and since my time with the Doors, but I've never played the same solo twice. Anyone who has ever heard the song live has experienced their own unique version of it, created by the specific chemistry of the musicians onstage and shaped uniquely by the moment.

Once "Light My Fire" was released into the world, it became an entity. A year after our version hit the charts, a blind guitarist I had never heard of named José Feliciano released a classical acoustic cover. It became his highest-charting song in the United States, and it charted even higher than our version in several countries. I didn't like José's version at first. It lacked Ray's trademark organ intro and Jim's trademark howl. It was more easy listening than rock 'n' roll. But the closer I listened to it, the more I appreciated his masterful playing, and I've come to truly love it over the years.

The success of José's version on the heels of the success of our version turned "Light My Fire" into a "standard," which is when a song becomes so widespread that it's part of an unofficial songbook that all musicians are expected to know. Its pervasiveness really hit me when, at some point in the seventies, I was riding an elevator in an office building and a Muzak version of the song came through the speakers. I remember thinking, "Oh shit. We made it to the elevator." It has been heartening, though, to hear "Light My Fire" covered by dozens of artists over the years, across a vast array of genres. Stevie Wonder, Al Green, Etta James, Johnny Mathis, Booker T. & the MGs, Nigel Kennedy and the Prague Symphony Orchestra, Minnie Riperton, Alicia Keys, Shirley Bassey, UB40, Isaac Hayes, Massive Attack, Nancy Sinatra, Nina Hagen, Jackie Wilson, the Ventures, the Guess Who, Martha and the Vandellas,

Boots Randolph, Mae West, Rick Moranis, the Beastie Boys, and—fittingly—Ananda Shankar (Ravi's nephew)...all of them found interesting and creative ways to make the song their own.

As a result, "Light My Fire" has become more financially valuable than all the other songs the Doors ever wrote. Combined. Do I ever regret not taking sole songwriting credit? Not for a minute. Well...I suppose we all have those dark and greedy minutes sometimes, right? But even though it's technically considered "my" song, it's indisputable that without Ray, Jim, John, and Paul Rothchild giving it lift, it never would've made it into orbit. And considering what money can do to a young band, Jim's suggestion of an equal split likely saved us from an early, greed-based breakup. It was, in the end, what was best for the Doors.

In the late eighties I was finally introduced to José Feliciano backstage at a taping of *The Pat Sajak Show*. I said, "Thanks for doing my song."

He replied, "Thanks for writing it."

"Why don't you do another one of our songs?" I joked. "How about 'Touch Me'?"

In response, he grabbed his guitar and effortlessly belted out a perfect, graceful, Latin arrangement of "Touch Me." It turned out he was planning to record a cover of the song at some point, but for one reason or another it unfortunately never happened. Apparently he was a much bigger Doors fan than I realized.

No matter how long you live or what path you've chosen, life will always surprise you. I never could've envisioned the journey my song would take when I first sat down in my room to answer Jim's songwriting challenge. And I still marvel at something Paul Rothchild pointed out about it: so many of the cover versions don't bother with the organ intro or the solo or any of the other elements that made up the original. They all survive off the strength of three simple words: "light," "my," and "fire." It's almost impossible to believe that somehow, in the entire history of music, no one had thought to put those three particular words together until a twenty-year-old kid from Pacific Palisades stumbled onto the idea. It's a constant reminder that music is infinite and there is always something new to discover. There are three words out there right now just dying to be strung together into a brand-new phrase for a brand-new song. There is freedom to be found between the staves. Pick up an instrument. Find your three words.

The Doors at the London Fog

BETWEEN CLARK AND HILLDALE

The first show I remember playing with the Doors was in a massive airplane hangar full of well-dressed, middle-aged couples who worked for the Hughes Aircraft Company, but I was in a haze of Methedrine, so most of the details escape me. Ray's dad worked for Hughes, so he got us a gig performing a set of mostly jazz standards for some sort of annual company party. The stiff atmosphere, the cavernous venue, and the fact that it was our first official show must've been weighing on our nerves because Jim and I both took a bunch of my study aid pills to get through it. Ray tried to cope by dropping a huge dose of acid, but it backfired and he nearly forgot how to play. We had brought in a bass player to fill out our sound, but he had broken at least two of his strings and couldn't afford to replace them, so he really had only half a bass. I don't remember the set, I don't remember what we played or how we sounded, I don't even remember the bass player's name. But we survived.

Our second show was at UCLA's famous Royce Hall, which is an eighteen-hundred-seat venue that bands usually play after they're much more established. Ray had recruited us to provide musical accompaniment for his entry in the UCLA student film showcase. I had my Ramírez acoustic, Ray had a melodica, and I think John and Jim had tambourines and maracas. It was a purely instrumental performance; we all just stood onstage and improvised sounds as we watched the film. It barely qualifies as a Doors show, but it was interesting to see how confident Ray could be when he wasn't under the microscope of his dad's colleagues. Most of the students introduced their films by standing up and meekly saying a few words. When Ray stood up, it was a show. He spoke boldly and held the crowd in the palm of his hand. It was the first time I got a sense of Ray's flair for the dramatic. After all, he was the only student who went so far as to bring in musicians to create a live film score.

In most film footage of the Doors, Ray is hunched over his keyboard, playing an unassuming, supporting role. That's not because Ray scorned attention. It's because he was smart enough to never take the spotlight off Jim. At our early practices and shows, Ray would sing along with Jim to help bolster his confidence. But once Jim grew into his role, Ray instinctively backed off so the audience would give Jim their complete focus. It's rarely talked about, but Ray was a natural-born showman. And his knack for stirring drama would serve the Doors' legacy well in later years.

Our third show can be credited to my parents. Some friends of theirs, Al and Nancy Isaacson, were having a New Year's Eve cocktail party and my mom recommended us as the entertainment. We set up in the backyard and played a mix of covers and originals. Even though it was another audience of square grown-ups, they actually seemed to dig us. It was beyond the polite applause we had gotten from the Hughes Aircraft workers; we played "Louie Louie" and "Moonlight Drive," and they got down! We made my parents look good in front of their friends, which is probably one of the reasons they forever held on to a high opinion of Jim, regardless of what they'd later hear about his behavior. A girl at the party named Andrea—a friend of the Isaacsons' daughter—seemed to dig us the most, though. She was a hippie before hippies became commonplace. Jim tried to impress her by flipping a quarter in the air and swallowing it. I don't know if it worked out for him, but it was certainly one of the most original pickup attempts I've ever seen.

A few months later, my parents would make one more historic contribution to the band. We had been having trouble finding a bassist we could work with, and we liked the dynamic we were creating as a foursome, so Ray suggested he could fill out the low end of our sound with a Fender Rhodes piano bass. It was a pricey item. But since I was the kid from the Palisades, I asked my dad to give the band a loan. He made a big deal about how he expected us to pay him back in full, but he let us borrow the money. The tone of the Fender Rhodes became a defining element of the Doors' sound, and it shaped the way our songs were written. Since Ray's left hand had to be on autopilot while his right hand played more complex melodies, he wrote bass lines that tended to be simple and repetitive. Those low notes droning in loops underneath the other instruments made our songs subtly hypnotic. We usually dubbed in a traditional bass guitar on our albums, but when we were writing and rehearsing and performing live, the bass lines all came from Ray's left hand on that sinister Fender Rhodes.

In the end, my dad never asked us to pay back the loan. Our band, and our fans, will always owe him.

Like any band, we took whatever gigs we could get in those days. Lewis Beach Marvin III—a wealthy animal rights activist who was the head of the Moon Fire Temple and was always surrounded by a harem of younger hippie girls—hired us to play at an outdoor party at his communal ranch, and at an anti-war event at Will Rogers State Historic Park. And a friend who had a connection with the

Ford Motor Company hired us to provide an improvised instrumental soundtrack for one of their sales training films, which had the sublime title *Love Thy Customer*.

John and I were assigned to hunt down better gigs. We hit up every sleazy venue in Hollywood, some of them more than once, but no one was interested. I wasn't even allowed inside a few places because I was still below drinking age. When we walked into a bar on Sunset called the London Fog, we were expecting yet another rejection. It was formerly called Jesse James's Opera House, but they changed the name and tossed some pictures of British bands on the wall in a transparent attempt to capitalize on the hip factor of England at the time. The bar was sparsely furnished with a few tables and barstools, a go-go cage, mirrored walls, and a tall but cramped stage near the entrance. The staff was limited to a couple of waitresses and the lovely Rhonda Layne, a slightly overweight go-go dancer with frizzy blond hair. The depressing lack of patrons was immediately noticeable and was probably why I was never asked for proof of my age. The Fog wasn't anything like the always-packed, scene-making Whisky a Go Go just half a block down the street, but it wasn't the worst place John and I had found on our gig quest. It was, at the very least, a place to start.

I would estimate that the owner and bartender, Jesse James, was about forty years old at the time, but then again, when you're twenty, everyone older than you seems forty. He was tall, blond, snappily dressed, and most likely gay (but of course he couldn't be out at the time, even in Hollywood). We approached him with a copy of the first demo, lied straight to his face that we were still signed to Columbia Records, and asked for a gig.

He didn't say no.

We happened to walk into the London Fog at the exact right moment. Had we handed the demo to Jesse James a few months earlier, he might not have been desperate enough to give us a shot. Had we started our band a few months later, the bar would have already gone out of business. There was no other band onstage when we stopped in. No one else was begging Jesse to play the Fog. He had nothing to lose. So he gave the Doors their shot: a single weeknight gig.

John and I put the word out to every friend we had, and Ray and Jim rounded up practically the entire UCLA film school. For the first time ever, the London Fog was packed from wall to mirrored wall with a young, rowdy crowd thirsty for a good time. Jesse had never sold that much beer in his life. With dollar signs in his eyes, he immediately hired us as the house band.

When we showed up to play the next night, it was just us, Jesse, the waitresses, and the lovely Rhonda Layne.

We acted surprised, but soon enough Jesse accepted that the full house was a fluke. He said, "I don't give a shit. Just keep playing real loud. Someone will come in." For the next two months we played real loud six nights a week, four sets a night, for five bucks each. It wasn't the most lucrative gig, but it was a priceless opportunity. With no one watching, we could play whatever we wanted. With so much time to kill, we could work out new songs and improvise instrumentally. It gave us the freedom to jam and the discipline to rehearse. It fostered our chemistry, both musically and personally. Every band should be lucky enough to have a London Fog. The first Doors album was written in that bar as much as it was written in our practice space or in Jim's head or in my parents' living room.

In Oliver Stone's *The Doors,* the London Fog is depicted as a happening place filled to capacity with a line out the door and people begging to get in to see us.

Nope.

We gradually gained a few fans along the way, but I don't think we ever had a crowd of more than a dozen people during our residency. But again, this was a gift more than a hardship. Jim Morrison wasn't hatched into this world a perfect front man. As shy as he had been at our practices, he was even more introverted onstage. The rest of us weren't exactly seasoned professionals, but we had at least all been in bands before. Jim's only experience onstage before the Doors was drunkenly stumbling through "Louie Louie" with Ray's previous band, Rick and the Ravens, at a UCLA hangout called the Turkey Joint West. Taking his own lyrics out of his poetry books and sharing them with the world was a much more harrowing prospect. He needed time to find his voice, both literally and figuratively. The Fog is where Jim abandoned the lightweight head voice he used on the original demo and built up the full-chested howl he became known for. By the end of our run, Ray didn't need to prop him up with excessive backing vocals anymore. Jim could fly on his own.

Young musicians sometimes complain about paying their dues. Pay them. They will, eventually, pay you back. You need to play the backyard parties and the empty dives just as much as you need to rehearse and write good songs. The first night at the Fog when our friends packed the place? That was an illusion. If you want to create something that will last, you have to earn your fans one by one.

When we were ready for the next step, the next step found us. In the form of a bold young woman named Ronnie Haran.

Ronnie was the booker at the Whisky a Go Go, which had opened just two years earlier and had seamlessly transitioned from the most popular dance club on the Sunset Strip to one of the most famous rock clubs in the entire world. Ronnie was a straight-up New Yorker: all business, take-no-prisoners. She had been to see us once or twice before but was understandably unimpressed. Word had been growing about Jim's performances, though, so she came by the Fog one more time. She brought British guitarist Peter Asher with her, which made us even more impressed with her clout. According to her version of events, I was the one she approached about playing at the Whisky, and I replied coolly with something like "We'll get back to you." On one hand, it's strange to think she'd approach me, the guy with the least seniority in the band. On the other hand, I had been unofficially appointed as the band's business manager, collecting and distributing our gig payments and dealing with the promoters. The band's logic was probably, "Let the rich kid deal with the money: he must know something about it we don't." I don't remember balking at Ronnie's offer, but if I did, it wasn't because I was playing a clever game of hard to get. It was because I honestly didn't know if we were ready.

As much as our timing was lucky for getting the Fog gig, the timing of Ronnie's offer was even more fortunate, considering that Jesse James fired us the same night. Had Ronnie waited even one more week to come see us, she would've walked up to a permanently closed club, the Doors would've missed their shot, and we would've had to establish ourselves all over again somewhere else.

The Whisky was owned by a former Chicago cop named Elmer Valentine and a professional gambler named Phil Tanzini, and it was managed by one of Elmer's Chicago buddies, Mario Maglieri. There were rumors about their Mob connections, and Elmer later opened up to the press about how he used to collect payoffs and was once indicted for extortion, but we never saw that side of them. They didn't muscle us around or wear pinstripe suits. They were lovable guys who dressed like ex-cops trying to blend in with hippies. I don't know if we were their cup of tea, but Ronnie lobbied hard for us and we soon became the house band. Step one was joining the musicians' union: instead of the five bucks a night we had been making at the Fog, we were making a standard rate of eighty dollars a night, each. It was enough for me to move out of my parents' house, but more importantly, it was enough for us to hold our heads up high and call ourselves professional musicians.

Throughout the summer of 1966, we made the Whisky our home, playing two sets a night and opening for all the touring acts and headliners. We were playing live so much we didn't have any more need (or spare time) to rehearse. And we were getting a master class in stagecraft from watching incredible bands like Buffalo Springfield, the Turtles, the Chambers Brothers, Captain Beefheart, and Love. Van Morrison's band, Them, played a two-week run with us, and at the end we joined them onstage for a twenty-minute version of their song "Gloria," which to me is one of the greatest rock songs ever written. It was a cover we played from the very beginning, and it's something I still include in my solo sets today. The two Morrisons, Van and Jim, had startlingly similar personalities: quiet and introverted one minute, loud and extroverted the next. I can't pinpoint an exact moment when Jim's true confidence as a performer took hold, but playing alongside Van definitely seemed to have an effect on him.

Whether it was Captain Beefheart's acid-drenched unpredictability or Van Morrison's propensity for smashing mic stands or the Chambers Brothers' taut musicianship or Love's sense of style, we absorbed ingredients from each band. But mainly we learned to be ourselves. Our goal every night was to blow away every other band on the bill, but even though there was competition, there was never any rivalry. Since our sound was so different, no one ever thought of us as a threat, even if we sometimes got more applause. We never consciously discussed it at the time, but subliminally we were learning that our greatest asset was our individuality.

The irony is that I, personally, was actually trying my best to sound like everyone else...and failing. Unlike Ray, I wasn't a technical player, but I was foolishly ambitious. By punching above my weight class in terms of musical ability and haphazardly incorporating my unorthodox influences into a rock context, I stumbled assbackward into a unique style. It wasn't a conscious effort to sound different. I was just too lazy to properly learn how to sound the same.

Thanks to that spring at the Fog and that summer at the Whisky, we improved individually and as a group, but Jim's transformation was the most noticeable, and the most crucial. He didn't exactly conquer his shyness, but night after night, set after set, it weighed him down less and less. He let himself be himself. When you went to see a Doors show, you saw the real Jim Morrison. There was no difference between Jim on- or offstage. There is a long list of iconic singers throughout the history of rock 'n' roll, but almost all of them were putting on a show. A great show! But a show all the same. Mick Jagger is a consummate performer and has rocked audiences around the globe. But when he walks offstage, you won't see him pursing his lips and strutting around like a chicken. Elvis was one of the greatest entertainers of all time and one of Jim's biggest influences, but he didn't wear those rhinestone jumpsuits around the house. Chuck Berry changed my life with his energetic stage presence, but the duck walk would've been an inefficient way to get around. I'm pretty sure Iggy Pop doesn't roll around on glass in between trips to the supermarket, I doubt Jimi Hendrix ever set his guitar on fire just to keep warm, and I've played golf with Alice

Cooper dozens of times and he's never once showed up at the course caked in horror makeup. I don't mean to diminish or insult any of those guys. They are absolute masters of their craft and they put their entire souls into their performances.

But the magic of Jim is that Jim was just…Jim.

The audience may not have known Jim personally, but on some level they could sense that he was being genuine. People have attempted to analyze Jim Morrison's appeal over the years and have found it impossible to truly pin down. It's something even I still struggle with. But I think it lies in the way he offered himself up with complete, unflinching honesty. You didn't know what he was going to do next onstage, just like you didn't know what he was going to do next in real life, and you were always on the edge of your seat waiting to find out. Even if you were in the same band with him. It may have occasionally made him a challenge to deal with, and it may have made the practicalities of planning a career more difficult, but it drew you in. It couldn't have been simpler, and yet it couldn't have been more powerful. And it's why he's still drawing people in to this day.

UNKNOWN SOLDIERS

When you're of draft age, and your friends are all of draft age, and there's a military draft in effect, it permeates every conversation and always weighs on you. The dead soldiers on the news aren't statistics. They may as well be your neighbor or your cousin or the kid you always played basketball with.

Or you.

Thankfully I didn't lose any close friends or family in the Vietnam War, but a classmate from Menlo named Jim Odriozola went over there and was hit with Agent Orange. He's battled cancer ever since. Another friend from Menlo, Phil Lehman, also served and thankfully survived intact, but he never wanted to speak about what went on over there. I didn't need the details: I knew I never wanted to go.

I wasn't alone. No one I knew gave any credibility to the idea that Communism was coming from Vietnam to destroy America. There was no shame in avoiding such an obviously unjust war. Thousands of people were fleeing to Canada, inventing fake medical conditions, calling in political favors, taking calculus at UCLA...Maybe if you're having that hard a time getting people to agree to fight, you shouldn't be fighting in the first place.

Just as the Doors were gaining steam at the Whisky, John, Jim, and I all got our draft notices. Ray was the only member of the band who could breathe easy. He was several years older than the rest of us, and after college he had enlisted in the army. He was stationed in Thailand and Japan for a couple of years, but when he realized he'd rather be studying film at UCLA, he convinced the military that he was gay. It was a bold move. There was a reason every draftee didn't immediately claim he was gay for a quick dismissal. Homosexuality was literally illegal. Even if you avoided arrest, your discharge paperwork would follow you and prevent you from getting hired at any "respectable" company. Ray must've known he'd never have a straight job: otherwise he never would have pretended not to be straight.

John tried to act crazy at his induction appointment but it didn't work, so he also resorted to saying he was gay, but it only got him a 1-Y classification, which meant he had to report back a year later. Luckily there was so much bureaucracy that he never got a second notice, but he spent a long time waiting for that other shoe to drop. The goal was 4-F: registrant not qualified for military service. But as long as you had life and limbs left to lose, the military generally considered you qualified.

I reported for my draft physical and gave Uncle Sam a sample of my urine and blood. Then, reminiscent of the time I was in jail, they lined us up naked and had us bend over. My student status at UCSB had gotten me a deferment earlier, and this time, thanks to my enrollment at UCLA, I got a 1-Y, just like John. It wasn't ideal, but it bought the Doors some time. A lot can happen in a year. Maybe the war would be over by then?

John and I took Jim to the induction center for his appointment and waited patiently outside. He wore his favorite green welder's jacket, down the spine of which he had sewn a patch of lizard skin.

Since neither John nor I had gotten lucky with a 4-F, we asked Jim what his plan was.

"Don't worry. I got it figured out."

John and I were definitely worried. Jim's appointment seemed to take forever. We didn't remember our own physicals taking that long. When Jim finally emerged, John turned to me and said, "What do you think? He doesn't look happy."

I said, "You never know what he's thinking."

Jim strolled over to us and we asked him what had happened. He said, "I got a Z."

There is no such thing as classification Z. John asked Jim what that meant. Jim said, "I think it means I'm free. Anyway, I'm not hanging around to find out. Let's get out of here."

Jim never told us what his actual draft status was, or what had gone on inside that induction center. Whatever happened, the military never sought out Jim Morrison again.

All was quiet until the spring of 1968, when the Doors were at the peak of their popularity. We were about to release our third album, we had multiple hit singles on the charts, and we were headlining arena shows around the country. That's when the government decided my 1-Y was up and sent me another draft notice.

More than half a million soldiers had been sent to Vietnam, over thirty-five thousand of them had died, and tens of thousands of others had been horribly wounded. Many more would follow. It didn't matter that I was successfully living my dream. The war was hungry and it demanded to be fed.

Bill Siddons recommended a lawyer who specialized in helping people get out of the draft. The lawyer referred me to a psychologist, Dr. Isidore Ziferstein, who was so vehemently opposed to the war that he was one of the speakers at the massive UC Berkeley Vietnam teach-in, alongside Dr. Benjamin Spock, Norman Mailer, Alan Watts, Paul Krassner, and Dick Gregory. At the time I was chasing after a girl named Lynn (who I would later marry). She was living on Horse Shoe Canyon Road, which was lined with houses full of musicians. Everyone at her house was constantly stoned, jamming, and partying. Lynn also had a bunch of gay friends. One of them, a three-hundred-pound bear who went by the name Boom Boom, had a major crush on me. I told Dr. Ziferstein all about the crazy characters and the debauched parties and Boom Boom, and he said, "That's perfect!" He wrote up a letter detailing my experiences and promised it would help.

The lawyer who had gotten me the appointment with Dr. Ziferstein recommended that I do my induction outside California, since the growing anti-war movement had numbed the California draft boards to excuses. I told him my uncle Sonny worked as a dermatologist in Scottsdale, Arizona, so he said I should use my uncle's address on my registration and take my exam out there.

"They've never seen anyone as screwed up as you in that town."

Just nine days before the Doors were set to headline the Hollywood Bowl, I drove out to Arizona to meet my fate. My clothes were unwashed, my hair was unkempt, and right before my appointment I gulped down several tiny balls of aluminum foil (about the size of what you'd have left over after eating a Hershey's Kiss), which urban legend claimed would simulate ulcers at a routine physical. When I got to the induction office, I checked in with a no-nonsense military guy, handed him my letter from Dr. Ziferstein, and waited.

And waited.

And waited some more.

I didn't want to jinx anything, and I didn't know if they were watching me, so I just sat there for hours, bored out of my mind, worrying about what those little balls of foil might be doing to my digestive tract. Finally, when I couldn't take it anymore, I went up to the guy I had checked in with and pointed out that I hadn't been called in for my physical yet.

He said, "Are you Krieger?"

"Yeah."

He shoved a piece of paper into my hands. "Get out of here! We never want to see you again!"

I pretended to be disappointed and shuffled out of the building. I never read Dr. Ziferstein's letter—it was sealed when he gave it to me—so I'll always wonder what kind of tales he wove to provoke that kind of response. I kept up my disappointed act until I was at least a block away from the induction center and then looked down at my paperwork.

4-F: Registrant not qualified for military service.

It was, with no exaggeration, one of the happiest moments of my life. Thanks, Dr. Ziferstein. And thanks, Boom Boom.

I've since played more than a few benefits for veterans because if I had ended up in Vietnam, I'd hope someone would do the same for me. For several years my friend Scott Medlock and I hosted a charity golf tournament and concert to give scholarships to vets through the Pat Tillman Foundation. I may not agree with the idea of war itself, but I don't have anything against our soldiers. So many guys were either sent to Vietnam against their will or sold a lie by our government. I don't feel an ounce of shame for dodging the draft, but I will always have reverence for those who served. Like Jim Odriozola and Phil Lehman.

Scott Medlock and me at a Medlock-Krieger charity event

The first vet benefit I played was a star-studded event in 1986 called Welcome Home. It was held at the Forum in L.A. and was a perfect time capsule of the mid-eighties, with guests like Whoopi Goldberg, John Ritter, Kris Kristofferson, Ricardo Montalban, Catherine Bach from *The Dukes of Hazzard,* Ed Asner, Jon Voight, and *Night Court* star Markie Post. The music was provided by Stevie Wonder, Neil Young, Richie Havens, and Chris Hillman of the Byrds. I played "Roadhouse Blues" with actor Steven Bauer on vocals, and then sang "Love Me Two Times" on my own.

It was a little overwhelming, looking out at the thousands of vets who had seen unspeakable things and made unfathomable sacrifices, thinking about how different my fate could have been if I hadn't gotten that 4-F. I dedicated "Love Me Two Times" to them, explaining that I wrote it about a soldier who was trying to get some last-minute affection from his girl before shipping out to Vietnam.

That wasn't true. It was simply a song about sex. I was just caught up in the moment, wanting to make some sort of connection with the soldiers after what they had all been through. That explanation of the song has lived on since that night, though, for better or worse. It has even been perpetuated by my own bandmates. I probably should've heeded Jim's advice and left the interpretation open.

Countless veterans have approached me over the years to tell me how our music got them through Vietnam. Oliver Stone's infatuation with the Doors began when he first heard us during his tour of duty with the army. Dan Rather told me that when he was covering the war for CBS News he only ever heard two types of music over there: country and the Doors. On one hand, it's disturbing to think of our songs as the soundtrack to so much violence and bloodshed. On the other hand, we've been told repeatedly that our music helped a lot of guys through the absolute worst moments of their lives. When you're eight thousand miles from home and facedown in the mud with bullets screaming past your head, the last thing you probably want to hear is "All You Need Is Love." They were literally staring down The End. They spent every waking hour in arm's reach of The Other Side.

Some people may still have preferred it if I had picked up a rifle, but I have no regrets about picking up a guitar instead. Between all the civilians and soldiers on both sides of the Vietnam War, the tally was over 1.3 million dead. I don't know what we all gained from that. But I know for sure it represents a lot of music that the world never got to hear.

A QUEST FOR ENLIGHTENMENT: PART I

I believe there's more to this universe than what we can see or measure, but I don't think any one particular religion has ever gotten it right. My parents were both technically Jewish, but they were never big believers, and they didn't want us to be known as "that *Jewish* family" in our very WASPy Palisades neighborhood, so they never pushed religion on my brother or me. Every year we had a Christmas tree in our house, but we celebrated the holidays with a secular spirit. My dad in particular was hoping he could sneak under the radar enough to join the prestigious Los Angeles Country Club, which didn't allow Jews, but I guess they know a Jew when they see one over there: he ended up joining the Riviera Country Club instead. My brother and I attended Hebrew school for a while but we goofed around so much that we got kicked out and never had our bar mitzvahs. I popped into church services with some Catholic friends here and there, but I found it equally as boring as sitting in a synagogue. Traditional religion just seemed like something for old people.

I don't feel like I missed out on anything with my spiritually lazy upbringing, but as I grew up, I naturally wondered about life's big mysteries, and I went on my own search for answers. Unencumbered by dogma, my mind was open to Eastern philosophies by writers like Alan Watts. I wanted to explore higher states of consciousness, like the Indian concept of samadhi and the Japanese notion of satori. I was on a quest for enlightenment.

So of course I turned to drugs.

I was never much of a drinker beyond those stolen kegs in high school and a few overindulgent nights in college. It got boring pretty quickly. And watching Jim drink later erased any lingering appeal it might have had. Marijuana felt like it served more of a purpose in terms of providing a new perspective, but the legal repercussions weren't worth it. And besides, I was looking for something more.

In what could be seen as a moment of fate, I came across a book called *The Doors of Perception*. In it, Aldous Huxley details mankind's eternal search for transcendence and offers up an account of his personal experiences with mescaline. He philosophizes that the human mind has been trained to filter out true reality and that psychedelic substances have the power to remove those filters. The book repeatedly references William Blake, and Huxley adapted the book's thesis and title from a line in Blake's *The Marriage of Heaven and Hell:* "If the doors of perception were cleansed, everything would appear to man as it is: infinite."

It was pretty boring.

I figured I'd be better off doing psychedelics on my own than reading about other people doing them, so during my year at UCSB I got ahold of some real Sandoz acid imported from Switzerland. Strong stuff. I went down to the beach and saw faces and animal shapes emerging from the cliffs along the shore. But the hallucinations paled in comparison to the sense of cosmic understanding and oneness with the universe. I wanted to share my revelations with the world, so I became a proselytizer for the experience. I spread LSD around to all my friends like I was Johnny Acidseed. But then my friend Kenny took some and went on a horrible bummer.

"Do you feel samadhi? Do you feel satori?" I asked him.

"Sorta. But why do I have all these feelings of guilt about my parents?"

"Wait...that's not supposed to happen..."

Another time, I was driving around with the guys in the Psychedelic Rangers when Grant freaked out and tried to bury himself in the back seat. He was snorting like a gopher and digging at the floor of the car with his hands.

"Grant, what's wrong?"

"Don't worry about it!"

I learned that everyone is different, and what might be a good trip for one person might be a bad trip for somebody else, so I decided to stop being an off-brand Timothy Leary and dialed back my acid evangelism. In an ideal world I'd recommend that everyone try acid at least once, but these days you never know what kind of formula you're getting, and even under the best circumstances a trip can uncover deep-seated emotional problems in nightmarish ways that can leave permanent scars. I never had any horrible bummers myself, but everyone I knew had a story of a trip that went bad. Before I met my wife, Lynn, she was hanging out with her friend Peggy at the New York apartment of a guy forebodingly known as Danny Overdose. Peggy found Danny's supply of liquid Owsley acid (a particularly potent formula) and said, "Let's have a tea party!" Instead of placing a single droplet on their tongues, Peggy and Lynn filled up half a teacup each and started sipping. A normal acid trip kicks in after about a half hour; the Owsley hit them almost instantly. The people outside on the street suddenly appeared to have bizarrely long necks, and their heads were bobbing around like they were in some sort of spooky cartoon. Despite Danny coming home and trying to level them out with Seconals, they were freaking out over the idea that they'd never see normal-necked people again. Just when Lynn thought she was mellowing out, Danny went to fry up some ham, and Lynn heard the ham scream. She was inconsolable as she shouted "Oh my God! They're crying!" over the tortured squeals. Today, it's a funny story, and Lynn laughs about it, but imagine if you had to watch someone fry up some actual living pigs and you had to listen helplessly to their actual death squeals. As far as Lynn's brain on acid was concerned, those pigs were real, their screams were real, and the ensuing trauma was real. When it was all over, she swore off acid—and ham—forever.

In hopes of finding a new way to look inward, I tried an alternative to acid: morning glory seeds. I had heard that by eating the crushed seeds I could achieve a similarly psychedelic high. So off I went to my local florist.

I arranged to eat the seeds with two sisters I knew named Georgie and Josie Newton. Georgie was definitely attractive, but my sights were set on Josie, who was slightly older and slightly hotter. Both Newton sisters had long, straight, black hair and dark complexions, with sweet but quiet demeanors that were equally unsettling and alluring. Imagine Disney's version of Pocahontas if she came back as a vampire.

Josie, Georgie, and I ground up the seeds and swallowed them down. And then immediately threw them back up. But an intense high followed. The universe became crystal clear, and for some reason I started speaking in an English accent. I convinced myself I had been British in a previous life. I thought my newly posh diction would help me charm Josie, but all the vomiting kinda ruined my shot.

I had tickets to see Bob Dylan that night at the Long Beach Municipal Auditorium, so I invited Josie and Georgie to go with me. They weren't feeling up to it (again, the vomiting) so I went by myself. Dylan had "gone electric" at the Newport Folk Festival a few months before, and was touring with a full rock band backing him up. It was a controversial move, but I loved it. I was struggling with my musical identity at the time, and I saw myself in Dylan. I came from a background of acoustic folk but had just joined the Doors to play electric rock. Dylan's show that night was a revelation: I didn't need to be defined by a single style. It was a beautiful moment of clarity for me personally, but all the folk purists in the crowd were booing Bob's new sound. Maybe they needed some morning glory seeds to understand how fantastic it really was.

Jim and I did acid together a few times during my first year in the Doors, but I was always chasing that first high, when my ego was shattered into a million pieces and my entire self was redefined. Subsequent trips still showed me colors and other fun stuff but always left me feeling a little disappointed. And the more acid you do, the higher your tolerance gets. Jim claimed to have done five thousand micrograms when he went in and scuttled our Columbia deal, even though one thousand would be almost enough to drive a normal person insane. Maybe he was exaggerating or miscounting, but he did so much acid so often that he might have been able to handle a dose like that due to the tolerance he'd built up.

Or maybe it actually did drive him insane and none of us could tell the difference.

One night during our stint at the London Fog, Jim and I took out the two waitresses who worked there and he persuaded us to take acid with him. We went over to Venice Beach to gawk at the waves and drink in the moonlight. Ray had somehow talked the Doors into paying half his rent at a house in Venice, right on the sand. He and his girlfriend, Dorothy, lived there and the band rehearsed in the living room, which had huge picture windows looking out on the ocean. Jim proposed the idea of dropping in on Ray and Dorothy, but it was after 3 a.m. so I suggested it might be a little late for a social call. Jim insisted they'd be happy to see us. When we showed up on Ray's doorstep all wet, sandy, and high, he was certainly surprised, but I wouldn't say he was happy. Since we were subsidizing Ray's rent in order to use his house as a practice space, he couldn't argue with letting us in to party. He went back to bed and Jim started flipping through Ray's neatly organized record collection, pulling the discs out of their sleeves, and hurling them across the room. One classic album after another, sailing into the walls and smashing into pieces. I was deeply embarrassed by Jim's behavior, but at the same time the acid made it seem hilarious, so when Jim finally found a record he liked and cranked up the volume, we all just laughed and danced around like fools on a carpet of shattered black vinyl.

I felt horrible about it the next day, but Ray never held the incident over our heads. Everything was business as usual, no apologies necessary. Ray was paternal toward all of us since he was several years our senior—he was almost seven years older than I was—but when it came to Jim, the father-son dynamic was especially pronounced. Ray, the indulgent father, was patient, protective, and forgiving, even when Jim, the wayward son, rebelled against him. So Jim got away with smashing all those records just like he got away with everything else. But my conscience couldn't handle it the way Jim's could. I was supposed to be on a quest for enlightenment, not a crusade of destruction.

A couple of months later, Jim and I took acid together again, this time in Tempe, Arizona. It was the first time the Doors played outside California. A moment worth celebrating. But it doesn't take much to steer an acid trip into the abyss. In this case the catalyst was our opening act: an Elvis impersonator with an apparent developmental disability. I think maybe the owner knew him and generously gave him some stage time now and then. The crowd seemed to know him, too, and was supportive with their applause. In the sober light of day I probably would've thought it was all very sweet. But you can imagine how my fried brain and dilated pupils processed the whole scene.

The venue was dark and cramped, with a stiflingly low ceiling. I learned early on that one should always do psychedelics outdoors and away from crowds, in a space where nature can help you feel free. Even the tiniest sense of claustrophobia can ruin a trip. Not only did the low ceiling make me feel boxed in, but when we took the stage, it squashed our sound, and the acid mercilessly accentuated the bad acoustics. And, like Ray at the Hughes Aircraft dance, I suddenly forgot how to play.

I struggled through the set, freaking out about the loss of my musical ability, freaking out about the squashed sound pummeling my ears, freaking out about the stifling darkness, and freaking out about the haunting vision of the Elvis impersonator, all while a single thought kept circling through my mind: *This is definitely the last time I do acid.*

Ronny and me (or me and Ronny?)

RONNY

In the mid-seventies, I owned a gleaming white 1953 Buick Skylark convertible. Gorgeous curves, glistening chrome, whitewall tires, V8 engine. One of only 1,690 ever made. The quintessential classic American automobile. It turned heads wherever I went.

One day I was driving through West Hollywood with the top down. I pulled up to a stop sign on Hilldale Avenue, a side street off Santa Monica Boulevard. A guy with scraggly long hair and dark sunglasses approached the passenger side of the car while I waited to make my turn.

"You're Robby Krieger, right?"

"Yeah." I smiled, thinking he might ask for a handshake or an autograph. Instead, his voice dropped low, and he grimly intoned:

"We have to take acid together and die."

I politely replied, "Well, I'm pretty busy this week... Try me later," and quickly drove off.

When you're a member of the Doors, you collect a lot of stories about the acid casualties who cross your path. It's entertaining when you don't know the person and you can laugh off the encounter, but it cuts deeper when acid claims your own brother.

We spelled our names Robbie and Ronnie, but sometimes we'd mutually agree to switch to Robby and Ronny, or switch back, depending on our mood. My brother and I weren't identical—he had slightly darker skin and slightly lighter hair—but we came out of the same womb on the same day, and there's a closeness between twins that I doubt other siblings share. Ronny and I were both athletic and popular as kids, but we both suffered through awkward phases in our teenage years. I got fat and broke out in zits, but Ronny's problems were more emotional. He retreated into himself and became a loner. Kids have a way of sniffing out weakness, and due to the arbitrary jungle laws of adolescence, my friends picked on my brother and not me. Instead of standing by my brother's side, I let it happen. Acceptance is everything to a teenager. I wasn't willing to risk mine to help him get any. I still beat myself up over it. I would give anything to go back and act differently, now that I have more perspective. But that's not how life works.

When I was sent to Menlo, Ronny was sent to the Stevenson School, near Monterey. Our dad got both of us into golfing at a young age, but Ronny really excelled at it, and Stevenson was known for its golf team. It was an easy walk from the campus to the world-famous Pebble Beach Golf Links, so when I'd visit him at school we'd get to play there. It cost only five bucks for a round back then. It's roughly a hundred times more expensive today (not including tax, tips, and caddie fees).

Ronny and I were competitive when we golfed as kids, but he far surpassed me as we got older. He couldn't hit very straight, but he could hit far. At his best he was a scratch golfer, which meant he could play most courses without any handicap. As a teenager he would shoot about a 70, sometimes even less. I've kept up with golf my whole life and even on my best day I'd be lucky to hit a 75. He

Captain Krieger at Pebble Beach

From Ronny's high school yearbook

was one of the top two golfers at the Stevenson School, and he aspired to go pro one day. He didn't quite get there.

When Ronny was eighteen, someone gave him some bad acid. He was overcome with a deep sense of dread, and he refused to come out of his room for a couple of days. Looking back, it's clear that something was wrong with Ronny from a young age, but his bad trip seemed to amplify it. He retreated into a shell and developed a one-track mind: play golf all day, sit home alone all night. The aftermath of his bad trip was one of the reasons I stopped being so cavalier about supplying acid to all my friends. And it marked the point where our roads diverged.

Ronny went to Cal Western University in San Diego—known back then as a safety school for kids who couldn't get into UCLA or San Diego State—but he dropped out after a year or two to take a job on the grounds crew at the Riviera Country Club, where my dad was a member. My dad wasn't wild about Ronny forgoing higher education, or defying Riviera's dress code by walking around the club in shabby clothes, but Ronny was still pursuing his goal of going pro. He won a couple of club contests for the farthest drive, once hitting the ball over three hundred yards with a set of old wooden clubs, but he still couldn't manage to make a living through the sport, and he didn't have a degree or any other career aspirations to fall back on.

I tried to break Ronny out of his always-darkening spiral by bringing him on tour with the Doors as a roadie when we first started, and it helped a little. The band welcomed him and enjoyed his company. We were all weird guys anyway, so he fit right in. But as we entered our twenties and the Doors became more successful, I was constantly recording and touring, and Ronny couldn't tag along forever.

It almost felt like the more I succeeded, the more Ronny suffered. While I was playing guitar onstage in front of thousands of fans, he was trimming the grass at Riviera. He was able to find work, and he even got married before I did, but his demons never retreated completely. I tried to help him financially as the years went by, but I couldn't help his mental condition, which gradually declined to the point of frequent short-term institutionalization.

Twins have the unique experience of growing up parallel to another human being. You learn about life at the exact same pace, and you can, if you want to, literally walk in each other's shoes. Yet even with the exact same experiences and environment, two twin brothers can still end up in starkly different places.

A QUEST FOR ENLIGHTENMENT: PART II

When I went looking for an alternative way to achieve enlightenment, I found Maharishi Mahesh Yogi. I didn't even have to go to India; he was hanging out within walking distance of my parents' house.

My friend Keith Wallace and his older brother, Peter, had read their share of Alan Watts and were on a journey similar to mine. Peter had set off on a trip to India to find a guru, and he found quite a few, but he thought the Maharishi was the most compelling. The Maharishi was traveling the world to spread his teachings, but this was still a full two years before the Beatles thrust him into the global spotlight. When the Maharishi came through Los Angeles in 1965, he held a meeting at Keith and Peter's parents' house in Pacific Palisades. Only about a dozen people attended. Three of them would go on to form the Doors.

It's a fortunate coincidence that Ray Manzarek's confidence in acid happened to be shaken at around the same time mine was because the Maharishi's meeting at the Wallace house was where Ray and I first met. Dick Bock, the head of World Pacific Records, had financed some of the Maharishi's trip and had been working with Ray's first band, Rick and the Ravens. World Pacific would later produce the first Doors demo, but they had previously released a lot of Indian music, including the bulk of Ravi Shankar's catalog, so I assume that's how Dick was introduced to the teachings of the Maharishi. Dick brought Ray to the meeting. I brought John Densmore.

I didn't get to know Ray that first night beyond a handshake and some small talk, but John and I kept ending up at meditation classes with him. Ray and I never had any significant conversations until after I auditioned for the Doors, but in class he always stuck out as an interesting character. Our instructor was Jerry Jarvis, the Maharishi's right-hand man. One day, at the end of class, Jerry asked if anyone had any questions. Ray's hand shot up.

"No bliss!"

It wasn't really a question so much as a formal complaint. Ray seemed to expect the effects of meditation to kick in as quickly as a dose of LSD. When the class stopped chuckling, Jerry Jarvis explained that it would take time and discipline. Ray didn't like that answer. But before he stopped attending classes he traded phone numbers with John because Rick and the Ravens needed a new drummer. Meditation may not have brought Ray bliss, but it ultimately brought together the Doors.

John and I still wanted to achieve the transcendence the Maharishi had promised us, so we continued to take classes and meditate regularly. The Maharishi was this soft-spoken, giggly, happy guy. On the outside he appeared pretty damn blissful. You couldn't help but want what he had. And he would spout philosophical ideas that at least sounded better than what you'd hear in a standard church or synagogue. He was a maverick among other gurus because he didn't preach sacrifice or guilt, just meditation. Usually you'd expect an Eastern philosopher to tell you to give up all your earthly possessions and live barefoot in a cave or something. The Maharishi believed you could be rich in spirit and in bank account at the same time. That sounded much better to me! And that's probably why he caught on with so many celebrities, and Western culture as a whole. Just twenty minutes of meditation twice a day and you can have it all.

John and I got so deep into meditation that we even went to a few retreats. One was at a mountain resort near Lake Tahoe, where we brought some instruments and jammed in front of our fellow meditators with vibraphonist Emil Richards and jazz flautist Paul Horn. The Maharishi introduced our performance personally. Other than that, the Maharishi gave talks every day, but most of our time was spent meditating. Hours and hours a day, sitting in silence. And yet even with all that focus, and with direct access to the Maharishi himself, I still wasn't experiencing the enlightenment I was yearning for. I was a little bored, to be honest.

One day I was meditating with John at his house and he swore he felt a golden light radiating between us.

"Did you feel that?!"

I didn't.

The only mystical experience I ever had while meditating was much later, in the seventies, when I saw a vision of a glowing green skull. I was sitting on my bed, repeating my mantra, when the skull appeared out of the darkness, all electric and fluorescent. It wasn't scary, but it wasn't the kind of peaceful, spiritual vision everyone else seemed to have. I rode it out, waiting to see what might come next, but nothing did. After a while the skull vanished, and I went on with my day. I never came up with an answer about what it was supposed to mean, but I was happy to see anything after several thousand hours of sitting still.

Despite my wife Lynn's negative experiences with acid, she had no interest in meditation and rolled her eyes whenever John or I talked about it. For all my dedication and practice, she said she never saw much of a difference in me. I was already a mellow guy. According to her, if I got any mellower I would drop off the face of the earth.

Jim was never into astrology or psychics or any of that stuff, but John and I talked about meditation so much that he was intrigued. We picked up the phrase "Take it as it comes" from one of the Maharishi's lectures, and we used it so often that Jim and I built it into a song on our first album. (Jim's lyrics were more about sex than spiritual enlightenment, but he liked the double entendre of the word "comes.") After the Beatles turned the Maharishi into a celebrity, the whole meditation thing became a bit of a circus, but we took Jim to hear one of the Maharishi's lectures at the Wilshire Ebell Theatre. By that point my old friend Keith Wallace was working full-time for the Maharishi's organization, so after the audience left we got to stay behind with a small crowd, and everyone surrounded the Maharishi to shower him with admiration and inquiries about higher consciousness. Jim weaved through the group and got right next to the Maharishi, studying him up and down and staring deep into his eyes. The Maharishi smiled and returned his gaze. They didn't exchange a word. When Jim was satisfied, he walked away.

"Well, what happened?" I asked him.

"Nothing, man. No vibes at all."

He never went to another lecture after that. And I never did achieve the enlightenment advertised by the Maharishi. No golden glow. No transcendence. No bliss. But I still meditate from time to time. Sitting quietly and breathing deeply for a few minutes may not unlock all the mysteries of the universe, but it's still a good way to relax. And at least it's safer than acid.

Sunset Sound Recorders

ELEVEN MINUTES, FORTY-ONE SECONDS

I was sitting in the pitch black of the Hollywood Cinerama Dome when the silence was broken by the ghostly, muffled whirring of helicopter blades. The screen faded in on a tropical jungle. And then the theater was filled with the distinct sound of my Gibson SG Special.

Expectations were high for the release of Francis Ford Coppola's *Apocalypse Now,* but I was already entranced within the first minute. My guitar line for "The End" danced over rising orange smoke. Jim's echoing voice cued napalm explosions in the trees. John's rattlesnake tambourine ushered helicopters across the frame. And Ray's Vox Continental organ gently awakened Captain Willard. An irrefutable epic of a film played out, bookended by "The End," playing once more over an intense, bloody finale that I'm sure Jim would've absolutely loved.

It was the first time our music had ever been featured in a movie.

We had recorded "The End" twelve years earlier and performed it live with Jim for the last time eight years earlier. Now it was washing over me like a tidal wave in glorious six-track Dolby Stereo surround sound. Funny to think it started out so humbly as a half-written love song in my parents' living room.

We all assumed Jim wrote the song about his first serious girlfriend, Mary, a stunning brunette who followed him when he moved from Florida to L.A. to attend UCLA film school. She worked as a go-go dancer at Gazzarri's but wasn't the wild and crazy type. Jim's wildness and craziness was apparently too much for her after a while, so she broke up with him, but they stayed in touch. We could tell she had broken his heart, but he never admitted it out loud. When he first showed me the lyrics to "The End," he said only that it was about the end of a romance.

Since we thought we'd have to stretch out the song to reach the three-minute run time necessary for radio, I figured a raga would be perfect. Ragas stretch out endlessly by their nature, holding on to a single chord or scale. Like Ray's left-handed bass grooves, it was another way to hypnotize the listener. Once we started our residency at the London Fog, we had nothing but time to kill, so the raga for "The End" was as fertile for musical improvisation as the raga solo in "Light My Fire." Night after night Jim gradually added lyrics about the king's highway and the blue bus and the weird scenes inside the gold mine, and the idea of a three-minute run time vanished in our rearview as we rode the snake to the ancient lake.

During our tenure at the Whisky we sometimes played after-hours gigs at a place called the Warner Playhouse. We were booked there by the same guy who got us the job scoring the Ford Motor Company training film. In an effort to spice up our still-evolving live show, he hired a belly dancer to join us onstage one night. When we played "The End" and got to the part where the tempo speeds up, she spun and swayed and jiggled furiously, trying to keep pace. We showed her no mercy, extending the solo longer than usual. By the time we finished the song she was too dizzy to stand, and afterward she loudly declared she'd never dance with us again. We hadn't meant to upset her; I thought it was a perfect song for a belly dancer!

Other than "Light My Fire," "The End" always got the best reaction when we played it at the Whisky. We always closed the set with it because, well, obviously, "The End" goes at the end. Except for the one time when we famously played it at the beginning.

We were ready to take the stage at the Whisky one night, but Jim hadn't shown up. He may not have been the most responsible guy we knew, but he had never missed a show before. The only other time he had failed to report for duty was when he had been arrested in Blythe, so naturally we were worried. We had no choice but to play our first set without him, so we fumbled our way through some jazz and blues covers. Between sets we split up to scour the city for Jim. I checked all his favorite bars while Ray and John headed over to the Tropicana Motel. Jim occasionally stayed at the Tropicana because it was a hive for Whisky groupies and a party hub for touring bands. Ray and John found Jim in one of the rooms, cowering under the bed and babbling about how he had taken ten thousand mics of acid. Again, I couldn't tell you if he was exaggerating, bad at math, batshit crazy, or all of the above. But Ray and John managed to get Jim back to the Whisky for our second set. A song or two into it, he demanded we play "The End."

"The killer awoke before dawn..."

When we got to the middle of the song, Jim launched into a new lyrical improvisation we had never heard before.

"He put his boots on..."

We didn't know where he was going, but as always we were dying to find out. As Jim wove his narrative, the Whisky came to a standstill. Everyone held their breath as the killer walked on down the hall.

" 'Father?' 'Yes, son?' 'I want to kill you.' "

The moment kept building.

" 'Mother . . . I want to . . .' "

Many people recall being scandalized the first time they heard Jim's Oedipal scream on the first Doors record. Imagine hearing it unexpectedly for the first time while sharing a stage with him.

Ray, John, and I took Jim's cue to explode, and we brought the song to a cacophonous, cursing climax, and then a calm conclusion. Jim didn't collapse on the stage like you see in the Doors movie. He just stared, stone-faced, out at the crowd. It was pin drop silent for a moment. And then there was the loudest burst of applause we'd ever gotten.

Legend has it that the swearing and Oedipal imagery got us fired that night, but I don't remember anyone being angry or yelling at us. The crowd loved it, and we played the Whisky for at least a few more nights after that. It doesn't even make sense that we'd be fired for such a thing: the place was owned by a self-described corrupt cop and a professional gambler who both had Mob ties. They were offended by *crude language*? I'm pretty sure it was simply the end of our contract that ended our residency. We remained friends with Elmer, Phil, and Mario and went back to the Whisky for subsequent shows the following year. How upset could they have possibly been?

Either way, we knew that "The End" finally had its last missing piece, and we needed to get it onto vinyl as intact as possible.

Sunset Sound Recorders is one of the most historic studios in the world, having produced everything from *Exile on Main Street* to *Purple Rain* to the soundtrack to *Mary Poppins*. But it was a workshop. No frills. White acoustic tile on the ceiling, gray linoleum on the floor, bare walls, fluorescent lights. We knew we couldn't achieve the vibe we needed in a space like that, so we brought in our own lamps, turned off the fluorescents, and lit some candles and incense. But mood lighting got us only so far. If Jim wanted to re-create that inspired night at the Whisky, he figured he needed to re-create his acid intake as well. I heard him chanting and pounding on a table in the vending machine area:

"Fuck the mother, kill the father! Fuck the mother, kill the father!"

I tried to calm him down. "Yeah, right on, man..."

"Fuck the mother, kill the father! Fuck the mother, kill the father! That's it! That's where I'm at!"

He seemed ready. We were all experienced enough with acid that we weren't alarmed or afraid. We were excited. Two takes turned out to be all we needed. We all went home satisfied.

Except Jim.

Still flying on whatever monster dose of acid he had taken, Jim somehow snuck back into the studio when everyone was gone and sprayed the whole place down with a fire extinguisher. He coated our gear in sticky, chemical foam and overturned a couple of those big, standing, sand-filled ashtrays, which combined with the foam to create a disgusting paste all over the floor. Thankfully the mixing console and the master tapes weren't damaged, but the studio owner wanted to call the cops. Our record label, in a moment of baffling generosity, agreed to cover the cost of the cleanup. And once again, Jim got away with it. I don't remember him even apologizing for that one, but we were so relieved that we hadn't lost our record deal we never dared to mention the incident again.

When it came time to join our two takes of the song together, Paul Rothchild and engineer Bruce Botnick created a "window edit," which is one of the most fascinating feats of analog studio wizardry I've ever seen. One of the notes from Ray's piano bass didn't match up at the point where the takes would naturally be spliced, but how do you remove a single note from a single instrument without scrapping all the other sounds recorded around it on the same stretch of tape? First, Paul gently brushed some sort of solution onto the tape, which made the waveforms from each track temporarily visible. With a grease pencil, he marked off the spot where Ray's bass note appeared, and then he used a razor blade to surgically remove a very narrow inch-long and eighth-inch-wide rectangle from the center of the half-inch tape. Paul then took the tape of the other take and lined up the correct bass note in the "window" he had created, and adhered it all together with splicing tape. If he hadn't done it exactly right, there would've been a noise on the track, which would've been especially noticeable on a relatively quiet song like "The End." Bruce tells me the edit is somewhere near the beginning of the Oedipal section, and he says if you listen to the song with headphones you can hear a subtle change in the tone of Ray's piano bass when the second take kicks in. But I've listened to that song a million times in my life, and to this day I couldn't tell you where that edit is.

Paul Rothchild and Bruce Botnick

All the cost, chaos, and painstaking effort that went into "The End" was well worth it. It has a certain power that eclipses all our other songs. It brought the Whisky to a standstill. It nearly killed a belly dancer. It possessed Coppola to use the same song twice in a landmark film.

Once, before I started dating my wife, Lynn, she and Jim and a few other friends needed a ride to a party, so they were hitchhiking on Sunset. Car after car passed by their freakish crew until, out of nowhere, a blue bus appeared.

"The blue bus...is calling us..."

It was like an old Greyhound bus, but it had been customized and given a shiny blue paint job. Jim had already been working on the "blue bus" section of "The End" around that time. I always assumed he was referring to the Big Blue Bus transit line that carted him around Venice, but again, Jim never confirmed nor denied this.

"The blue bus...is calling us..."

The blue bus pulled to a stop and opened its doors. The driver was a white-haired hippie with a bushy beard, and the only passengers were a pack of beautiful Dalmatians. The interior of the bus had been given a psychedelic treatment, and the seats had all been removed and replaced with overstuffed pillows. The driver welcomed Jim, Lynn, and their friends on board. They petted the dogs and chatted with the friendly driver until he dropped them off at their party—at which Jim stole a bottle of booze and the host kicked them all out. They were now stranded in some residential neighborhood in the middle of the night, wandering, lost, and trying to hitchhike home.

"Driver, where you takin' us?"

I always think about that story when I hear "The End." Call it a coincidence if you want, but there's part of me that wants to believe Jim conjured that blue bus out of thin air. Sometimes a song is just a song. Sometimes it's an incantation.

PAIN IS SOMETHING TO CARRY, LIKE A RADIO

Jim loved to get into fights, but he would always lose. Most guys who pick fights are doing it to look tough or prove something. Jim didn't care about dominating people physically. He never threw the first punch; instead, he provoked people with words or acts of destruction until they finally took a swing. He wasn't a weakling—he could've defended himself if he wanted to—but then again, he was usually so wasted that a stiff breeze could have knocked him off his feet. Was it masochism? Manipulation? Pushing emotional limits? Symbolically striking back at his authoritarian father? I used to chalk it up to drunken stupidity—which it was—but now I recognize it as *calculated* drunken stupidity.

Liquor was always the catalyst. Jim wouldn't even think of saying or doing something to start a fight when he was sober. He was always a perfect gentleman, even to cops. Underneath it all he never wanted to actually hurt anybody. Once, he accidentally kicked a stage light at a show in San Bernardino and it flew into a girl's face and left her bloody. Jim felt horrible about it. He brought the girl backstage and stayed with her while she received first aid. She sued us later on, but he did his best to apologize.

There was his biker bar brawl in Blythe. There was the time he challenged the cops with my brother. There were a couple of public wrestling matches with Janis Joplin. I don't want to defend or glorify his behavior. The fights he got himself into were usually avoidable and always obnoxious. But the nature of how each battle started and ended seemed to reveal something about his personality.

Once Jim and I were eating at a diner when some navy boys came in and started picking on us about our long hair. The standard taunts: calling us girls and so forth. I muttered something back under my breath, probably a smart-ass remark about their sailor suits. Whatever I said, Jim repeated it loudly for their benefit and then took the insults to the next level. They grumbled back at us, but things died down and we finished our meal in peace.

As we were leaving, Jim went to make a call from the phone booth outside. The sailors followed us out. They tried to grab me but I shook them off and ran. I turned to see Jim pinned inside the phone booth, with one of the sailors strangling him and bashing his face against the glass. Jim shouted, "Call the cops!"

The sailors got in a few more licks and left Jim in a bloody pile on the ground. I ran back to help him and offered to take him to the hospital. He shrugged it off and said he was okay.

The incident was hardly his fault, but it was yet another example of Jim being a magnet for violence, and reveling in it. I'll never fully understand the psychology of what drove him to fight, but I'll also never forget the look on Jim's face when it was being flattened against the glass of that phone booth.

He was smiling. Ear to ear.

THE FIRST ALBUM

If you tap along with the tempo at the end of "Light My Fire," you'll notice that after the instruments drop out John comes back in on the three instead of the four. On the last note of "The Crystal Ship," I play a minor chord and Ray plays a major chord when we technically should've been hitting the same notes. On the first chorus of "Break On Through," Jim sings "Break on through to the other side" three times, but on the second chorus he sings it only twice. If our first album was recorded today, John's snare would be quantized to match perfectly with a tempo grid, the notes Ray and I hit would be pitch-corrected, and Jim's vocals would be digitally cut and pasted to fit a more uniform structure. But we had no computers, and only four tracks to work with. Organ and guitar on the first track, drums and piano bass on the second, vocals on the third, overdubs on the fourth. No click track, no Auto-Tune. Technology has opened up so many creative possibilities and streamlined the recording process in miraculous ways, but the ability to endlessly mix and tweak and fine-tune everything to death has created way too many albums that sound way too perfect. I'm glad we recorded all the Doors albums when and how we did. The imperfections are what make them feel alive.

Both Arthur Lee from Love and Ronnie Haran have taken credit for bringing the Doors to the attention of Jac Holzman from Elektra Records. I don't know who has the stronger claim, but I thank them both for their efforts. Our shows at the Whisky were getting us noticed by the music industry. Phil Spector, Terry Melcher, Lou Adler, and even Frank Zappa expressed interest in producing us. But none of them seemed quite right. Elektra was an unusual choice since they were mostly known for putting out folk, flamenco, and jug bands. I don't know about the other guys in the band, but that was a dream label for me! And Jac wanted to pair us with producer Paul Rothchild, who had previously worked with two of my all-time biggest influences: the Paul Butterfield Blues Band and Koerner, Ray & Glover. Coincidence? Or fate?

Jac cut a striking figure with his tailored Brioni suits and tall, slender frame. I already respected him since Elektra had become one of the biggest folk labels in the world and since he had put out tons of records by artists that might've been otherwise overlooked. He was a hip, intellectual type, bordering on snobbish genius, so of course Jim respected him as well. And Jac had signed Love—who we all idolized—earlier that year. Elektra would turn out to make all the difference in the story of the Doors, and the Doors would end up making all the difference in the story of Elektra.

Our debut album was recorded in the perfect amount of time: not so fast that we didn't have time to get the energy right, but not so slow that we second-guessed ourselves. After months of playing multiple nightly sets at the Fog and the Whisky, we were able to just hit Record and go. Jac had unwavering confidence in the results. He took a major gamble by blowing up the photo on the album's back cover to create the first ever rock 'n' roll billboard, which overlooked the Sunset Strip. His logic was that it would catch the attention of every music industry professional in town on their way to work. Jac took us down to where they were making the billboard and had photos taken of us watching them lay it out, and later, when they put the billboard up, he had photos taken of us pretending to help. In an era when everyone was striving so hard to play it cool, it was a little embarrassing for us to pose as if we were saying, "Oh boy! We're so excited to help put up our billboard!" But Jac had spent so much money on the whole thing we couldn't say no. And I have to admit: once it was up, I might've gone out of my way to drive by it once or twice.

Jac innately understood the power of imagery and marketing. I was always a fan of Elektra's album covers. Their in-house art director, Bill Harvey, presented us with several options for our band's logo, and the one we picked became so integral to our visual identity that I later had custom windows shaped like Bill's version of the letter *O* installed on the front and garage doors of my house. After our billboard went up it became practically a requirement for other labels to put up billboards for their bands as well—a trend that persists today. Jac also sprang for a "promotional film" for the song "Break On Through" long before the term "music video"—let alone a TV channel on which to play them—existed. We may have felt a bit self-conscious about the marketing barrage, but those feelings were overpowered by our deep appreciation for all the time, money, and resources Jac was putting into helping us.

And then we let him down.

The band and the label mutually agreed that "Break On Through" should be the first single, but despite the billboard and the promotional film and all of us calling radio stations with different voices to repeatedly request the song, it didn't even crack the top one hundred. I've always suspected that it failed because it was originally mastered at a low volume and didn't come across as powerfully as it should have on people's radios. But either way, it hurt. I felt like we had recorded a great album and now no one was ever going to hear it. Jac, thankfully, gave us a second chance.

I thought "Twentieth Century Fox" was the ideal choice for a second single. Maybe it should've even been the first single. Maybe we shouldn't have used the song with the bossa nova beat to introduce ourselves to the world. Maybe we should've gone with "The Crystal Ship," which had some of Jim's strongest lyrics. Maybe we should've gone with one of our covers, like "Alabama Song," which was catchy and unique, or "Back Door Man," which was fun and familiar. "Twentieth Century Fox" had clever wordplay, a good beat, a radio-friendly run time—everything we could want in a single. Thankfully Dave Diamond convinced us otherwise.

Dave hosted a radio show on KBLA-FM called *The Diamond Mine*. Back then, FM was the underground and AM was the mainstream. You needed special equipment to receive FM stations—most cars didn't even include FM radios yet. Since Dave didn't have to worry about the stricter standards of AM radio, he was able to play an eclectic mix of artists, and, most importantly for us, he didn't care about run time limits. He was likely the first DJ to play the original seven-minute version of "Light My Fire" on the air in its entirety. Dave told us that every time he played it he would get tons of phone calls from people asking him to play it again. He said it was the only song in his rotation that got such a reaction, and he pushed us hard to consider cutting down the solo part so AM stations would play it.

We knew that "Light My Fire" was strong since it always got the best crowd response at the Whisky, but we really didn't want to cut out the solo. Bob Dylan had gotten a pass with over six minutes of "Like a Rolling Stone"; why couldn't we get away with the same thing? And we had already cut the word "high" out of the single version of "Break On Through" to make it more radio friendly, and where did that get us? But in our guts we knew Dave was right. We had to either cut the solo or roll the dice with "Twentieth Century Fox."

But even sacrificing the solo wasn't enough to appease the radio gods. We had to play a show at the Cheetah in Santa Monica, promoted by KHJ's "Boss Radio" DJ Humble Harve. We packed in over three thousand fans, and Harve (who later "accidentally" shot his wife) kept almost all the ticket money. Our payment was that Harve would *consider* playing "Light My Fire" on the air. The thrill of playing our biggest headlining show up to that point was dampened a little by the knowledge that we were Humble Harve's humble servants.

A few months later, I was having dinner at my parents' house. I had moved out by then, but I tried to drop by regularly to be a good son. And their cook, Clarence, made much better meals than I could manage on my own. Humble Harve had indeed been playing "Light My Fire" regularly on KHJ, and through the spring of 1967 we watched it slowly climb the charts. By early July we had cracked the top twenty, by mid-July the top ten, by late July the top three. My parents and I were listening to the weekly countdown, wondering if the song would go higher, hold its position, or begin its descent. When the DJ announced that number three was "Windy" by the Association, we knew "Light My Fire" had gone up at least one notch, and when he announced that number two was Stevie Wonder's "I Was Made to Love Her," we burst into celebration. My mom was the loudest and most expressive, of course, but my usually reserved dad still went a little crazy. Even Clarence joined in the revelry.

It's interesting to think that if "Break On Through" hadn't

flopped, we wouldn't have had a reason to put out "Light My Fire" as a single, which means our first album may not have done as well, which means the first song I ever wrote may not have become a standard. The potential ripple effects are staggering to consider.

I still think "Twentieth Century Fox" could've been a hit, though.

ME AND WILLIE

Until the early nineties, Willie Dixon was unaware that the Doors had recorded his song "Back Door Man." So many artists had covered him over the years that it was probably hard to keep track. Even our version was a cover of a cover. I had brought John Hammond Jr.'s album *Big City Blues* into an early Doors practice without realizing it had several Willie Dixon covers on it, and we based our version of "Back Door Man" on his. Ray played us the Howlin' Wolf version of the song, but we liked Hammond's bouncier feel. The song became a staple of our early live sets, and by playing it night after night we molded it into something that felt like it was our own.

As much as Willie wasn't aware of our cover, I was unaware for a long time how much of an influence he was on me. When the Doors covered "Little Red Rooster," it was because the Stones had done it — I didn't realize Willie had originally written the song for Howlin' Wolf. When I lifted the guitar part for "Break On Through" from Paul Butterfield's version of "Mellow Down Easy," I didn't realize Paul was covering Little Walter, who was playing a song that

Willie had written. It's a strange thing to be influenced so heavily by a songwriter and not even know it. But Willie was in there all along.

After a *Los Angeles Times* reporter mentioned our cover to Willie in 1991, I got a call from Willie's daughter. She was managing his business affairs at the time and she told me Willie wanted to meet me. And she suggested I bring my guitar.

By that point I had put all the puzzle pieces together and come to appreciate what a musical giant Willie was, so I was ecstatic. I went over to his house in North Hollywood, where he welcomed me inside. He had put on a lot of weight by then; my hand disappeared inside his when he shook it. He thanked me for the cover and we chatted for a while, and then he said, "Why don't we write something?"

He set up a cheap cassette recorder and told me to play some guitar. I happily obliged. I assumed he'd play bass since that was his main instrument, but instead he decided to play drums. And by "drums" I mean he took a piece of cardboard, laid it across his enormous stomach, and pounded out a beat while he sang. He made up some words, I made up some chords, and we wrote ourselves a silly little song.

Willie died a few months later. I was extremely grateful to have had a chance to spend an afternoon laughing and jamming with the songwriter who had—whether I knew it or not—been such a crucial influence on me. I've had the pleasure of recording music in professional studios with some legendary performers over the course of my life, but one of my favorite collaborations resides on a lo-fi cassette tape stashed away somewhere in a dusty storage space, featuring Robby Krieger on guitar and Willie Dixon on cardboard stomach drums.

LOVE STREET

Laurel Canyon is a focal point of folk folklore. It's nestled in the hills about two miles north of the Sunset Strip, and the cottages along its twisty mountain roads were famously home to Joni Mitchell, Neil Young, Carole King, Crosby, Stills, and Nash, and members of the Byrds, the Monkees, Love, and so many other bands that defined the California sound of the mid-sixties. The rent was cheap, the air was quiet, and the views were stunning. There were parties, of course, but Laurel Canyon was more about hanging out than getting crazy. The hard-core party animals lived down in Hollywood. Those of us who were playing in loud clubs every night enjoyed having a peaceful retreat during the day.

In the summer of 1966, John Judnich, the soundman from the Whisky (and the guy who discovered Lenny Bruce's body after his overdose), was vacating his old house on Brier Drive in Laurel Canyon, so John Densmore and I took over the lease. We spent our days meditating and occasionally jamming with our neighbors, the Mothers of Invention. The house was perched on one of the Canyon's many cliffs, and it was where Jim first scared the shit out of us by exhibiting his fondness for dangling off balconies. Jim was still spending most of his nights at random girls' houses, but officially he had moved into the house next door, so he and I were able to easily get together for songwriting sessions. Unfortunately, we all had to give up our Laurel Canyon addresses when we spent six weeks in New York for our residency at Ondine's. When we returned to L.A., I ended up in an apartment a few blocks north of the Whisky, on Clark Street. I shared it with a few thousand bedbugs and, occasionally, a married woman with whom I was having an affair.

Back when I had my first real Sandoz acid trip, the high lasted for something like sixteen hours. I was with Bob Cranson, the harmonica player who used to jam with Wolff and me during our folk wannabe days at UCSB. We decided to drop in on Bob's friend Wardie Ward, whose family had a sprawling Spanish Revival mansion in Carpinteria, surrounded by a seventeen-acre avocado grove. We often barged our way into Wardie's parents' place back then. Sometimes we'd steal amphetamine-based diet pills from his mom's medicine cabinet and put them in a blender with fruit juice to make stimulant smoothies. On the day of the Sandoz trip, we walked from the avocado grove down to the beach, which is where I watched the cliffs shift into faces and animal shapes. The Wards had a small guesthouse on the beach, separate from the main residence. When we entered, I saw a radiant woman bathing her cherubic baby. A Renaissance vision of *Madonna and Child*. It was Wardie's older sister, Happy. She was gorgeous even without the acid, but the Sandoz left me with an unforgettable first impression.

Happy was five years older than me and married with two kids, so I didn't think I had much of a shot with her. But after I started taking classes at UCLA, she and her husband moved down to Beverly Glen, which wasn't far from the UCLA campus. Their place became a hangout spot: Wardie was always there, Bob Cranson would drop in when he was around, and Jim and John would come by with me sometimes. The Doors even practiced at Happy's house a few times before we rented our spot in Venice.

The more I got to know Happy, the more I realized she wasn't... happy. Her husband was nice to us, but he was always putting Happy down and making her feel worthless. Happy always saw us doing acid and wanted to try it, so one day Wardie gave her some— he just didn't tell her first. He slipped it into her morning coffee, and the confusion over the new sensation mixed with the negative vibes from her husband created the perfect recipe for a bummer trip. The room became distorted, her family's faces turned into evil caricatures, and she saw flashing lights and dragon-like creatures all around her.

Wardie called me since I was the foremost acid expert in our circle of friends, and I agreed to be Happy's Sherpa through the darkness. I thought about how my best trips were always outdoors, in natural spaces. It made sense that if you were attempting to connect with the universe you didn't want to be inside a man-made structure. I drove her to a cliff overlooking the ocean, where we sat on a bench and calmly watched the sun go down and the waves roll in, and the monsters disappeared. It was an emotional day and a romantic moment, but I didn't feel right making a move on a married woman. At least not yet.

After Happy's trip, she found some clarity and knew she had to change her life. We became friends, and soon enough we became more than friends. She saw the Doors at the Whisky a few times, she came on some of our road trips, she was in the studio for some of the *Strange Days* sessions, she booked us a New Year's Eve gig at a party in Montecito, and she and I spent a lot of time together at my bedbug-infested Clark Street apartment.

We used to make out on the beach near the Doors' Venice rehearsal space because it was such a desolate spot. No one ever hung out on that particular stretch of sand, so we figured no one would ever catch us there. But one day, in a coincidence I still struggle to explain, Happy's sister-in-law happened to walk right past us. She never spoke to Happy again after that. Happy's husband must've heard about it. At the very least he probably suspected something was up when Happy brought home bedbugs. But there was never any confrontation. Her husband either didn't care or was pretending not to care. It was the sixties, man.

John and I moved back to Laurel Canyon, this time splitting a house on Lookout Mountain Avenue, which is the street where Neil Young, Frank Zappa, and John and Michelle Phillips from the Mamas and the Papas all lived. Happy would drop by early in the mornings while her kids were at school and her husband was at work. John lived on the ground floor and I lived on a lower level, so John, barely having fallen asleep after our late-night gigs, always had to wake up to let her in. It was a minor strain on my relationship with John, but nothing a little meditation couldn't fix.

Jim also returned to the Canyon, moving into a house on Rothdell Trail with a redhead named Pam Courson who he had been dating steadily (relatively speaking). They lived behind the Canyon Country Store, which was a central hub for groceries and socializing. The store sold produce from the gardens of Canyon residents and its simplistic charm completed the illusion that we were all living out in the sticks even though we were just up the road from the bumper-to-bumper cruising traffic of the Strip.

Jim immortalized Pam's "house and garden" and the "store where the creatures meet" in the lyrics to our song "Love Street." There was something about Laurel Canyon that drew creativity out of people, as evidenced by the staggering amount of classic American music that came out of its hills. Jim wasn't exactly an aspiring folk singer enamored with acoustic love ballads, but the Canyon managed to inspire him all the same. Late one night John and I were entertaining some girls at our Lookout Mountain house when Jim dropped by. I had seen Jim in every type of mood, but I had never seen him so depressed. He kept saying things like "What's the point, man?" At first I thought it might be a pity play to get the girls to feel sorry for him, but it soon became clear that this was genuine despair. I don't know what was weighing on him. He wasn't drunk, as far as I could tell. He didn't specifically say he wanted to end it all, but his attitude was heavy enough that it seemed like that might be on the table. We all tried to cheer him up, but nothing was working. As the predawn light filtered through the windows, I suggested we all take a walk up to Appian Way to watch the sunrise.

It worked. The sun brightened both the sky and Jim's mood. When we got back to the house he explained the revelation he'd had: "When *you're* strange…*people* are strange!" It's your own mind that makes everything seem fucked up, even when it isn't. It doesn't come from the outside; it comes from within.

Jim immediately scribbled down some rough lyrics, I added a guitar part, and within the week we recorded "People Are Strange" for the *Strange Days* album. I thought it was a nice, quirky little song, but I had no clue at the time that the Laurel Canyon sunrise had just inspired one of the Doors' biggest hits.

Happy and I eventually parted ways. She left her husband while we were together, but I was constantly traveling and gigging and she needed something more stable. Plus we were both dating other people. And it didn't help when I caught the clap from another woman. Or when I contracted crabs. What can I say? It was the sixties, man.

As the Doors became more successful, John and I realized we could afford to live without roommates, so he moved to a little cabin next to Neil Young in Laurel Canyon and I moved to a house on Topanga Beach. Last I heard, Happy had remarried and moved to New Mexico.

In 2018, fifty years after the release of "Love Street," the city of

Los Angeles placed a historical marker outside Jim and Pam's former home on Rothdell Trail and officially renamed part of the road Love Street. The dedication ceremony was held during the annual Love Street Festival, which brings together Laurel Canyon enthusiasts and alumni for a day of music, art, food, and memories in the parking lot of the Canyon Country Store. John and I were on hand to make speeches, and Michelle Phillips, Micky Dolenz, and I each played a few songs and reminisced with the crowd. I hope that historical marker will stand long after we're all gone, to remind people of that fleeting cultural moment when music and free love reigned. Thankfully the idyllic Eden of the Laurel Canyon scene has been memorialized in photos and on album covers and in multiple documentaries. If you take the time to really gaze at all those hazy, sun-dappled images of young people hanging out, smiling, and playing music in what seems like a perpetual golden hour, you can see what it means to really live life, and to be free.

Just remember: they all had crabs.

1967

After our first show at the Fillmore Auditorium in San Francisco, a young fan helped himself to some balloons that had been tied to one of the speakers by the stage. The promoter, Bill Graham, came barreling across the venue floor and tackled him to the ground.

"You tryin' to steal my goddamn balloons?!"

San Francisco: the city of peace and love.

Our debut album was released in January of 1967. Up until that point, we had played only in Southern California, New York, and that one venue in Arizona with the developmentally disabled Elvis. Ronnie Haran from the Whisky was helping us book our out-of-town gigs. After our album came out, she and Elektra sent us north to try and make an impression on San Francisco and hopefully on Bill Graham, who was the kingpin of the Northern California music scene. Despite San Francisco always turning its nose up at anything from Los Angeles, we managed to win over a few fans when we opened for the Young Rascals one weekend and the Grateful Dead the next. Trips to the Bay Area became a monthly ritual for the rest of the year. During one of our Fillmore shows, Jim accidentally clocked Bill Graham on the head with a microphone while swinging it around like a lasso. Jim had been in perfect control, but Bill was worried Jim would hurt someone so he lunged into the path of the mic and fulfilled his own prophecy. Jim made amends on our next trip by gifting Bill with a hand-painted helmet to prevent any future injuries.

In March of '67 we played two packed weekend shows at the Avalon Ballroom with Country Joe and the Fish and then followed it up with several weeknight gigs at a much smaller club called the Matrix. They had a decent live recording setup and they happened to roll tape while we were in town, so years later we were able to release a rare live album from their archives. Of course we didn't draw much of an audience as an out-of-town band playing on a Tuesday, so it almost felt like we were back at the London Fog. If you listen to our album *Live at the Matrix 1967* you can get a sense of what it was like. We play the big finish for "Light My Fire" and then: *clap...clap...clap...*

It's crazy how two cities in the same state can be so culturally different. In Los Angeles, everything was Beatle boots and miniskirts. In San Francisco, it was long hair and tie-dye. But as much as they might have been skeptical about us, the San Francisco crowd seemed much more serious about music, and more willing to really pay attention to a new band. The Fillmore and the Avalon were sold out every weekend, no matter who was playing. And during our first trip we went over to Golden Gate Park to attend the first Human Be-In, where we saw tens of thousands of hippies united by music, poetry, and LSD.

One day we showed up for a Fillmore gig and there was a strange-looking woman in our dressing room who reeked of booze and was swigging from a bottle of Southern Comfort. I thought she was a homeless person who had wandered in off the street. She greeted us with a cheery "Hi! I'm Big Brother!," which made me even more confused. But after a moment it finally clicked that she was talking about Big Brother and the Holding Company. I don't know why she didn't just introduce herself as Janis Joplin, but we were charmed all the same.

We got to talking and she invited us to see her perform at the Avalon Ballroom later that night. I'm not even sure if she really knew who we were; I think she was just being friendly. I had heard the name Big Brother and the Holding Company before, but they hadn't put out their first album yet so we had no clue what they sounded like. After our set that night we took Janis up on her invitation and headed across town to check them out. They played "Summertime" and my jaw hit the floor. This tiny, unassuming woman took complete charge of the room and overpowered every instrument in the band with the power of her voice. If you never saw Janis perform in person, there's no way I can possibly convey the sensation of walking into a venue without a clue as to what to expect and being greeted by her mind-blowing presence. Even on the Big Brother albums you can't really get a sense of how great she was; the guitars hog too much attention. Paul Rothchild came as close to doing her justice as anyone could when he produced her *Pearl* album, but nothing will ever quite live up to my memory of that night at the Avalon.

We got to know Janis pretty well and hung out with her whenever our paths led us to the same city. Jim even ended up going home with Janis one night soon after we met her. All was well until they heard a motorcycle pull up.

"That's Frank! Get out of here! He's gonna kill you!"

Frank was Janis's boyfriend. Better known as Freewheelin' Frank, the secretary of the San Francisco chapter of the Hells Angels. Jim snuck out and, as far as I know, Frank never found out he had been with Janis that night. Yet again, Jim managed to escape certain death.

The Hells Angels were woven into the fabric of the Northern California scene. They semiofficially provided security for the Fantasy Fair and Magic Mountain Music Festival in Marin County, where, in June of '67, we were on an all-day bill sandwiched between Canned Heat and Dionne Warwick. The Angels wouldn't let Jim up onstage at first because they didn't believe he was with the band, so we had to argue with them—carefully—to get him access. Other than that they didn't cause any real problems, but you could feel the weight of their presence. When the news broke about Altamont two years later, I wasn't the least bit surprised.

The Fantasy Fair Festival wasn't as well-documented as the Monterey Pop Festival or Woodstock, but it was actually the first major outdoor music festival of its kind. Tens of thousands of people, thirty bands, multiple stages, art installations, vendors, food, drugs, and a big inflatable Buddha. It's largely forgotten about now, but we had never seen anything like it. And of course I forgot to bring my guitar. Happy had come on the trip with us and we got into an argument about something, probably involving her husband. My mind was preoccupied with the fight so I left my guitar in our motel room and ended up borrowing a red Gibson ES-335 (the Chuck Berry guitar I coveted when I first bought my SG) from one of the other bands. We were building a name for ourselves but we were still rookies at this game.

The Monterey Pop Festival took place one week later, but we were "overlooked" by the bookers. At least that's the explanation we were given. I never bought it. Sure, we weren't at the top of the charts yet, but Big Brother and the Holding Company played even though their album wasn't even out. Jefferson Airplane played even though we drew the same size crowds as them. John Phillips from the Mamas and the Papas and Lou Adler were the organizers. One of them lived up the street from me and the other had offered to produce us when he saw us at the Whisky. My theory has always been that Lou purposely snubbed us because we didn't sign a record deal with him. But even if we had been invited to Monterey Pop, we couldn't have gone. We were committed to dates on Long Island that weekend. We were actually originally booked in Manhattan at Steve Paul's the Scene, but the shows were moved to Long Island because Steve Paul abruptly decided to close the club for a couple of days...so he could attend the Monterey Pop Festival.

Every year as a member of the Doors was a strange year, but 1967 was especially weird. For the first half of the year, we were touring in a van as unproven unknowns. For the second half, we were being flown to headlining gigs as number one artists. Before "Light My Fire" hit, we were playing high school auditoriums and teen centers and skating rinks and American Legion halls. We were booked alongside the Coasters at one high school show, which was an interesting choice of lineup. And we commanded no respect outside the boundaries of Los Angeles County. When we opened for the Grateful Dead at the Earl Warren Showgrounds in Santa Barbara, we were hoping to borrow some of their gear. Everyone borrowed amps and equipment back then. We didn't think it would be a big deal, especially with such a laid-back, easygoing San Francisco band like the Dead. Their keyboardist, Pigpen, played the exact same Vox Continental organ that Ray did. But he refused to let Ray touch it. I don't know what they had against us, but I couldn't believe a peace-and-love band that was on the bill at the Human Be-In could be so uptight. Maybe I should've tracked down Bob Weir and appealed to him as a Menlo alum, but the whole band wanted nothing to do with us. I read an account somewhere that we supposedly did acid with the Dead that day. Believe me: we were not in the mood. The Grateful Dead's PA system was a wall of Altec Lansing 604E speakers, which were top-of-the-line studio monitors with fifteen-inch woofers that could push out superior-quality sound for miles. They wouldn't let me plug into them. My guitar went out to three thousand people that day via a microphone dangling in front of a five-watt practice amp.

Of all the San Francisco bands we played with, we were probably the most friendly with Jefferson Airplane. We shared a stage with them often, and our careers ran parallel in the beginning, so we had a bit of a friendly rivalry with them, spurred on by Bill Graham. Bill was managing the Airplane, and I was still the guy who settled shows and dealt with our band's money. Whenever I settled up with Bill, he'd poke at me: "How many records did you guys sell last week?" And then he'd contrast my answer with the numbers for his clients. When we played Humble Harve's show at the Cheetah to get "Light My Fire" off the ground, we headlined over the Airplane. Bill stopped poking soon after.

I was dealing with promoters directly because we had no management yet. And we couldn't afford a crew so we recruited my brother, Ronny, to serve as our roadie and cart us around in his beige Volkswagen Microbus. We shared motel rooms. Sometimes we shared beds. It wasn't glamorous or comfortable, but it was probably the most fun we had as a touring group. There was no real pressure, and there were no hangers-on trying to get Jim drunk yet. It was pure. If we'd known how quickly and drastically things were about to change, we might've taken the time to appreciate those days a little more.

The second half of 1967 was when things got more exciting, but more complicated. "Light My Fire" was climbing the charts through the summer, so we were suddenly in demand all over the country. But we still had commitments to play smaller shows that had been booked before the song became popular. A week before we broke into the top ten we played a high school auditorium in the L.A. suburbs, once again billed with the Coasters. The next night we played a huge arena in Fresno with Janis Ian as the headliner. The billing probably made sense when the show was first booked and her song "Society's Child" was doing better than "Light My Fire." But as talented as Janis was, can you imagine trying to follow Jim Morrison's Oedipal screams with a soft voice and an acoustic guitar? On the other hand, when we opened for Simon & Garfunkel a month later, Jim's Oedipal screams were met with awkward stares from an audience that had paid specifically to hear soft voices and an acoustic guitar.

We headlined new cities in the Pacific Northwest and the Atlantic Northeast. Some were sold out, some were nearly empty, some were still high school auditoriums. Instead of the VW Microbus there were planes and limos and occasional flocks of screaming fans. It was a thrill, but it quickly became a grind, with haphazard tour routings that would take us directly from L.A. to New Jersey to Texas to Utah to New York to Illinois with barely any time to recover from the whiplash.

Ronny hadn't signed on to be a professional roadie; he was just helping out for the fun of joining us at the shows. Sometimes he enlisted his friends as extra muscle, most notably Rich Linnell, who would later go on to promote quite a few Doors shows, and Bill Siddons, who would soon after become our tour manager. One night at the Avalon we had to load in quickly because we were running late. Ronny slowly trudged up the long stairwell to the stage with a single piece of gear in his hands, but a moment later I saw Bill Siddons flying up the same stairs with an amp in each arm. That was the kind of professional-level hustle we needed, so we hired Bill on the spot as our sole official crew member.

Bill joined right as things were changing. Not just in terms of our career, but in terms of Jim. Acid was always Jim's drug of choice, but after a while acid fucks up your brain, so Jim started drinking more to balance himself out. I've done my share of drugs, and they all have their downsides, but alcohol is really one of the worst. Different drugs have the ability to unleash different monsters. Booze will release the meanest among them. And like any drug, the more of it you do, the more of it you need to overcome your tolerance.

A month after Bill started working with us, he hitchhiked all the way to New York—while fending off the sexual propositions of a preacher who picked him up along the way—to join us at the Long Island shows when everyone else was at Monterey Pop. Bill and I watched helplessly as Jim pounded shot after shot of whiskey at the bar before we went on. Jim wasn't mad or anything: he had just made a decision to get wasted, and he was sticking to that decision. I couldn't keep track of how much he actually drank, but it was at least enough that any other mortal human would've had to get their stomach pumped. Surprisingly, the show went well. Until I was in the middle of a solo and Jim thrust his hand into my crotch and grabbed my balls.

Hard.

In junior high my friends and I called it "goosing" and did it to each other all the time, but I couldn't believe Jim did it to me onstage as a grown man. I nearly broke his arm with my guitar neck, and he recoiled like an injured puppy. That sobered him up pretty quick. I wasn't quite as mad as when he tackled me naked during the previous year's trip to New York, but I was still pissed. In the dressing room afterward he immediately went into his sheepish routine:

"Man, I'm so sorry, I'll never do that again..."

"You're goddamn right you won't ever do that again!"

He knew he had fucked up, and I knew he had drunk so much he didn't know what he was doing. He was so contrite, and his apologies still worked on us back then. I let it go.

While Bill Siddons was put in charge of things on the road as our tour manager, our attorney Max Fink recommended we hire two slick Hollywood characters as our career managers: Sal Bonafede and Asher Dann. Sal had previously managed Dion, and I'm pretty sure he was the one who advised him to split from the Belmonts and go solo (a tactic he later tried with Jim). Asher was a real estate agent — Beverly Hills used to be wallpapered with ads for Asher Dann Realty — and he occasionally crossed paths with my dad on the golf course at the Riviera Country Club. He didn't have any experience managing bands, but he was a good drinker, which was an essential skill when dealing with Jim. Sal and Asher's theory was that if we got Jim totally drunk the night *before* a show, he would wake up the next day all contrite and humble, and therefore he wouldn't drink as much on show night. This, of course, did not work. Asher took Jim out and got him hammered one night before we played at the Scene in New York. The next night at the show, not only was Jim drunk, but when he started swinging the mic around like a lasso in the same fashion that had taken down Bill Graham, Asher jumped onstage to try and stop him and our show suddenly turned into a wrestling match. We bought Sal and Asher out of their management contract early the next year.

If it wasn't drunken wrestling it was drunken hide-and-go-seek.

Toward the end of '67, we played several shows in Colorado, and it was one of the rare times that Happy was able to get away from her family and join me on a trip. Jim got plastered and was lumbering around backstage, trying to find us. Happy and I were giggling as we avoided him, ducking around corners, running around outside the venue, and hiding in a car. Ray caught us and chewed us out for not taking care of our singer. We felt a little bad when he put it like that. It was Ray's protective paternal instincts kicking in again. But Jim was impossible to deal with when he was trashed like that. Why should it be our responsibility to humor him? We were all adjusting to a new dynamic, but in general Jim's drunken episodes were sporadic, so we tried to shake them off. Later that night, though, Happy and I stayed in a hotel room that shared a wall with Jim's. Fans were gathered on the street outside, and Jim would occasionally go to the window and get them all riled up. As the night went on, we heard him throwing things across the room, making all kinds of thumps and bumps and noises. Rumbles of thunder indicating what was to come.

Over the course of 1967, we had graduated from the Fillmore to the Winterland and from high school shows to college shows. In between all of it we recorded and released our second album, *Strange Days,* which hit number three in November. We should've been enjoying the ride, but between crisscrossing the country every week and Jim's drinking, we were already starting to feel burned out. We had only been a band for about two years. And in December: New Haven. Apparently, we were just getting started.

LET'S FEED ICE CREAM TO THE RATS

I don't know why Jim didn't like ice cream. Maybe he had some bad experience with it in his childhood. Maybe pushing away the dairy element was a subconscious rejection of his mother's milk. Or maybe I'm overthinking it and he actually loved ice cream and I just never noticed. All I know is that when we were on our way to a show at the University of Michigan in Ann Arbor in October 1967, we all wanted to stop for ice cream and Jim got mad.

The Doors always had a very dour public image, but we were human like everyone else. We were happy that day. With our second album in the top ten and our crowds getting bigger, we had every reason to be. So when we saw an ice-cream parlor on the way to the gig, we decided to stop in for a cone.

Jim grumbled something about us being children and went to find a liquor store instead. In the time it took us to finish our ice cream, Jim had finished most of the bottle he had bought. It was a revenge move. We were in a good mood and he wasn't, and misery loves company. I wasn't too worried about the show—there had been plenty of times when we had played well with Jim completely drunk.

This would not be one of those times.

Ray kicked things off with the intro to "Soul Kitchen," and John and I came in on cue as usual. But...no vocals. In fact: no Jim. He hadn't even joined us onstage. Again, this wasn't shocking. Jim had taken the stage late before, so we kept repeating the intro over and over, figuring Jim would eventually join us. But it went on so long that the audience started to boo.

It's pretty rare for a band to leave the stage before even finishing their first song, but what else could we do? "Soul Kitchen" wasn't working as an instrumental. It took us about a half hour to find Jim and drag him onstage. But it's like that old saying: You can lead a horse to water, but you can't make him sing. Jim didn't want to do any Doors material; he just wanted to jam the blues. We tried to appease him for a while, but then we'd say, "Come on, 'Break On Through,'" and he would just growl and pout.

He swore fiercely at the audience, and this was during an era when we weren't even allowed to say "high" on the radio. It was barely our crowd to begin with, considering that it was the university's annual homecoming concert. Most of the kids were clean-cut preppies who had probably heard "Light My Fire" on the radio but didn't really know what to expect from a Doors show. Then again, the entire time we were a band even I never knew what to expect from a Doors show. On good nights it would be illuminating. On nights like this it was humiliating.

I met eyes with John and we signaled to each other that we'd had enough. This wasn't Jim breaking new ground with some inspired psychedelic improvisation. This was a tantrum. John and I, for the first and only time in our career, abandoned Jim and walked off-stage. Ray soldiered on with Jim—he even picked up my deserted guitar at one point and tried a few blues riffs. But the booing only grew louder and Ray, too, finally gave up.

What never made sense to me is that Jim was always such a

prankster. He wasn't above impish behavior now and then. When we visited the Empire State Building in New York, we got on one of the local elevators to go to the top, and as soon as everyone else boarded, Jim swiped his hand across all the buttons, to the annoyance of all the other passengers who then had to wait as the elevator stopped at every single floor. He was like a big kid. So why was he so upset about some good old-fashioned ice cream?

Even though it's a night I wasn't too proud of, the University of Michigan show had a significant impact. As the crowd around him booed, one young man was captivated by Jim's defiant attitude and sneering contempt for the audience. It was the exact opposite of what all other musicians were doing at the time. That fan later went on to say that our unhinged performance that night inspired him to sculpt his own anarchic stage persona. Back then he was known as Jim Osterberg, but the world now knows him as Iggy Pop.

And that's why we always put up with Jim's erratic behavior. People ask me sometimes if I ever got angry when Jim caused chaos or threw a wrench into a show, but I almost always took it in stride.

Because even at his most challenging, he still had the power to draw people in.

Iggy Pop, of course, went on to heavily influence the punk scene of the seventies and countless musicians beyond, so I'm left wondering how different the course of music history might have been if we hadn't made the fateful decision to stop for ice cream that one night in Ann Arbor.

Good thing Iggy didn't catch us at one of our better shows.

James Brown and the Famous Flames in The T.A.M.I. Show

THE TEENAGE AWARDS MUSIC INTERNATIONAL SHOW

Since Jim and Ray were both UCLA film students, they were always eager to introduce John and me to their favorite directors. In the very earliest days of the Doors, we would go on band outings to a theater on Western Avenue that held midnight screenings of foreign and art films on Friday nights. I wasn't much of a Truffaut fan, but I liked Fellini. One Friday, though, the theater took a break from French New Wave and Italian surrealism and screened a concert film called *The T.A.M.I. Show*, which made the deepest impression of all.

The movie documented a single concert featuring a dozen acts, including Chuck Berry, the Supremes, the Rolling Stones, Lesley Gore, Jan and Dean, Smokey Robinson, and Marvin Gaye. It was a stellar lineup, and yet, as impossible as it sounds, there was one artist who managed to outshine them all.

The Godfather of Soul…Mr. Dynamite…the Hardest Working Man in Show Business…

James Brown.

We all knew his songs, but none of us had seen him live before. The footage from *The T.A.M.I. Show* is out there—I encourage you to watch it for yourself and see what we saw. The performance still holds up today. The music was great, of course, but the energy with which it was delivered really struck us. James was dramatic and acrobatic and explosive and emotional, all at once. He controlled his entire band as if they were one single instrument, and as if that instrument was an extension of his own body. For four young musicians just starting out, it was an unforgettable lesson in showmanship.

The Rolling Stones made the unfortunate decision to try to follow James at the concert. They were unable to compete. When the two acts were next to each other, it became painfully obvious how much Mick Jagger was trying to imitate James Brown, and it was laughable how poorly he measured up. It was a potent reminder to always be yourself. And never try to follow James Brown.

Soon after seeing the movie, I asked a girl named Elyse from my UCLA psychology class on a date to see James live at the L.A. Sports Arena. The cloud of weed smoke we waded through in the parking lot was thick even for the sixties, and we were the only white people in the audience from what I could tell. We were seated way in the back, but James still blew us away. He floated back and forth across the stage and had three drummers who sometimes played simultaneously and sometimes relieved each other when James wore one of them out. *The T.A.M.I. Show* wasn't some Hollywood trick. He really was that intense.

You can hear James Brown's influence on practically every one of our albums. The guitar part on "Soul Kitchen" loosely resembles the horns on "Papa's Got a Brand New Bag." The punctuations in the chorus of "Love Me Two Times" were taken from "Out of Sight," and they feature those signature James Brown E raised 9 chords. And "The Changeling" is consciously infused with the feel and attitude of "Say It Loud—I'm Black and I'm Proud."

I got to meet James only once, in the early eighties. I was playing guitar with a singer named Helena Springs, who looked and sounded like a post-disco Donna Summer. Sal Marquez, who played trumpet in Jay Leno's *Tonight Show* band, had recruited me to play live with her and help her write a few songs, but she was never able to break big and is now mostly known for being one of Bob Dylan's backup vocalists and Robert De Niro's ex-girlfriend. Helena opened for James at the Reseda Country Club. It had been over fifteen years since I'd last seen him live. He and his band had gotten older, naturally, and age gets the better of all of us eventually. The crowd seemed to enjoy the show, but compared to the high bar set by *The T.A.M.I. Show* and the L.A. Sports Arena, the night was a bit of a disappointment.

After the show, Helena and our band and I squeezed into James's dressing room to say hello. I don't think I even mentioned the Doors—I just told him I was a big fan. He was polite enough, but by that point he had probably grown numb to musicians telling him what an influence he was. Understandably, he was tired after his performance, so I excused myself and went back to our dressing room. I didn't want to bother him too much.

A few moments later, Helena came into our dressing room very upset. She had stayed behind to talk to James a bit more, and he had tried, in some uncouth way, to put the moves on her. Like I said: the night was a bit of a disappointment.

In the studio during the Strange Days *sessions*

STRANGE DAYS

We wanted to freak out the members of Jefferson Airplane. They happened to be in town when we were mixing the *Strange Days* album, so we invited them to drop by Sunset Sound and take a listen. They entered to darkness aside from the glow of candles and VU meters. Paul Rothchild always carried a briefcase full of electronic components and extremely potent weed, so we got them nice and stoned on Paul's stash and hit Play.

We had specifically cued up our weirdest composition, "Horse Latitudes," featuring eerie artificial wind noise, overdubbed screams of anguish, Ray clawing at piano strings, and Jim's shouted lines about animals being jettisoned into the sea. The Airplane played it cool and didn't say much beyond "Nice piano sound." But I heard later that we had, in fact, been successful in our mission to freak them out.

We started recording *Strange Days* pretty soon after the release of our debut album and before "Light My Fire" had even been released as a single. Sunset Sound had upgraded its equipment, so we now had eight tracks to work with instead of four, which was almost inconceivable just a year earlier. We were inspired—as all bands were at the time—by the recent release of *Sgt. Pepper's Lonely Hearts Club Band* and by the way the Beatles experimented in the studio, so we indulged in noises and overdubs, and Ray played piano parts backward. And Paul Beaver, a friend of our engineer Bruce Botnick, brought in a phalanx of knobs, switches, and wires that comprised a brand-new thing called a Moog. We were among the first rock bands to ever use one on an album. There's still something to be said for moving fast and not having time to second-guess yourself in the studio, but it was exciting to have more time, money, and technology to play with.

Most of the material on *Strange Days* was stuff we had written when the band was just beginning. Jim and I were working on the title track back when he was staying at my parents' house. "Horse Latitudes" was a poem that dated back to Jim's high school days. "My Eyes Have Seen You" and "Moonlight Drive" were from the World Pacific demo—although we rearranged "Moonlight Drive" significantly and incorporated the bottleneck guitar that had helped me pass my audition. I recorded the song with Ray's brother's National Town and Country guitar (the one I used in the "Break On Through" promotional film) after smashing several wine and champagne bottles to get just the right slide tone.

Ray has claimed that "You're Lost Little Girl" is about Frank Sinatra marrying Mia Farrow, but I wrote it and it's not. It was actually my second attempt at songwriting ever. I came up with the bass line first and built it from there. The lyrics are simple but it took me a while to come up with them. I wanted Jim to add a second verse, but he said, "No, man, it's perfect the way it is," and just sang my verse twice.

Even though some of the songs predated our first album, we were only able to play them to their fullest potential after putting in so much time together as a group and building our chemistry. As with the first album, most of *Strange Days* came together quickly since we had been playing the songs live for a while. The solo on "People Are Strange" took me only one take, and the solo on "You're Lost Little Girl" took me only two (well, it took more than that, but after Paul kicked everyone out of the studio and got me to relax, it flowed out of me in a matter of minutes). We released "People Are Strange" and "Love Me Two Times" as singles, and they both did well, but they didn't reach the same dizzying heights as "Light My Fire." Compared to our first album, *Strange Days* felt like a commercial failure, but artistically it represents us at a high point.

Of course, when you're making a Doors album it can't ever go smoothly. In the smallest possible hours of the night before we were supposed to record "When the Music's Over," I was in bed, asleep, when my phone rang.

"We're dying here! We're dying! You gotta come over!"

It was President Lyndon Baines Johnson.

Just kidding. Who the fuck do you think it was?

"We took too much acid! You gotta help us! You gotta save us!"

I almost hung up. But there was something serious in Jim's voice that differentiated this from his usual unsolicited wake-up calls. I drove bleary-eyed to some house in Atwater Village where he and Pam were staying. I almost expected to find the walls covered in blood...or other bodily fluids. I was half relieved and half disappointed to find Jim and Pam completely intact. And completely naked.

(I was used to Jim's nudity by then. Back in the Whisky days I once picked him up at Ronnie Haran's place and when she answered the door Jim was stalking around naked behind her. She said, "Can you get Elephant Dick out of here?" That was my first of several peeks at the reason Jim had so many girlfriends.)

"So what's wrong?" I asked.

"We took too much acid! We're lost and you're the only one who can help us," Jim responded. Pam was drooling and incapable of speech, but Jim pressed me to accompany them on their acid trip. "Come on, take some of this! Join us!"

"Ah, that's okay. No thanks."

My previous experience with Happy's acid bummer had confirmed that taking them out into nature would help. "Let's take a walk over to Griffith Park."

"Yeah, yeah!" They were like little children, putty in my hands.

"But first, let's put some clothes on."

Their moods improved drastically once they saw the stars in the sky, the flowers on the ground, and the shimmering water in the Mulholland Memorial Fountain. They kept pestering me to drop acid with them, but I kept reminding Jim that we both needed sleep before our recording session. After an hour or so they seemed to be in a better place, so I left them there and made Jim promise me he would show up at the studio the next day.

Jim, of course, did not show up at the studio the next day.

I told Ray and John what had happened and we concluded that waiting around for Jim would be pointless. Since we were set to record "When the Music's Over," we weren't sure what to do, because when we did the song live we always took subtle cues from Jim and never played it the same way twice. Ray decided that this time Jim would have to follow us instead of the other way around, and we pressed forward, with Ray laying down a temporary vocal track to guide us through.

When Jim finally came by the studio we got the standard apologies. We may have wanted to hold a grudge, but it didn't last long once he started to sing. He summoned all his intuition, followed the flow we had created for him, and nailed the vocal track perfectly in only two takes. How could we stay mad at him after that?

When I went in later to record the guitar solo for "When the Music's Over," I had a very specific tone in my imagination. I wanted sustain from Hell, but my Maestro Fuzz-Tone was too jagged. I wanted it to sound smooth, like a violin. Bruce Botnick fed the sound of my guitar amp into a mic, into a mic preamp, into a fader, into another mic preamp, into a line amp, and into another fader. Paul Rothchild, meanwhile, dug into his briefcase and pulled out a diode or a resistor or some other small piece of mysterious circuitry that looked like a little baby firecracker. Bruce incorporated the baby firecracker somewhere in the signal chain and rode the faders until the tubes inside the preamps glowed so much they lit up the control room. When they were finished they had created not only the exact sound I had in my head but my favorite sound on a solo ever.

Once we had locked in the right sound, we had to lock in the right mood, so we all indulged heavily in some weed from Paul's stash. I cranked up my amp and went to work. The foundation of the solo was a single E minor chord, which left me free to chase a psychedelic Coltrane vibe, going as far out as I could in a total stream of consciousness. After the third or fourth take, I went into the control room to listen to the playback, but Bruce Botnick, still reeling from Paul's weed, had forgotten to mute my previous take. As a result, two versions of my solo came out of the speakers simultaneously. Both takes were different, but they intersected at enough points to naturally complement each other. We were all blown away by the trippy sound, so we left it on the album like that.

Those happy accidents are the best moments one can hope for in the studio. And symbolically that solo encapsulates the Doors as a whole: disparate parts coming together in a way that somehow sounds natural. A mysterious, musical, stoned accident.

LYNN

When Lynn Ann Veres was about ten years old, she and some neighborhood kids snuck into the local playground after hours. While they were playing on the swings, a creepy man approached them holding a huge ring of keys in one hand and a pair of little girls' panties in the other.

"I have to see whose underwear this is!"

He wanted to check and see which of the kids were wearing underwear to solve the mystery, like they were in some sort of kiddie porn version of *Cinderella*. Thankfully one of Lynn's older friends yelled at the guy to get lost. He took off, and everyone got home safely. But when Lynn's mom found out about the incident, she blamed Lynn for the whole thing and punished her.

Lynn's mom was a fanatic Catholic who dragged the family to regular church services and forbade any of her eight children to curse, even though she herself cursed all the time. Lynn's dad was generally laid-back, but her mom had wild mood swings and kept the whole house on edge. When Lynn was a teenager, her brother told their mom that Lynn had gone on a date with Sammy Davis Jr.

It was an absurd story, intended to inflame their mom's simmering racial prejudice, but it worked better than expected. Lynn's mom not only flipped out in the moment but held it over Lynn's head for years, no matter how many times Lynn and her brother attempted to explain that it was a joke.

Lynn had to get out. Her family lived in an Archie Bunker–style town called Fords, New Jersey, about an hour outside Manhattan. If her mom had had her way, Lynn would've gotten a job as a secretary, married well, and stayed in Fords for the rest of her life. Lynn said no. She couldn't take the pressure and the hypocrisy and the oppression, so she escaped into New York City to go clubbing whenever she could. At only sixteen years old she moved into an apartment on the Upper East Side with one of her closest companions, a gay hairdresser named Kenny. The owner of the apartment building was in an iron lung so they had to be quiet all the time, but she was free.

Kenny introduced Lynn to New York's pre-Stonewall gay scene, and they would vacillate between uppers and downers so they could party all night and sleep all day. She got a job as a go-go dancer at the Wagon Wheel, and then at the Peppermint Lounge, where the twist had been invented just a couple of years before. Kenny would sometimes join her onstage for choreographed routines. She later moved into a gargoyle-adorned building with neighbors like Dave Budge from the Druids and a fashion designer named Lennie Barin, who threw extravagant, star-studded parties. (He once painted himself gold from head to toe to look like an Oscar statuette when he hosted Halloween.) Lennie gave Lynn dresses he had made so she could show off his creations around town, and he encouraged her to get into modeling. With her skinny frame and blond hair she had the looks to score a couple of catalog shoots, but unfortunately she was too short to work the runways. Once after getting a pixie-style haircut, though, she was chased down the street by some people who were convinced she was Twiggy. Her modeling career never took off, but she supported herself with a cushy job as a hatcheck girl at a Mafia-owned Spanish restaurant. It was a little scary seeing holster-shaped bulges under all the patrons' suit jackets, but she was clearing $400 a night in tips, and all the wiseguys loved her.

Lynn was, without a doubt, having way more fun than everyone else living back in Fords, New Jersey.

By the time Lynn was eighteen, she had friends at clubs all over the city, so she had no trouble getting into the Ondine Discotheque when the Doors made their New York debut in 1966. I didn't meet her that night, but Jim Morrison did. She met the humble, gentlemanly version of Jim and was predictably charmed by him. She invited him back to her building to check out the wall mural she had painted with her roommate. That night, with the enthusiasm of a tourism board member, Jim told her all about Los Angeles, and how the West is the best. Palm trees, sunshine, beaches…she was sold. She and her friends drove cross-country and saw that Jim wasn't lying.

Or at least not lying about the L.A. atmosphere. But he hadn't been too forthcoming about his relationship status. One day during her visit, she was hanging out at Jim's house on Rothdell Trail in Laurel Canyon when Pam walked in and shrieked, "Jim!"

"Who's that?" Lynn asked.

"Oh, this is Pam, my girlfriend."

Jim had failed to mention Pam before then. Lynn wasn't naive; she knew Jim was seeing other people. But a secret, official, live-in girlfriend?

"Fuck you!"

Lynn ran out of the house and down the steps past the Canyon Country Store. Jim chased after her, shouting, "Don't go!"

"How could you do this?"

"Stop! Don't go!"

"Why didn't you tell me?"

"She's, like, my *old* girlfriend."

Lynn wasn't stopping, and Jim needed to get her attention. So when he spotted a car heading up the road, he threw himself onto the hood. He bounced off and flopped to the ground. The car came to a screeching halt and the driver jumped out.

"What the fuck is wrong with you?!"

Lynn went to check on Jim. He stood up. And laughed.

She stormed off and he let her go. She spoke to him a few days later and it was as if he had no memory of the whole event.

"How are your ribs? Are they okay?"

"Why shouldn't they be?"

Somehow, even after that, Jim convinced Lynn to keep hanging out with him. She went back to New York and they met up whenever the Doors traveled east, and she saw him whenever she took trips out to L.A. with her friends. It was the beginning of the hippie era, and L.A. wasn't as crowded or as noisy as Manhattan. At first it was almost too peaceful for Lynn, but after a while—convinced that she could maybe solidify things with Jim if she lived a little closer to him—she finally made the move to Laurel Canyon.

Lynn originally moved into a house near the burned-out ruins of the Houdini mansion (it's never actually been proven to be Houdini's mansion, but that's what everyone called it). The house was full of Tiffany lamps and had a hidden elevator that went down into a secret tunnel under the street, and one of her housemates was Tandyn Almer, who wrote "Along Comes Mary" for the Association. Lynn tutored the owner's children in exchange for room and board, and spent her nights dancing at clubs on the Sunset Strip and getting thrown out of parties with Jim.

Jim didn't drive much when we first formed the band, but once we started making money, he got himself a 1967 Shelby GT500 that he lovingly called the Blue Lady. Bill Siddons subtly influenced him to choose that specific model because it had dual shoulder-harness seat belts and was the first American car to include a factory-installed roll bar. It didn't take a psychic to predict that Jim would be getting into multiple accidents. Once he even crashed the Blue Lady on the lawn outside a police station. I always heard the details of his crashes secondhand because Jim was too embarrassed to tell us about them himself. We would just occasionally notice that the Blue Lady was conspicuously missing and that Jim had arrived somewhere in a rental car.

Lynn was driving Jim home in one of his rental cars one night on a rare occasion when he admitted that he was too drunk to drive. The only problem was that Lynn was drunk, too. Plus she was a New Yorker, and New Yorkers don't drive. Lynn didn't even have a license. As she wove her way down Lookout Mountain Avenue, the driver's-side door was rattling, so she attempted to pull it closed, but instead she unlatched it and the door flung completely open. She swerved and banged the door into something—a pole, a tree; who knows?—and the door became stubbornly stuck in its open position. Jim was no help, flopping from side to side in a barely conscious state, and Lynn didn't have the presence of mind to simply stop the car, so she kept swerving her way through Laurel Canyon, screaming, with her door wide open, clipping anything in its path.

The police pulled them over. Lynn heard them say, "It's that Morrison guy again," and they arrested him instead of her. Lynn was the one who miraculously got away without consequences this time.

Jim said "Call Max!" and went without a fight. The cops took the car keys, so Lynn had to walk to the Canyon Country Store to call our lawyer from a pay phone and then walk home from there.

Jim tested Lynn's limits just as he did with everyone else. Once they were at a party at a fancy Malibu beach house, with a deck that stretched out over the sand. Lynn was leaning over the railing when

Jim grabbed her ankles and hoisted her over the edge. He held her dangling there as the blood rushed to her head. She screamed, "Get me up! Get me up!"

He made a single demand: "Tell me you love me."

She could barely sputter out the words because she was so furious, but she told him what he wanted to hear and he pulled her back onto the deck. Then he went on a drunken rampage and trashed the house. Lynn dragged him out of there in such an embarrassed rush that she left her purse behind.

At first it was easy for Lynn to cope with Jim's behavior because she had been surrounded by one type of craziness or another her whole life. But he kept pushing. On one of their last "dates," Jim drove her over to Marymount High School, an all-girls Catholic school near UCLA. He parked outside and cracked open a beer. He just sat there like a creepy old man, watching the girls and nuns go by. There was no agenda, other than being in a place where he didn't belong and inviting trouble. Lynn had dealt with enough Catholic wrath in her life and begged Jim to leave, but it took over an hour of nagging before he listened.

Lynn ended up moving to a house on Horse Shoe Canyon Road with my draft savior, Boom Boom; another gay guy, named Gwen; Laurie Sullivan (who claimed to be Ed Sullivan's illegitimate son); and a guy named Jerry who was known as the Green Lantern because he would tie a sheet around his neck like a cape and leap around on the roof like a comic book superhero. There was always a party going on there, or across the street at her neighbor Micky Dolenz's house. One of the rooms in Micky's house had padded walls and a padded floor, probably for meditating? Or in case they needed to lock up a mental patient? And Micky was building a single-seat airplane in another room. It was easy enough for him to get all the individual parts inside, but he never explained how he planned to get the finished plane outside once it was done. He always said, "I'm gonna get it up there someday."

One of Lynn's housemates at the Horse Shoe Canyon place was a girl named Gin, who was known for having very audible sex. Everyone could hear her through the walls, screaming her carnal catchphrase: "Get in there!" Lynn and Jim were already on the outs after their Marymount date, but the split was solidified one night when Jim was hanging out at the Horse Shoe Canyon house and Gin walked in. She took one look at Jim, grabbed his arm, and dragged him into a downstairs bedroom. Everyone did their best to ignore the telltale moans, but Gin was putting on a real show, likely as a way to prove to Lynn who the queen of the house was. Lynn's relationship with Jim officially ended for good the moment she heard Gin bellow, "GET IN THERE!"

That's when ol' Krieger moved in...

I may have terrible eyesight, but I'm not blind: I noticed Lynn's good looks immediately. But she was dating Jim and I was dating Happy, so we didn't pay much attention to each other. By early '68, though, we were both officially single, and her hilarious sense of humor, her East Coast edge, and her fearless spirit set her apart from other girls and made her irresistible. So one night when I found out that Lynn was going to be at a party at a mutual friend's house, I made sure to attend. I had recently bought a burgundy Porsche 911S, so I gallantly offered Lynn and her friend a ride home. Like every dumb guy, I tried to show off by gunning the engine and taking corners at dangerous speeds. As stupid as it was, it actually worked. Nothing physical happened that night, but it was the first chance Lynn and I had to really get to know each other, and we started hanging out at her Horse Shoe Canyon house after that. In spite of the reckless driving, Lynn said I was like a little Scottie dog, which was probably a swipe at my hair as much as a description of my personality. I was mellow. I was easy to talk to. I was the opposite of the guy who used to dangle her off balconies and jump in front of cars. Turns out women don't really like that—at least not when they're looking for something long-term. Lynn started bringing her friends over to my house on Topanga Beach to hang out, and finally one night her friends got the hint and left us alone long enough to... officially become a couple.

We grew very close very quickly. We used to take my yellow raft out on the ocean all the time. I would fish for bonitos while Lynn sunbathed. I actually learned that I lived two houses down from Lee Marvin because we saw him on TV mentioning how he had recently seen a beautiful woman with no top on in a yellow raft near his house. Lynn also joined the Doors on our first trip to Hawaii. We spent a couple of days on the Big Island before our show and a couple of days on Maui afterward. We snorkeled and surfed and sailed, but I got pretty upset when Lynn got plastered with Jim and the guys filming our *Feast of Friends* documentary. She was climbing coconut trees and staying up all night with them. Her breakup with Jim wasn't that distant a memory, and I got the feeling Jim was probably trying to coax her into revisiting the past, but I wasn't allowed to be jealous because it was the sixties, man. I never asked Jim how he felt about me dating Lynn because back then he wasn't allowed to be jealous either. And besides, he still had Pam, so it seemed like everything had worked out well for everyone.

About a year later, Lynn and I moved into a house in Benedict Canyon that would later become the inspiration for the song "Hyacinth House." Jim and a few friends were over one night, and he found an excuse to be alone in the kitchen with Lynn. He asked her if we had any wine. We had some fancy bottles of Château Latour, but Lynn knew that Jim was more interested in the fortified variety that could be found at only the finest gas stations. She offered him what we had and he changed the subject to the idea of them maybe starting things up again.

When Jim first met Lynn, she was just a silly kid. As time went on, she held on to her fireball spirit, but she had matured and grown. She and I had something good going. Jim saw that and felt like he had missed out, but she made it clear that her time with him had ended forever. Later that night, Jim complimented me on my choice of partner. He never went after Lynn again. And she and I remain together to this day.

Performing with Eddie Vedder at our Rock & Roll Hall of Fame induction
ceremony

LIFETIME ACHIEVEMENT

The Doors never won a Grammy when we were still together. We weren't bitter or disappointed about it—we never expected any different. They just didn't give Grammys to guys like us back then. They gave them to Frank Sinatra and Herb Alpert and James Taylor. We didn't even get a Grammy for "Light My Fire," even though José Feliciano did. At some point in the nineties, though, it seemed like trophy factories started working overtime to churn out Lucite plaques and gold-plated statuettes to make up for lost time.

In 1993 the Rock & Roll Hall of Fame hadn't opened its museum yet, so we weren't sure how big of a deal it would turn out to be, but our induction was our first major music industry honor. Backstage, they told us to keep our speeches very short, and they specifically told us not to thank anyone. Jim's sister spoke first, offering up only two quick sentences. I decided I'd bend the rules with a quick thank-you to my parents since they were in the audience and I'd never had an occasion in my life to thank them publicly. I spoke for less than forty-five seconds, John offered up a thank-you to his parents and bandmates in half that time. But when Ray got up he defiantly rattled off eight thank-yous right off the bat, and then went on to discuss fascism, the Summer of Love, psychedelics, the influence of the Beat Generation and jazz, and the idea of bringing all the races together as one, after which he read one of Jim's poems in full, explaining the poem's meaning in detail along the way.

Later that night, Lynn was furious at me for not thanking her.

"They told us not to thank anyone!"

"Ray thanked *his* wife!"

"But that's Ray! I didn't know he was gonna do that!"

"You thanked your parents!"

We've had multiple versions of that argument ever since. I've never won.

Ray, John, and I reunited to play a few songs at the Hall of Fame ceremony, with Eddie Vedder on vocals and Don Was on bass. It was certainly one of our best post-Jim performances, even if it was in front of people in formalwear seated at fancy tables instead of the chair-breaking hippies we were used to. We were all middle-aged by then so we were a little out of the loop in terms of the grunge phenomenon, but in 1993 everyone on the planet knew who Eddie Vedder was, and we were excited that he wanted to sing with us. We were supposed to practice together a few times before the show, but Eddie was driving down to L.A. from Seattle and he got caught in a major storm along the way, so he didn't make any of the rehearsals. The rest of us got together without him, after not having played together in about twenty years. You would think there'd be some rust to work out, but as soon as we plugged in, it was as if no time had passed at all. No matter what separate directions we've taken since the band ended, and no matter what petty disputes we've engaged in along the way, the musical chemistry between the members of the Doors will always bond us. It's almost scary.

Eddie made it to L.A. in time for one quick rehearsal at soundcheck on the day of the ceremony. Turned out he didn't need much practice—he walked in and nailed the songs. Except for the first line of "Light My Fire," when he sang, "*I* would be untrue" instead of "*it* would be untrue." Everyone makes that same mistake for some reason, so I doubt anyone in the room noticed. Unless they happened to be the guy who had written the original lyrics.

Eddie was a true Doors fan. Between our soundcheck and our performance, I hung out with him in his hotel room, where he peppered me with questions about Doors history. He wanted to know everything I could tell him about Jim Morrison, and I was happy to share as many stories as I could. It was a nice compliment to be inducted into the Rock & Roll Hall of Fame, but talking to Eddie and seeing the tangible influence the Doors had on a musician of his stature was an even more meaningful honor.

One of the other highlights of the evening was finally getting to meet my musical idol, Bob Dylan. After years of being a fan of his I had no idea he was a fan of ours. He dropped by before the ceremony to say a quick hello, and I did my best to hide my awe. I didn't take the opportunity to tell him how much his music meant to me, or how big of an influence he was, or how I had spent so many nights with a harmonica holder around my neck at the Red Rutabaga, trying to pay tribute to his songs. I was still programmed from the sixties to be cool and aloof. He's the one guy I've always wanted to collaborate with, though. Later on I was kicking myself for not trying to make more of a connection. Oh well. Maybe some other time.

In 2007, forty years after the release of our first album, the Doors were finally invited to the Grammys to accept a Lifetime Achievement Award. Even though we had never yearned for that kind of validation, it was pretty cool to be involved in all the pomp and circumstance. Lynn and I walked the red carpet and got interviewed by Joan and

Melissa Rivers on the way in, and later I got to chat about jazz and Coltrane with Ornette Coleman.

I got so swept up in the glitz of it all that for a moment I dropped my too-cool sixties attitude and gushed to Joan Baez about what a fan I was and how I've never asked anyone for an autograph except for the time I saw her play at Stanford during my Menlo days and got her to sign the back of my hand. She was polite but seemed unimpressed. I told her how I had lifted the line "'til the heavens stop the rain" from one of her songs when I wrote the lyrics to "Touch Me," but she didn't seem to care, or even really know what I was talking about. Years later I realized I was quoting the wrong lyric. The line I actually stole was "'til the stars fall from the sky," which was from an old English folk ballad called "Fare Thee Well" that Joan had covered. But Joan used different lyrics and never sang that line. No wonder she was confused. Maybe it was for the best that I stayed quiet when I met Dylan.

Left: Joan Baez smiling politely, right: me embarrassing myself

When I took the stage to accept our Grammy, I wanted to finally put an end to the always-smoldering argument I had unintentionally started with Lynn at the Rock & Roll Hall of Fame ceremony. The spotlight hit me, the applause died down, and I began my speech with, "I better thank my wife or I'll be in the doghouse." The crowd laughed, but when I got back to my seat, Lynn said, "That wasn't funny!" She was even angrier about that speech than the first one, and a new argument was born.

I'll never win.

PAM

Pamela Courson was no Yoko Ono. She never tried to put a wedge between Jim and the band. She never meddled in our creative process. I always thought she was good for Jim. Their relationship may have been tumultuous at times, but they never had any major fights when I was around. They made their own rules. It was clearly an open relationship since they were both seeing other people, and that incited trouble from time to time. But they genuinely seemed devoted to each other. A true couple. And even their unstable version of stability was better than Jim bouncing from girl to girl every night.

Pam used to date Arthur Lee from Love, who called her Yellow Tooth due to her discolored incisors. But her sweet looks outweighed her dental shortcomings enough that John hit on her at the London Fog before Jim ever did. Her squeaky voice and goofy demeanor made her appear sweet and innocent, but she was crazier than Jim in some ways, taking up with weird guys and doing heroin. To many men that would be a negative, but Jim had finally met someone who could walk on the edge right alongside him. Pam was too flighty and flaky to get into poetry or literature on the same level as Jim, but she was smarter than most people realized. Some people question whether she was calculating the cost-benefit of dating Jim in the name of a financially comfortable future. I can't say that wasn't a factor, but she still legitimately loved him. It was a complex coupling, to say the least. The bottom line is that she was weird, he was weird, and they were lucky they found each other to be weird with.

The red hair was the cherry on top. Jim's mom was a redhead, and I realized in the studio when we were recording "The End" and Jim was repeatedly screaming "Fuck the mother, kill the father!" that his Oedipal complex was for real. He confided in me once that he saw his mother's face in the moon when he took acid. I only met his mother once, very briefly, when she showed up at one of our shows in Washington, DC. Jim told our crew he didn't want to see her, so everyone was running interference to keep them apart. She and I politely shook hands and exchanged some small talk and I didn't see why Jim was so upset by her presence. After the show, though, Bill Siddons told us how her kindly facade had disappeared. She had been bossing around our crew and complaining angrily that the lights weren't good enough for her son. An erratic, volatile redhead swinging dramatically between selfless affection and selfish aggression? Freud would've had a field day with the whole thing.

Pam and I were both Capricorns so we always got along well. She seemed to get along with the other band members and all our girlfriends, too, even after Lynn's awkward introduction to her at the Rothdell Trail house. But Jim and Pam were often in their own little bubble. I don't think Pam ever consciously tried to separate Jim from the rest of us. She just hung out with all these junkies and oddball Europeans, and the separation naturally evolved. I can't say for sure that moving to Paris with Jim in 1971 was her idea, but I've always believed that her long-standing affair with a French count/

heroin dealer must've factored into her enthusiasm for the idea. Either way, we unanimously agreed that Paris would be a good thing for Jim. A chance to relax and put the pressures of the world and the band behind him. A chance to center himself and come back with a renewed passion for making music.

Paris did, by all accounts, provide those chances for Jim. But it also famously became his final resting place thanks to a heart attack or a heroin overdose—depending on which reality you choose to live in. After Jim died, Pam returned to the States, exited the airport, got in a cab, and entered into a heroin-fueled fling with the driver, who happened to also be a drug dealer. I saw her only a few times after that. She was still the same Pam, but her silly side had been blunted by obvious and severe depression. She never wanted to talk much about what had happened in Paris, of course. The last time I ran into her was when Lynn and I met Ray and John and their wives for dinner up in Sausalito. Pam coincidentally walked into the same restaurant with another new boyfriend—who happened to look like a shorter, younger version of Jim. She sat with us for a few minutes and made chitchat but then excused herself to eat at a separate table.

There has always been speculation about whether Pam's fatal overdose was accidental or intentional. I couldn't possibly say. I just know she was sad. And one way or the other, the grief took her.

The Doors on The Ed Sullivan Show

A REALLY BIG SHOE

The Ed Sullivan Show was an American institution—a signpost for entertainers that read, "You Have Arrived." Or at least that's what it was when Elvis, the Beatles, and the Rolling Stones made their first appearances. By 1967, Ed seemed corny and out of touch. It was a show your parents watched. But it was still an institution, and still a signpost we wanted to pass.

On the outside we played it cool, but in the privacy of our dressing room we were giddy. We were in New York City, in the CBS studios, on Broadway, about to be transmitted into millions of living rooms. We had done TV before, but only local channels. This was our first national broadcast. For some reason, I channeled all my pent-up excitement into entertaining my bandmates with my impression of Curly from the Three Stooges. I dropped to the floor and did that thing where Curly makes whooping noises and "runs" in a circle on his side. That's when Ed Sullivan happened to walk through our dressing room door.

We had done a rehearsal earlier; Ed was stopping by to wish us luck before going on the air. Ed caught the Doors in a rare moment when our guard was down and we were all laughing. Seeing our lighter side inspired him to tell us how good we looked when we smiled, and that we should wear those same big smiles when we went live.

"Live" was what made our *Sullivan* appearance stand out. Most of our previous TV performances had been lip-synched, which was lame, but it was just how music shows were done back then. And all of them had been recorded ahead of time, which came in handy when Jim didn't show up to a taping of a short-lived show called *Malibu U,* hosted by Ricky Nelson. Ray, John, and I were sitting on Leo Carrillo State Beach, surrounded by actors and crew members staring at us and checking their watches. A fire truck had been brought in as a backdrop and all our instruments were set up on it, but we had no lead singer. Being on TV was a big deal for us back then. We couldn't believe Jim had stood us up. After a while we faced the reality that Jim wasn't coming, so we played "Light My Fire" while my brother Ronny faced away from the camera and did his best impersonation of Jim Morrison's back. The next day the crew tracked down Jim and filmed him singing while wearing Ronny's shirt. The whole incident seems more absurd every time I think about it. Can you imagine Mick Jagger not showing up for a TV taping and the Stones filming Keith Richards's brother from behind instead?

We had also done Dick Clark's *American Bandstand,* which, like *Sullivan,* was struggling to stay hip as the Summer of Love changed the cultural landscape. Dick greeted us in our dressing room before the taping, and he was friendly and welcoming. But he swore like a sailor. He wasn't angry or bitter; it was his awkward attempt to seem cool. Being on *Bandstand* was, overall, a surprisingly forgettable experience. But I'll always cherish the memory of hearing Dick Clark repeatedly say "fuck."

Since Clark and Sullivan were the old guard, we were more

excited about appearing on *The Jonathan Winters Show.* Jonathan hadn't built up a legacy like *Sullivan* or *Bandstand,* but we loved his frantic, unpredictable comedic style. Which is maybe why our frantic, unpredictable lead singer launched himself into a piece of scenery and tangled himself in a bunch of rubber webbing at the end of "Light My Fire." But Jim was out-crazied that night by our host. At the end of the show, Jonathan came out and improvised a monologue for the studio audience. Among other things, he took out a folding carpenter's ruler and bent it into different shapes like it was a balloon animal, pretending it was a puppy dog or a machine gun. It was cool to see him do some unpolished comedy, but he went on and on, and soon the crowd started to thin out. For over an hour he never let up, even though people kept leaving. We hung out and watched him out of morbid curiosity to see how long he could go. Eventually the entire audience had disappeared. The cameras were off. He was making jokes to literally no one. I don't even remember him stopping. As far as I know, he stayed there talking until the next week's taping.

Our episode of *Jonathan Winters* aired later that month, when we had a gig at the Winterland Arena in San Francisco. Back then, of course, there was no way to record a show and watch it later. So in the middle of our set Bill Siddons brought a TV onstage. We stopped playing, put a microphone up to the TV speaker, and sat down to watch ourselves. We thought it would be a treat for the audience, but the screen was only about nineteen inches wide. I doubt anyone past the first few rows could see or hear anything, so we just awkwardly watched the show and then awkwardly resumed our set. This was only a couple of weeks after our New Haven show, when our fans had learned to expect the unexpected from the Doors. I don't think any of them expected that!

When we played "Light My Fire" on *Sullivan,* we didn't trash the set and we didn't swear and we didn't use my brother as a stand-in for Jim, and yet it was the most controversial TV appearance of all. The narrative, according to the supposedly canonical Doors biography *No One Here Gets Out Alive,* is that a producer told us not to sing the word "higher," and we all conspired to contravene the order after the producer left the room. According to Oliver Stone's movie *The Doors,* Jim mugged for the camera and over-enunciated the word "higher" on air to protest the attempted censorship. According to Ray's autobiography, the producer shouted at us after the show and told us we'd never play *Sullivan* again, and Jim coolly replied, "Hey, man. So what? We just *did* the *Ed Sullivan Show.*"

But in the dressing room we weren't offended by the suggestion to change our lyrics: we thought they were joking. "Light My Fire" had been number one for weeks, playing on every major radio station around the country. We had performed it on half a dozen other TV shows. No one cared about the word "higher." They couldn't possibly be serious. As for Jim's delivery, the original footage is out there and you can see for yourself how he hardly moved for most of the song. Jim never moved on TV the way he did at our concerts. The bright lights and the cameras and the artificial atmosphere of a TV studio always made him feel self-conscious. We never conspired about not changing the lyric ahead of time, and we never talked about why he didn't change it afterward, but my guess is he was just nervous. It was *Sullivan.* It was national. It was LIVE. He went on autopilot and sang "Light My Fire" the same way he had a million times before. He may not have even been listening when they suggested the change, but if he did do it on purpose, it was probably because he didn't think it would be a big deal. Bill Siddons might've gotten scolded by the show's staff when we weren't around, but I don't remember anyone yelling at us or telling us we'd never play *Sullivan* again, and I definitely don't remember Jim's perfectly scripted badass response to the frazzled, square producer. The way Ray told stories, I'm surprised his version didn't end with us strutting in slow motion down Broadway while the CBS studios exploded in the background.

The other thing the retelling of the Sullivan Legend always gets wrong is my smirk. After Jim sang "higher," the camera cut to a shot of me and Ray, and people have since interpreted the look on my face as a sly grin in reaction to Jim's act of defiance. In truth, I was just the only member of the band who took Ed's preshow advice to smile. It wasn't until long after the show aired that I was finally able to see a clip of our performance. Ray, John, and Jim all looked so cool, playing on that historic stage with their serious, stoic faces.

And there I was... smiling like an idiot.

CARRY ME, CARAVAN, TAKE ME AWAY

On a September afternoon in 1968, we set up our instruments in Frankfurt's historic Romer Square, and we drew more stares than autograph seekers. We were there to film a performance of "Hello, I Love You" for a local TV station, and if there hadn't been cameras there I'm pretty sure we would've gained as much attention as a group of random street performers. The pedestrians who stopped to watch us badly lip-synch our hit single weren't fawning over Jim or even tapping their toes to the beat. They were mostly older men in business suits and disapproving older women with their arms folded. Our show in Frankfurt later that night drew a large contingent of U.S. service members from a nearby military base. While many soldiers reported listening to our music during their tours of Vietnam, it seemed like the troops stationed in Germany didn't have the same taste. They only came to the show because their options for American entertainment were otherwise limited. They mostly milled about in the audience and hardly paid us any attention. Most of our songs were met with silence.

The world wasn't as connected back then as it is now. Our music was popular enough to bring in an audience on our first European tour, but we still had to prove ourselves. Being a curiosity was an asset in London, where it fueled us to play one of our best shows ever at the Roundhouse. And it was an even bigger asset in Amsterdam, where we had to beg the crowd for forgiveness.

In the dressing room before our Amsterdam show, we thought Jim had drunk too much, as usual. He was barely able to stand, so Bill Siddons's wife, Cheri, was using all her strength to prop Jim up over the bathroom sink while Bill splashed water on his face. Jim gradually went limp and then (as the song goes) he slipped into unconsciousness.

Bill and Vince Treanor, our equipment manager, tried to revive him but were getting nowhere. Jefferson Airplane was touring with us as an opening act and one of their roadies told me someone had handed Jim a block of hash earlier in the day, which he immediately gulped down. (Bill and Cheri have since informed me that it was Bob Hite from Canned Heat who gave Jim the hash—his band happened to be touring Europe at the same time.) I also found out that while the Airplane was playing and we were backstage preparing to go on, Jim had wandered onto the stage and done some sort of flailing dance. Who knows what else he had taken?

He was breathing, but he was out cold. An ambulance took him to the hospital and we were faced with the difficult decision of whether or not to play without him.

Other than that one set at the Whisky, Jim had never missed a show before. And at the Whisky we were an opening band playing a small club. This was a headlining show in a foreign country in front of two thousand people. We deliberated over what to do and ultimately figured we'd let the crowd decide. We sent Vince out to explain the situation and offer the crowd a choice between a refund and a Doors concert without Jim Morrison. They chose the concert.

Most Dutch people probably weren't reading *Life* magazine, so they likely hadn't heard about New Haven. *Ed Sullivan* didn't air in Europe. I doubt the news of our riot shows had hit their newspapers. Jim Morrison wasn't JIM MORRISON over there. He was simply the singer for the Doors. Having grown weary of the expectations of American audiences based on our image, we found it a breath of fresh air to finally play in front of an audience that was genuinely interested in the music. It's a shame Jim Morrison missed it.

We played a commendably tight set that night. Normally we had to be on our toes at all times onstage, watching Jim for cues and trying to follow his sudden improvisations. That tension is part of what made our live show so unique, but without having to worry about any sudden twists or turns, we could play with more musical precision. The crowd seemed to dig us and the show was reviewed well in the papers. I was just happy we got through it without anyone throwing anything at us for not having Jim there.

I've never hungered for the direct spotlight. I love performing, but I was never a flashy guitar player. Having Jim there to always soak up all the attention was perfect for me. Without him, there was a void of energy. Ray did an admirable job of filling it by singing most of our songs that night. I sang "Love Me Two Times" and a couple of other tunes that were in my range, and I jumped in on backing vocals to help out Ray here and there. I had fun pushing myself to be more animated than usual to make up for Jim's absence, but I was relieved when he rejoined us for the next show.

As always, Jim being wasted at one show meant he would lay off the booze at the next, but that didn't stop him from telling the crowd in Copenhagen to "shut up!" The Danish fans had a method of applauding in rhythmic unison, like they were doing a soccer chant or something. It was a sign of affection, but Jim hated it. Maybe it was too conformist? Or too distracting? Whatever the reason, there was no way to pull him aside and reason with him about it, so he just got more and more pissed off and kept berating the audience.

The tour ended on a mixed note, with a show in Stockholm that was well performed but poorly attended. My parents had flown over to Europe for a vacation and they specifically scheduled the trip so they could see us play. Thankfully they picked the half-empty show instead of the awkward Frankfurt show or the Jim-less Amsterdam show or the "Shut up!" Copenhagen show.

Despite a few stumbles along the way, we came home from Europe in good spirits. Maybe we hadn't proven ourselves at every show, but we had at least made an impression. We assumed we'd make it back for another tour soon after, but aside from one performance at the Isle of Wight Festival, it was the only time we played Europe while Jim was still in the band. Those poor bastards in Amsterdam came so close...

FEAST OF THE RESURRECTION

Roughly 2,012 years after the birth of Christ, I visited the site of his death. Ray and I had booked a show in Israel as part of our later-era reunion tours, so we scheduled a day to sightsee around Jerusalem with our band and crew. A private guide took us to the Church of the Holy Sepulchre, which was built around the fabled site of the crucifixion and burial of Jesus. I don't know how much proof they have that it's the right spot, but it was hard not to get swept up in all the religious fervor.

Right by the entry, tourists were gathered around a stone slab on the floor where the body of Jesus was supposedly laid after they supposedly took him down off the cross. I asked our guide if I could lie in the same spot to see if I could feel some Jesus vibes and experience what being resurrected as the Son of God might feel like. He cheerfully told me to go ahead. I flattened myself facedown on the stone. I didn't feel anything spiritual. But a moment later I felt a hand on my collar as a guy in monk's robes grabbed me and roughly dragged me out the door while yelling, "Blasphemy! Blasphemy!"

He dumped me outside, and as I collected myself I wondered if the next day's headlines would read "DOORS DEFILE CHRIST" or something. Ray, our guide, and the rest of our group were too afraid of getting in trouble themselves to stop the monk, but once the coast was clear they casually exited the church to find me. I didn't mean to cause any problems. The guide said it was okay! If only Jesus had been there. I'm sure he would've forgiven me.

It was a little embarrassing, but how many people can brag that they were kicked out of the holiest site in Christianity? It was one of many fond memories Ray and I made in Israel, like when, despite my usual indifference to my Jewish roots, I donned a yarmulke and said a little prayer to Jim at the Wailing Wall. We made memories in other countries as well, like when we got to walk through Red Square in Moscow, and when we saw the stunning collection of Rembrandts and van Goghs and Picassos at the Hermitage in Saint Petersburg. We had bats flying overhead and monkeys begging us for food in Brazil, and we got to hold koalas and pet a 175-year-old tortoise at Steve Irwin's zoo in Australia. This was touring in the new millennium.

After all the volatility and anxiety of our earlier years on the road, we were finally getting to actually enjoy ourselves. We flew first-class, we stayed in fancy hotels, we relaxed or went sightseeing during the day, and our road crew set everything up perfectly for us so we could breeze onto the stage and play at night. In London we filled the Wembley Arena, in Paris our show was oversold by thousands of tickets, in Italy we played in an outdoor piazza where the barricades buckled from the energy of the surging crowd, in Mexico we played a bullfighting ring with live chickens in a coop visible beneath the stage, and in Greece we played in a mountaintop amphitheater overlooking the lights of Athens. There were moments when I wished Jim could've been there with us. But, if I'm being honest, part of me was relieved he wasn't. If I can get kicked out of Christ's tomb, can you imagine what kind of trouble Jim might have caused in the Holy Land?

John repeatedly turned down offers to join Ray and me. Part of it was because of his tinnitus, but I sensed that the bigger factor was the long history of personal friction between him and Ray, which, in 2003, culminated in a bitter legal battle between all three of us. I understood, but it still would've been great to have him along for the ride. I kept telling John how great the shows were and how much fun we were having on the road and how all the stress of the old days was gone. Sure, it wasn't the same without Jim. But we also weren't playing high school auditoriums or using crappy borrowed gear or worrying about getting arrested midset. John wasn't interested.

There was only one original Doors show that John ever skipped. We were booked in Portland at the end of '67. I don't remember what exactly pissed off John—something with Jim fucking up a gig or a recording session, maybe. We were all a little fried and John always had the shortest fuse of all of us. So he called in sick. He may have actually been ill, but not so ill that he couldn't have played. I don't blame him for losing his patience with Jim, but it was a transparent excuse. I tried to talk him into coming, but he was really pissed about whatever Jim had done and he had made up his mind.

We didn't want to play without John, but canceling at the last minute would've caused all kinds of problems with the promoter, so we had little choice. We had previously played a few shows with a band called the Daily Flash, and their drummer, Jon Keliehor, lived near Portland, so he filled in with a few days' notice. Nobody in the crowd seemed to mind. In fact, they rushed the stage, so they must've enjoyed the show pretty thoroughly. John saw how little trouble we had replacing him and wisely reconsidered missing any more shows.

None of us wanted to admit it to John at the time, but the truth is, he wasn't as easily replaceable as it might've appeared. Even though the Portland crowd didn't notice the difference, those of us onstage knew an ingredient was missing. John didn't just keep the beat; he created a musical dialogue with Jim's lyrics, and he used clever fills to push Ray and me during our solos. He colored in our compositions with a range of dynamics, and he struck a perfect balance between foundation and flourish. I've played Doors songs with a bunch of different drummers over the years. Most of them are experienced, professional players who are given ample practice time to master the subtle nuances of each song. No matter who they are or how hard they try, no one plays those songs quite like John.

When Ray and I were touring, we played countries and continents that the original Doors never reached. We couldn't have taken Jim Morrison to Australia or Japan or Argentina: we never would have made it back! Everywhere we went, fans from around the world told us what a once-in-a-lifetime experience it was to see us play their favorite songs. I'm the first to acknowledge that the Doors aren't really the Doors without Jim Morrison fronting us and John Densmore backing us, but the fans don't need anyone to tell them that, and as long as there are people out there who still love our music, I will always love playing it for them.

WAITING FOR THE SUN

The standing accusation is that when we wrote "Hello, I Love You" we ripped off the Kinks. Nothing could be further from the truth: we ripped off Cream! The song's feel comes from me telling John to emulate Ginger Baker's rumbling tom-tom pattern from "Sunshine of Your Love." "Hello" was originally recorded for the World Pacific demo before I joined the band. We tried to rework it for our first two albums, but it always came out sounding too simple. By the time we got into the studio for *Waiting for the Sun,* we had burned through all our old material and it was one of the few songs we had left in our reserves, so we had to figure out something.

The fuzz tone on my guitar is maybe a little overdone, but along with the drum pattern, it was another one of my suggestions that helped the song stand out. And then there's the alien *beowwwwww-wwww* guitar break birthed from my Classic Doors Songwriting Theory: When in doubt, break out the bottleneck. We modified my slide with a tremolo and an echo effect and—even though I got the timing slightly wrong—we broke up the monotony of the song with a sonic curveball.

It is decidedly (and maybe a little embarrassingly) a pure pop song, but it was our only other number one hit. I can't take all the credit... but can I at least take a little?

Some of my favorite Doors songs are the less commercially appealing tunes on *Waiting for the Sun*. When I wrote "Yes, the River Knows," I tried to pull at the same inspirational thread that had brought about "Light My Fire": the four elements. This time it was water instead of fire, balanced out with lyrics comparing a breakup to a drowning death to once again keep up with Jim's darkness (he loved the line about "mystic heated wine" even though I only squeezed it in there for rhyming purposes). Ray gave the song life by playing a grand piano instead of his Vox Continental. It's my favorite thing Ray ever played. When I covered it years later on one of my instrumental solo albums, I altered almost every other element of the song, but I kept the piano part intact. And as much as Jim's voice is irreplaceable on any of our tracks, I'm convinced that no other human being could've sung that particular song any better.

I wrote "Spanish Caravan" as an excuse to finally use my Ramírez acoustic in the studio. The main lick was lifted from a classical guitar piece called "Leyenda," written by a Spanish composer named Isaac Albéniz back in the late 1800s. Lyrically I pictured a journey through the Spanish countryside, even though at that point in my life I had never actually been to Spain. Originally there was a much longer flamenco solo in the middle of the song. I spent hours perfecting it, but later we all agreed the song was too long, so the solo where I finally got to showcase all my years of classical training was cut out. I didn't mind changing the song, but I was heartbroken when I found out the master tape of the outtake was lost forever.

Jim initially wanted the entire B side of the album to be a seventeen-minute theatrical poem called "The Celebration of the Lizard." The rest of us weren't opposed to putting out a long, experimental piece—we took the time to record it and even played it live quite a few times. But if you're going to release a seventeen-minute song, you'd better be able to stand behind it, and we just didn't feel it was strong enough. A piece of it became the song "Not to Touch the Earth," which features warbly single guitar notes in favor of standard chords. I wasn't coordinated enough to bend the whammy bar while plucking the notes with my fingers and also triggering my echo pedal with my feet, so Paul Rothchild stood next to me with his hand on the whammy bar and bent the notes in time.

"Not to Touch the Earth" became most notable for its last line: "I am the Lizard King. I can do anything." Jim wasn't speaking about himself; it was a proclamation from one of the characters he had created in the poem, but it became Jim's eternal nickname. I chuckle inside a little every time I hear it. It always makes me think back to that green welder's jacket with the sewn-on lizard skin that he was wearing when I first met him. I wish Jim could witness the unintentional cultural impact of that single whispered lyric. It has been referenced in everything from *The Office* to *SpongeBob Square-Pants;* it became the name of a late-nineties pro hockey team in Jacksonville, Florida; and it even inspired some paleontologists to name a prehistoric species of iguana in Jim's honor: the *Barbaturex morrisoni,* or Bearded King Morrison. Jim always thought the Lizard King nickname was a little silly. It never bothered him, but he never embraced it. If he came back today he'd probably wonder why we were all still calling him that.

When it came to "The Unknown Soldier," Paul Rothchild approached it like a science project. Anti–Vietnam War sentiment was at its peak, so he thought Jim's lyrics could tap into the vibe of the moment and form the basis of a hit. When it came to the music, he decided to study hit singles to find common traits. What's the average tempo of a hit single? What's the average length of a hit single? What key is used most often on a hit single? We always trusted

Paul because he had guided us to the mountaintop with our first two albums, but when "The Unknown Soldier" barely cracked the top forty, it confirmed our suspicions that the scientific method was a terrible way to approach songwriting. No one really knows what makes a hit. Unless you're Quincy Jones.

The biggest problem with the album, though, was the production process. We were no longer bound by time or budget constraints, so Paul indulged by spending hours and hours dialing in drum sounds and tweaking everything obsessively in pursuit of a perfection that only he could hear. Our first record was fun and fast. Our second record was experimental and exciting. *Waiting for the Sun* was when recording turned into a chore. Paul's approach was to have us do endless takes, hacking and slashing at a song all night until we beat the life out of it, and then have us come in fresh the next day and nail it. Sometimes it worked, sometimes it didn't, but there was no talking him out of his methods. I can't argue with how great the album sounds, and I'm glad Paul cared enough to put in so much effort, but I don't know if it was worth the loss of morale and spontaneity. Every Doors fan has his or her own reason for preferring one album to another, but in all my life I've never heard anyone say "*Waiting for the Sun* is my favorite because it has the best snare tone!"

Drums were always done first and vocals were always done last, so with each passing hour that Paul spent on technicalities, Jim got more and more bored, and he would cure his boredom by drinking. The longer Paul took, the drunker Jim got. "The Unknown Soldier" was the first track we laid down, and we did over a hundred takes before Paul was satisfied. Jim's enthusiasm for the recording process was shot after that. So he started bringing his drinking buddies into the studio to keep himself entertained.

Jim was already on the outs with Lynn at the time, but she dropped by the studio occasionally with her friends Ron and Freddy from a go-nowhere band called the Magic Tramps. She had introduced them to Jim on the night she drove Jim home with the car door flying open. They would come into the studio wasted, feed Jim pills, and disrupt everything. I remember Jim hammering away on the studio piano trying to work out an early version of "Orange

County Suite" with Ron and Freddy, and they were fucking around so much that Paul finally snapped and kicked Jim's friends out. Jim threatened to leave as well; I don't know how Paul talked him down. Apparently at some point during the sessions John quit the band because Jim passed out and pissed himself. I seem to have blocked that incident out of my mind. But I think it's unfair for people to expect me to remember every time John threatened to quit. Or every time Jim pissed himself.

Relatively, Jim was on his best behavior when we recorded our first two albums. Sure, he hosed down the studio with a fire extinguisher, but we would've preferred that any day over dragging him through endless drunken vocal takes. The worst experience was when we were recording "Five to One," one of Jim's rare politically influenced songs, about the young outnumbering the old. On the finished album, a casual listener will hear an iconic vocal take. It's classic Morrison, howling for a long-awaited revolution. When he sings "Your ballroom days are over, baby," it's wonderfully anarchic, but in the studio we couldn't believe how out of time he was. If you close your eyes and listen closely, you can hear the tension. You can hear an exasperated producer and three cringing bandmates...who have all been dealing with the effects of endless technical tweaks... who have all been coping with the obnoxiousness of the Magic Tramps...who have been forced to sit through a bunch of completely unusable takes...who are staring daggers at their drunken singer...who are desperately hoping they'll get something that will work...

In a way, it's almost a tragedy that *Waiting for the Sun* ended up being our only album to hit number one. Because it normalized everything. It gave Jim an excuse not to change his behavior, and it gave the rest of us an excuse to ignore it. We were happy when we heard we had topped the charts. Maybe we shouldn't have been.

Outside the Doors workshop

SHIP OF FOOLS

The building at 8512 Santa Monica Boulevard has been repurposed several times over the years. Last time I was there it was a Mexican restaurant. Having tried the food, I can't say I'm surprised that they went out of business. But they had a picture of the Doors up on the wall, and now there's a plaque outside commemorating the time when it was our office and rehearsal space.

In early '68, after we fired our managers Sal and Asher, we promoted Bill Siddons from tour manager to manager. He helped us find an old building in West Hollywood near a strip club called the Phone Booth (where Jim often drank) and the Alta Cienega Motel (where Jim often passed out). Bill put his carpentry skills to work to build offices upstairs, a rehearsal space downstairs, a lounge area with a pinball machine, and a little workshop where Vince Treanor could tinker with our equipment to his heart's content.

My first Gibson SG went missing soon after we moved in. I've always suspected that one of the questionably qualified assistants Vince hired walked off with it. But it could've also been taken by one of the many oddballs the Doors tended to attract. We'd often enter the office to find a skinny, dark-haired homeless woman asleep inside. We dubbed her Crazy Nancy. She talked to herself, but she was harmless. There was also a trench coat–clad homeless man we called Cigar Pain who lingered outside the office and sang through the air-conditioning vents to get our attention. I believe Ray came up with his nickname after finding out the guy had purposely put a cigar out on his own vocal cords to sound more like Jim.

Being a musician is rarely thought of as a traditional job, but when we weren't on the road we spent most days at the office. If we weren't busy with press or tour plans or label business upstairs, we were jamming or writing downstairs. I don't want to take any credit away from Bill Siddons, but we were more hands-on than most bands when it came to business, almost to the point of managing ourselves. You'd think the dry day-to-day stuff would've bored the hell out of Jim, but he was actually at the office more often than any of us, usually because he'd spend the night crashed on the couch. But for a guy who regularly urinated in public, he was surprisingly attentive and involved. In fact, he was the only band member with his own desk.

A band meeting at Bill's desk during the L.A. Woman *era*

Around the time we opened the office, Jim had built up an entourage: Frank Lisciandro, Paul Ferrara, and Babe Hill. Frank and Paul
were his classmates at UCLA film school, so we hired them to tag
along with us on the road and shoot what would ultimately become
our *Feast of Friends* documentary. None of them were professional
filmmakers—Babe was a part-time stuntman brought on to do sound
and could barely operate his Nagra audio recorder—so the whole
project ended up unfinished and formless. We weren't thrilled about
spending band money to employ Jim's drinking buddies, but they
were a major improvement over some of the other slimy characters he
sometimes hung around with. And today their footage survives as
some of the most crucial visual evidence of the Doors' existence.

Jim wanted the Doors to be pirates—"Four guys drinking and
fucking their way across the country," as he put it. An armchair psychologist might say he was trying to compensate for growing up in a
fractured family, or that he was trying to cure some inherent sense of
loneliness. Whatever it was, we weren't able to provide it for him. It's
not that we were puritanical squares who refused to partake in drugs
or alcohol; we just couldn't possibly keep up with him. And if we had
tried, the artistic output of the Doors would've surely suffered. Frank,
Paul, and Babe were there to indulge him. They were nice enough
guys, and they were genuine friends to Jim, but we still saw them as
enablers. Jim would've been drinking every night either way, but they
always went with him, and they always let him pick up the tab.

As much as Jim valued his entourage's companionship, he valued
his bandmates' honesty. He knew we weren't sycophants. He
thought of us as equals. If all he wanted was constant praise, he
could've easily gone solo. When Sal and Asher were managing us,
they even encouraged him to do so. Instead of leaving us in the dust,
he was the one who suggested firing them. He could've hogged writing credit on the first few albums, but he was the one who suggested
a four-way split. When promoters tried to bill us as "Jim Morrison

and the Doors," he was the one who insisted the most loudly and stubbornly that his name be stricken from the marquee. No matter how famous he got, he never had an ego. So many bands break up because one member wants all the money, all the fame, all the control, or all of the above. Jim just wanted to be part of something.

When *Feast of Friends* wrapped, Jim and his crew wanted to make a feature film called *HWY.* Jim put up the money himself but as a loan from the band against future royalties. Based on how *Feast of Friends* had turned out, we weren't expecting much, but we thought it would be good for Jim to have a project to focus on so he wouldn't spend all his free time drinking. He rented a separate production space near the Doors office and went to work with Frank, Paul, and Babe. They planned some shots, they got drunk. They went on filming trips, they got drunk. They hacked together a rough edit, they got drunk. Follow-through was never Jim's strong suit.

For a while Jim also considered going into acting, but after one or two auditions he abandoned that pursuit as well. Some have theorized that Jim was exploring these nonmusical options as a way to leave rock stardom behind. But if he was so sick of his current career, why not put more effort into finishing his film? If he was so sick of the limelight, why go into acting, of all things? I never saw him wanting to leave the band. He wasn't shackled to us. He could've walked away at any point. He never cared about money, and even if he did, he had plenty of royalties coming his way. Filmmaking and acting and poetry were just other avenues for Jim to express himself. That's what creative people do: they create. I've always loved to paint, but no one has ever suggested that painting was my way of escaping the band. People can do, and be, more than one thing.

Jim was just easily frustrated. And even more easily distracted. The Doors worked only because the rest of us were able to remain relatively grounded when Jim's attention wandered. But we couldn't manage the rest of Jim's life for him.

There was some bad blood between the band and the entourage after Jim died. Obviously Jim's death wasn't their fault, but we felt like we had gone out of our way to pull Jim back from his bad habits while they steered him into the skid. I don't know if it was fair of us to look at it like that, because who knows how much worse things might've been if they weren't around? Either way, as with all grudges, I've done my best to let all that go. Frank and Paul shot a lot of classic Doors photos over the years, so we have friendly business dealings from time to time. Babe and I actually became pretty close friends, but it's been a long while since I've heard from him. He used to reach out to me for money every couple of years, and the fact that he hasn't asked for any in a while is a little worrisome. I never had his phone number, but he always managed to find mine. The last word I got was from his daughter, who told me he had gotten into some debt, someone was after him, and he was hiding out in Mexico.

Back in the day, Babe and I once talked about trying to turn Jim into an outdoorsman. I had convinced the band to buy a boat, and we christened it the *Ship of Fools,* after one of the songs on *Morrison Hotel.* Babe and I spent a lot of time on the boat, fishing and scuba diving together. We made a plan to take Jim out and teach him to fish. Get him out of the bars and into nature. He wanted to be a pirate: let's get him on the open sea!

Didn't work. When pirates get on the open sea, they drink. There's a metaphor in there somewhere about how you can steer a boat all you want, but the tides have the final say. When the Doors ended, I bought the boat from the band and hired Babe to live on board and be its caretaker. Due to some dim-witted act of negligence on his part, the *Ship of Fools* sank in its slip at the Redondo Beach harbor. There's probably a metaphor somewhere in there, too.

With the death of Jim Morrison the
remaining members of The Doors split
after a short attempt to stay together.
Guitarist Robbie Krieger and drummer
John Densmore came to England,
joined Bronco vocalist Jess Roden,
keyboard man Roy Davies and bassist
Phillip Chen: The Butts Band was born.

 **TOUR DATES**

June
15th Links Pavillion, Cromer
16th Greyhound, Croydon
18th Barbarella's, Birmingham
19th The Penthouse, Scarborough
21st University of Hull
22nd University of Reading

A NEW ALBUM

ILPS 9260 Cassette ZCI 9260 Cartridge Y8I 9260 Produced by Bruce Botnick

TIME TO AIM YOUR ARROWS
AT THE SUN

It took us longer than it should have to realize—or, more accurately, to accept—that the Doors weren't the Doors without Jim. After he died, we pressed on as a three-piece, and we thought the silver lining would be the ability to relax and not always be worried about our lead singer. But it turned out all that stress was as much of a blessing as a curse. Our band was like a Roman arch, with Jim as the keystone. All the tension was focused on a central point, which gave the structure strength and kept it intact. There was no room for the rest of our egos or individual agendas. Our energy was spent entirely on keeping the keystone in place. Without Jim, there was a spotlight vacuum. Ray—the former singer of Rick and the Ravens, and the showman who had captivated Royce Hall when screening his UCLA student film—was a natural to fill it. But with Ray's new position as a leader came the ego of a leader, which understandably rubbed John's ego the wrong way. I was always caught between them, with my own ego to tend to. Without our keystone, our arch was bound to fall.

After a year or so of touring and recording as the Doors without Jim, we decided the missing ingredient was a singer—ignoring the obvious conclusion that the missing ingredient was one singer in particular. We all moved to England to try and find someone to front the Doors. We didn't want some standard L.A. rock singer; we wanted someone who could theoretically take us in a bold new direction, and who would defy the inevitable comparisons to Jim. Plus we figured it would be good to get out of L.A. for a while. We rented rooms in an old London hotel where the hot water and electricity were shut off at a certain time every night. The city was suffering regular blackouts at the time, so electricity wasn't guaranteed during the day either. It was dreary and rainy and freezing all the time. Lynn and Ray's wife, Dorothy, joined us since we were planning to stay for a while. Lynn loved England and took to it well, but Dorothy was pregnant and having a hard time with the adjustment. Whenever we saw Dorothy, she was her usual quiet, sweet self, but Ray confided in us that the hormones were playing hell with her emotions, and it was wearing on both of them.

For years there has been a rumor that Iggy Pop was in contention for Jim's job. Our friend and advisor Danny Sugerman suggested the idea, but we never talked to or met with Iggy, or even seriously considered him. Iggy's whole persona had been modeled after Jim, so it seemed like almost an insult to bring him in as a replacement. Paul Rodgers of Bad Company and Joe Cocker were also suggestions that never made it beyond the brainstorming phase. We thought Paul McCartney would be an unorthodox choice since he was so obviously different from Jim, and he played bass, which would've been a plus. But again: nothing more than idle talk. The closest I ever came to interacting with a Beatle on that trip was jamming with Stephen Stills one day when he was staying at Ringo's house. But Ringo wasn't home.

The only singer I remember actually auditioning was Howard Werth from the band Audience. He was a nice guy, and talented, but we knew what real chemistry felt like, and it just wasn't there. It became harder and harder for us to ignore what was staring us in the face. The idea of an inevitably fruitless search started to weigh on us. And for Ray, all that pressure was on top of dealing with Dorothy's pregnancy-driven mood swings. One day John and I were talking to Ray about the musical direction of the band and I used the phrase "We think" in some context. Ray boiled over, taking it as an attack: "Oh, *you* think?! What about what *I* think?! Fuck this, I'm outta here!" He declared the Doors were done and made immediate arrangements to fly back to the States.

John and I were pissed that Ray had made the decision to end the band in such a unilateral way. It was a grudge that John would hang on to, but I tried to be forgiving. We've all been there. People break sometimes. Darkness and pregnancy and career uncertainty and weeks without reliable electricity or a decent shower. Ray broke. I couldn't blame him.

Jac Holzman had signed the Doors for several more albums after Jim died, more out of loyalty than as a sound business move. Elektra was relieved that they wouldn't have to ride out the rest of the contract. We finally admitted to ourselves what had been true since Jim died two years earlier: it was over.

So now what?

John and I still wanted to make music. We didn't want to go home yet. We settled in for a long stay, and Lynn and I rented a flat in a three-story walk-up in Brixton. The place was heated by a coal-burning stove, so every couple of days I had to drag a burlap sack full of coal up the stairs like a Charles Dickens character. It wasn't convenient, but I suppose it was quaint.

We set up a rehearsal space in the historic Garrick House in Covent Garden, and our British road manager, Davey Harper, connected us with a friend of his, a singer-guitarist named Jess Roden. Jess was skinny, with long blond hair and a soulful tenor voice. He had written some interesting original material, and we got along well. We asked him if he knew any bassists and he brought in Phil Chen, an incredible session musician who would later go on to play on Jeff Beck's *Blow by Blow* and tour with Rod Stewart. Phil brought in keyboardist Roy Davies, who would later go on to work with Freddie King, Madness, and Elton John.

Jess suggested the name the Butts Band, based on a road called Butts Lane in the town of Kidderminster, where he grew up. It wasn't until much later in life that I learned the history behind it: back in medieval times, archers trained with their longbows by shooting at mounds of earth known as butts, and their training grounds were traditionally located outside of town, in an area referred to as "the butts." Many English towns therefore have a Butts Lane today, as a nod to the spot where their archers used to practice. Jess intended the band name to be a reference to guys who hung out on the outskirts of town. He laughed with John and me when we explained that "butt" has a very different meaning in America. Yet—for some reason that I still cannot possibly explain—we went with the name anyway. I don't know why anyone gave me a vote. I was the guy who thought the Clouds, the Psychedelic Rangers, and the Back Bay Chamber Pot Terriers were all perfectly fine band names.

We started out jamming James Brown songs and ended up quickly writing an album's worth of soul/jazz-influenced soft rock material. John and I were eager to try something completely different from the Doors, and we were excited about the results. Bruce Botnick flew over to produce our debut album at the legendary

Olympic Studios in London, which is known for producing albums by an astounding list of artists: the Beatles, the Stones, the Who, Hendrix, Zeppelin, Queen...basically everyone all the way down to the Spice Girls. And then halfway through recording we uprooted everything and went to Jamaica.

Phil Chen was originally from Jamaica and had been talking it up the whole time we were working together. After I'd dragged one too many bags of coal up the stairs, it started to sound tempting. We moved the production to Dynamic Sounds in Kingston.

Reggae hadn't really become popular in the States yet, but it was huge in England. It poured out of bars and clubs and the many Jamaican restaurants in our Brixton neighborhood. We became fans of the genre and it influenced our songwriting. When we got to Dynamic Sounds we were excited to learn that Jimmy Cliff was recording in the studio next to ours, even though he didn't seem to care about our presence at all.

Jess had a connection with Chris Blackwell, the head of Island Records, who invited us to stay at his Strawberry Hill estate. It was a sprawling eighteenth-century plantation up in the Blue Mountains, where they grew coffee (and pot) and where Bob Marley would later hide out and heal from a gunshot wound after a 1976 assassination attempt.

In Kingston, white people were generally looked at with, at best, suspicion. After a few hundred years of oppressive British rule, which had ended only about a decade before we got there, it made sense. We were warned not to wander outside at night. We had a van and a driver to take us to and from the studio, which was surrounded by barbed wire and had a guard booth out front staffed by guys with guns. Whenever we were in the van, our driver had us slide down in our seats so no one could see us. Chris Blackwell said, "If you get in any trouble, just mention that you know Marley."

Sure enough, one day John and I were in our van on the way to the studio, and outside the entrance a group of four or five guys blocked our path and surrounded us.

"Um…we're friends of Marley's…"

They smiled. They may not have believed us, and they may not have had any ill intent toward us in the first place, but Marley's name took the tension out of the air, and they stepped aside to let us through.

When we got back to L.A., we took the finished album to Elektra, but our longtime champion Jac Holzman had retired, and the label had been acquired by Warner Communications and merged with Asylum Records. The new label was being run by some guy named David Geffen. My first impression of David was that he was full of himself. He wanted us to rerecord the entire album with Tom Dowd, the in-house producer at Atlantic Records who had revolutionized eight-track recording and had worked with everyone on Atlantic's luminary jazz roster—including Coltrane. In retrospect, we should've done it just for the honor of working with Tom and bugging him for Coltrane stories, but when David suggested it at the meeting, I took it as an insult. We had worked our asses off recording the album in first-rate studios, and we had done it with Bruce, who wasn't exactly a novice. I felt like David cared less about the album and more about trying to throw his weight around. Without realizing it, a sour expression crept across my face, and David noticed.

He said, "Well, you have as much enthusiasm as a half-dead worm."

He wasn't wrong. I said, "You're right. We fucking worked hard on this thing and there's no reason to redo it."

That was pretty much the end of our dealings with David Geffen. And it was the birth of my new nickname. When Phil Chen heard the story of what had happened, he permanently dubbed me the Worm. (My son later became Little Wormy, or if my son and I are together, we're the Worm and the Sperm.)

Bruce Botnick had some connections at a new, eclectic label called Blue Thumb Records, which welcomed the Butts Band with open arms. Bill Siddons signed on as our manager and set us up with our debut gig at the Roxy on the Sunset Strip and a quick tour of major cities around the U.S. He also got us a residency at Max's Kansas City in New York, where we opened for the nightly headliners, just as the Doors had in the Whisky days. Then we flew back to the UK, where we opened for the Kinks at the London Palladium and appeared on *The Old Grey Whistle Test*. We drew curious Doors fans who wanted to see what Robby and John were up to, and overall we got a warm response, even though we had to endure the occasional yell of "Play 'Light My Fire'!" But it was all on a very small scale, and upon our return to L.A., we suffered a drought of live shows. After a couple of months of sitting around and doing nothing while our album sales languished, the British half of the band got frustrated, quit, and moved back home.

We essentially formed an entirely new Butts Band, with John and me as the only original members. Siddons recommended a singer he had been managing, Mike Stull (who, aside from being a great vocalist, had also been the voice of the Wax Phantom in an episode of *Scooby Doo, Where Are You!*). We found a talented, versatile keyboardist named Alex Richman and a bassist named Karl Rucker, who had toured with the Jackson 5 and later went on to work with Nina Hagen, and we also brought in a second drummer (Danny "Splats" Spanos at first, and then Mike Berkowitz later) to play alongside John.

In contrast to the Doors, where things grew steadily and rapidly, with the Butts Band, everything felt stagnant and slow. Compared to what other bands go through on their way up, we had it easy due to our reputations and connections and resources. We should've fought harder to establish ourselves. But at that time in our lives John and I didn't have much fight in us. We had been spoiled by how quickly the Doors had rocketed to popularity. We were older, we had money, we had families. We weren't hungry kids willing to take on the world the way we were in 1965. And John had recently gone through a drawn-out divorce. It was his turn to break, just as Ray had in England. When we took the second incarnation of the Butts Band on a West Coast tour and came home having lost money, we finally admitted defeat.

The Butts Band was our first lesson in trying to escape the shadow of the past. If we had been judged as a seventies soft rock band and not as John and Robby of the Doors, I wonder how much further we could've gone with it. And if we hadn't been spoiled by our previous success, maybe we would've stuck it out long enough to break through.

Then again, maybe calling ourselves THE BUTTS BAND in the first place sealed our fate from the beginning.

Blue Thumb Records held a small release party for our first

album in a private room at Chasen's, a fancy West Hollywood restaurant where A-list Academy Awards after-parties were held and where the regulars were so famous you would know them by only their last names: Bogart, Sinatra, Reagan, Nixon, Hitchcock, Garbo, Monroe, Disney. By the seventies, the music industry had taken over and the restaurant had become a more casual spot, but when I was a teenager, we put on coats and ties for refined family dinners at Chasen's.

During our party, Blue Thumb hired three men to run through the restaurant, completely naked, with "the Butts Band" scrawled across their asses.

We never had a chance.

KEEP YOUR EYES ON THE ROAD, YOUR HANDS UPON THE WHEEL

I let Jim drive my van once.

Once.

We were on our way to the New Year's Eve gig that Happy had booked for us in Montecito. It was a costume party fundraiser for some charity her mom was involved with, and it was being held at a famous old mansion called Casa Dorinda, which is now a retirement home.

Jim kept pestering me to let him drive the VW Microbus my brother and I shared. He'd had a few beers but he wasn't drunk, so after enough nagging I finally handed him the keys. We were driving up the Pacific Coast Highway and enjoying its breathtaking views of the ocean.

And then Jim, for no reason at all, cranked the wheel to the left.

The tires shrieked, leaving skid marks behind us, and we were all thrown off balance as the van lurched into the path of oncoming traffic. He cranked the wheel back to the right, throwing us the other way. We had all our gear in the back — the whole van could've toppled from the shifting weight.

I shouted at him, "Hey! Do that in your own car!"

"Ah, no big deal." He straightened out the wheel and continued on.

I yelled at him to pull over and let me drive, but he said he'd be fine. And he was. He slowed down and drove responsibly after that. We all calmed down, but for the rest of the drive, there was a quiet, lingering anxiety that he'd do it again. We arrived at the gig intact, but I took over driving when it was time to head home.

It was such a small moment, but it perfectly encapsulated what it was like to know Jim Morrison. You would be cruising along with him, everything would be right with the world, and he would suddenly, without warning or explanation, swerve. You'd survive, and things would be fine, but your heart would be pounding from the shock. And you'd never fully relax again because — no matter how much reassurance he offered — you knew the next swerve could happen at any moment.

THE INCIDENT

I really didn't think our Miami show was that big of a deal. Yes, the air-conditioning was broken, and a restless, sweaty crowd of ten thousand people was generating unbearable heat. But we had played in shitty venues before. Yes, Bill Siddons was arguing with the promoters for overselling the venue and denying us a cut of the extra ticket sales while the promoters tried to hold our equipment hostage as leverage. But Bill was always putting out one fire or another, so I was more concerned with tuning my guitar. Yes, Jim had missed a connecting flight and gotten drunk at the airport and was running late. But he was on his way, and Jim being drunk was no longer newsworthy. Yes, things were a mess. But things were always a mess.

Yes Jim was drunker than usual, and yes Jim screamed and swore and derailed the songs to go on long, rambling tangents, and yes Jim encouraged the crowd, as he always did, to come up onstage, and yes our friend Lewis Beach Marvin III from the Moon Fire Temple was there for some reason and handed Jim an actual baby lamb while he was onstage to promote animal rights, and yes Jim joked about exposing himself, and yes our equipment manager, Vince Treanor, had to grab Jim's pants to prevent him from pulling them down, and yes Jim was at some point hurled into the audience, and yes the audience stormed the stage, and yes John and I had to jump ship when part of the stage collapsed, and yes the PA speakers toppled after that, preventing any possibility of an encore.

But to me it seemed like just another crazy Doors show.

The Miami Incident in March of 1969 would later become the most infamous episode in Doors history. But after we left the stage we shared beers with the local cops in our dressing room. There was no moral outrage. There was no scandal. There was no discussion about Jim exposing himself because it just plain didn't happen. No one got hurt. There weren't even any chairs to destroy because the promoters had pulled them all out to sell more tickets. The cops laughed with us about how wild the whole night had been, and when it was time for us to go they wished us well.

The next morning we all flew to the Caribbean, still not giving much thought to any of it. Miami was supposed to be the beginning of a long tour, so we had planned a preemptive vacation before hitting the road. Ray and Dorothy headed to one of those islands with a French name. The rest of us headed to Ocho Rios, Jamaica. Lynn and I shared a Tudor-style villa called Cary Island with John and his future wife, Julia. It was right on the beach, with a footbridge leading to a tiny private island that boasted great snorkeling. Jim, though, was all alone in a plantation house up in the mountains.

Pam was supposed to join Jim in Miami and Jamaica, but they'd had some big fight and she hadn't gotten on the plane with him. Jim didn't need an excuse to get drunk before a show, but it seemed like their argument drove him to drink even more than usual. The antagonistic nature of some of his ramblings at the concert was likely inspired by a play he had recently seen in which the actors got naked and confronted the audience. But if you listen to a recording of the Miami show, there's another theme woven in:

"I'm lonely. I need some love, y'all..."

"Ain't nobody gonna love my ass?"

"Nobody's gonna love me, sweetheart..."

"Nobody gonna come up here and love me, huh?"

"I'm getting lonely up here. I need some love..."

Loneliness. That's what Miami was really all about. And now Jim was sitting all by himself in an empty, cavernous plantation house while Pam was back in L.A. and the rest of us were having a romantic getaway with our significant others. Lynn and I felt bad for him, so we went up to his house for dinner.

When Jim and Pam booked the plantation house, I'm sure it sounded elegant and romantic, but the reality of it was a little creepy. Dinner was served on domed plates by a staff of about ten Black servants wearing tuxedos and white gloves. We sat at one of those extra-long dining tables while the servants stood quietly at attention behind us. The intention was to make us feel pampered, but we felt like colonial slave owners, which is the furthest thing from comfortable, so Jim gave the servants some paid time off and we invited him to stay at Cary Island with us for the rest of the trip.

Having a fifth wheel around put a bit of a damper on the romantic vacation John and Julia and Lynn and I had been anticipating, but we couldn't blame Jim for not wanting to stay at the plantation alone. What I did quietly blame him for, though, was convincing Lynn and Julia to get drunk with him and ruining our plans to enjoy the sun and sand. When we finally went snorkeling, Lynn was still pretty tipsy. She stepped on a sea urchin and we had to pull the spines out of her feet and take her back to the house for the afternoon. She was limping for the rest of the trip.

Hers wasn't the only injury, though. John was an active equestrian so Julia, Lynn, and I joined him for a horseback ride. The horses we rented were usually used for polo matches, so they were faster and more energetic than the mellow horses usually used for trail rides. And they gave us English saddles, which lacked the little horn that Western saddles have, and which I was accustomed to grabbing for stability. The horses took us through an orange grove and I quickly got the feeling they were intentionally trying to get rid of the American tourists on their backs. They galloped furiously under low-hanging tree branches and I had to keep ducking to avoid decapitation. At one point my horse raced down a hill and came to a sudden halt. I broke a stirrup, was thrown overboard, and got knocked the fuck out.

I awoke a minute or so later to the sound of Lynn screaming directly into my ear. Someone got a jeep to pick me up and take me to a local doctor's house. My head was swimming, but most of the pain was actually concentrated on my hip, which later blossomed into a patch of colorful bruises. The doctor was an older British man who didn't pay much attention to my potential traumatic brain injury. He was distracted by Lynn and Julia, who had gone riding that day in their bikinis. He tossed me some aspirin, but made it a point to closely inspect every square inch of the girls' bodies for ticks. I actually found a few ticks on my own body. The doctor didn't seem too concerned.

The whole trip was kind of a letdown. We couldn't even find good weed while we were there. And just before we were scheduled to return to the States to continue our tour, we got a call from Bill Siddons to tell us our concert in Miami had created a firestorm of controversy. Headlines. Criminal charges. Fifteen tour dates had been canceled and our songs had been pulled from the radio.

They were saying Jim had exposed himself onstage. Had I missed something? Lynn was at the show; she confirmed I wasn't crazy.

They were saying Jim had "simulated oral copulation" on me. I was the guy who had whacked him with my guitar neck when he grabbed my balls and threw him off me when he tried to wrestle me naked. I would've noticed if he had given me a fake blow job, and he knew better than to try. They were charging him with obscenity. For using the same language he had used at every concert we had ever played over the past three years? When Lewis handed him the baby lamb, Jim said, "I'd fuck her but she's too young." Come on... that's an objectively funny line! He would've said that even if he'd been sober.

The ensuing trial would hang over our heads for the rest of our career as a band and for the rest of Jim's life on this earth. For the first time ever, Jim was going to suffer the consequences of his actions. And yet it was the one time when those consequences were completely undeserved.

Janis Joplin and Paul Rothchild

THE 27 CLUB

Murray the K asked me, "Have you ever heard of Jimi Hendrix?" At the time, I hadn't. Murray was one of the biggest DJs of the sixties, having earned his musical credibility as an early champion of the Beatles. We were in his studio at WOR-FM in New York and he had a British import copy of Hendrix's debut, *Are You Experienced,* which hadn't yet been released in the U.S. He couldn't stop raving about it. He dropped the needle on the first track: "Foxy Lady." Murray's musical credibility remained firmly intact.

When I acquired my own copy of *Are You Experienced,* it rarely left my turntable for at least a full year. Unlike with most of my favorite guitarists, I didn't steal anything directly from Jimi, but of course I was in awe of his abilities. I went to see him at the Whisky in July of '67. *Are You Experienced* still hadn't been released in America, but the word was out and the place was packed. I had to stand on a booth in the back to see over everyone. It was the first time I had seen a guitarist use dual Marshall stacks—the volume was INSANE. After I saw that, I couldn't believe John and Ray dared to complain that I played too loud out of my little Twin

Reverb. I went to see Jimi again at the Forum a year and a half later, but he was disappointingly more subdued than the wild man I had seen onstage at the Whisky. I heard he was trying to change his image by going for more of a Miles Davis thing, but I got the impression he was emulating Miles pharmaceutically as much as musically.

In August 1970 the Doors headed to England for the Isle of Wight Festival, where Hendrix was also on the bill, so I was excited to catch him live again. When I walked onto the plane, I discovered that Jimi would be my seatmate for the duration of the flight.

If ever there was a conversation in my life where I wish I'd had a tape recorder rolling…I complimented his album, but of course I had to be all sixties cool and keep a lid on my praise. He knew about the Doors but didn't proclaim to be a fan or anything (I like to tell myself he was just being sixties cool, too). He was friendly and casual, a genuinely nice guy. We didn't talk much about music, except a little about our jazz influences. Mostly he wanted to know if I had any drug connections in England.

He said, "If you score first, call me. If I score first, I'll call you."

He didn't specify, but I knew he wasn't talking about marijuana. And he brought it up at least three or four times; he didn't want me to forget. In the end, I never "scored" anything he would've been interested in, and, unsurprisingly, I never got a call. I wasn't able to watch his set because he played the day after us and we were already on a flight home, but I figured I'd catch him on another tour soon enough. Maybe we'd get to pick up our conversation where we'd left off.

Three weeks later, Jimi was dead. They say he choked on his own vomit after taking too many sleeping pills. Based on our conversation on the plane, I always assumed heroin had something to do with it, but I'm not a licensed coroner.

A couple of weeks later, Janis Joplin was also dead. This time heroin was the official cause.

When Brian Jones drowned in his pool a year earlier, it was a shock to everyone in the music community. Jim wrote a poem about him, but we didn't know Brian personally, and we considered it a freak accident. When Jimi Hendrix died, I was sincerely upset since I admired his playing so much and since I'd shared such a nice moment with him on our flight. But Janis hit us the hardest. After welcoming us to San Francisco and embarking on a number of misadventures with Jim, she was more than just a fellow musician. She was our friend.

After Janis, Jim morbidly joked with people, "I'm number three." Of course he would say something like that. It was Jim being melodramatic as always. We were calloused to it.

But Paul Rothchild took Jim seriously. He was in the middle of recording what would become Janis's landmark album, *Pearl,* when she simply didn't show up at the studio one day. Just as Jim had done plenty of times before. Long before Janis passed away, Paul saw where Jim was heading, and he told us, "Boys, we better record as much as we can because he might not be around much longer."

We weren't blind. But we didn't have the emotional capacity to take Paul, or Jim, as seriously as we should have. The stupid calculation I made was that Janis had been taken down by heroin. Jim may have been a heavy drinker, and he may have been crazy, and he may have been self-destructive. But he'd never get involved with heroin.

Right?

CHASING THE DRAGON

Even as a little kid, I knew that something was wrong with my mom. She slept all the time. My grandmother was always over, taking care of me and my brother, and we had hired help that did most of the housework. Having twins must've thrown my mom for a loop. It's one thing to have a baby, get used to the idea of being a parent, and then have another baby. It's another to be thrown into the deep end with two at once.

My mom developed recurring migraines and her doctor prescribed codeine. As opioids go, codeine is relatively safe. But that doesn't mean you can't get addicted to it. I noticed that other moms weren't perpetually exhausted the way mine was, but it took a long time before I put the pieces together. When my brother and I got older, we were out of her hair, but the pills didn't stop. She managed her habit better, so even as an adult I didn't step in or say anything about her dependency, until I had a son of my own. When I realized she was driving her grandson around after downing ten codeine tablets, I got worried enough to confront her about it. Her doctor sent her to Hawaii for a couple of weeks so she could quit cold turkey, and shockingly, it worked. She never really owned up to the fact that she was a drug addict, but she had recovered, and that's what counted.

They say addiction runs in families. So maybe the drug problem that plagued me from my late thirties well into my mid-forties was something I inherited from my mom. Or even my grandmother, who popped a steady stream of red and green pills: one for going to sleep, one for waking up. My brother and I used to steal her meds here and there, but the more I saw the effects of narcotics on my mother and grandmother, the more scared of drugs I became. I went a little wild in high school and college for the sake of mischief, but by the time I was in my twenties I rarely drank, and I treated weed more like an occasional sacrament than a regular hobby. I left acid behind in the sixties, and I was barely smoking any weed at all by the end of the seventies. I never saw myself doing hard drugs.

Then I started doing hard drugs.

Cocaine was the drug that fueled the eighties. It was a party drug. It brought people together. And it was everywhere. I hadn't seen it take anyone down the way I had with alcohol, pills, and LSD, so it seemed relatively harmless. The only time I had a bad experience with cocaine was when I snorted something that wasn't cocaine. I was about to jam at some club when a guy gave me a bump of white powder. When I got onstage I couldn't move my fingers. I tried to will them to press down on the fretboard, but they kept sinking through the neck of the guitar like I was in a bad dream. After struggling through the embarrassing set, I asked the guy what he had given me. Angel dust. I figured as long as I didn't make that mistake again I could keep doing cocaine occasionally without any real consequences. I told myself I'd be fine, as long as I didn't start doing heroin.

Then I started doing heroin.

My usual coke dealer was a Middle Eastern guy everybody knew

as the King of the Valley. He was a skinny, bearded, shifty character, but he was also boisterous and entertaining. They called him
the King because he would always be holding court at his house,
regaling a circle of drug patrons with stories of his exploits. And he
always had the best stuff. His wife was a hilarious ballbuster, and
when we hung out socially, his teenage daughter got along well with
our ten-year-old son. The family allegedly came from great wealth
back in their home country, maybe even royalty (another reason for
the nickname).

One day Lynn and I were hanging out at the King's castle when
he taught us how to "chase the dragon." He used a lighter to melt
some opium on a piece of tin foil, and as it liquefied, he "chased"
the vapor with a little glass tube to inhale it. An amusing little party
trick from the King.

I didn't particularly enjoy the high. It was mildly relaxing, but
that was about it. But one night soon after that, Lynn and I went to
see Etta James at the Troubadour. We were friendly with the guys
in her backing band. All very talented. All junkies. Lynn and I went
to an after-party where everyone was chasing the dragon, but they
were melting heroin instead of opium. We felt so cool fitting in with
the jazz guys, and we loved the taboo vibe of the whole thing. Usually heroin is portrayed as a lonely, shameful drug that people do by
themselves in a locked bathroom stall. But we had a lot of friends
who were into it, and it was done openly in certain social situations.
Didn't seem so scary or dangerous. As long as we only did it at parties and not on our own, at home.

Then we started doing it on our own, at home.

Not every day. Maybe once a week. We didn't *need* it. We just
liked doing it every few days. And then every other day. Then I left
for a two-week tour with my solo band and got sick. I didn't realize I
was going through withdrawal: I thought I had some sort of stomach
bug. I'd wake up every day with cramps and diarrhea, wondering

why I didn't feel any better than the day before. I was miserable for the full two weeks, until I got home, took one puff of the magic dragon, and was instantly cured.

A non-stupid person might have said, "Oh, I was going through withdrawal. I better stop doing this drug before I develop an even deeper dependence."

But instead I said, "Oh, I was going through withdrawal. I better keep doing this drug so I don't get sick again."

Lynn and I were spending so much time with the King that at one point we invited him and his family to stay at our house for a while. Our kids hung out together and on the surface it was almost like we were living in a wholesome sitcom. But we soon realized that the King was more than a little crazy. We took a couples vacation with the King and his queen and there was some issue with the King's ticket at the airport. He threw a fucking fit. Today a Middle Eastern man screaming and throwing things and stomping around at a U.S. airport would be so harshly profiled by security that the whole country would go on lockdown. The eighties were a more innocent era, but even back then his tantrum had me convinced we were all going to get busted. The whole time he was ranting and raving he was in possession of a suitcase full of illegal narcotics. Somehow we were able to board the plane without being swarmed by federal agents, and we headed to Vegas. Or was it Tahoe? Didn't matter: once we arrived and opened the King's suitcase, we never left our hotel room.

After we got back, we found a polite excuse to kick the King and the royal family out of our house, and we made it a point to gradually lose touch with them. But spending time with them had kept up the illusion that drugs were all part of a fun, party lifestyle and not a descent into addiction. If, from the beginning, someone had said, "Hey, here's a needle; try this," I never would've touched the stuff. But it was all so innocent. Just friends hanging out. It's not like we were shooting up.

Then we started shooting up.

After the King moved out, we met a new dealer, Bhodi, which is not his real name because his dad was some powerful, politically connected figure from an unspecified Asian country and I don't want that guy mad at me. Bhodi was able to supply us with China White. The good stuff. You could snort it, but it was better to smoke it because you could tell how pure it was. The vapor didn't smell like burning sugar or any other cutting agents, and there was no telltale residue left on the foil. So it made us feel safe injecting it.

We started using so much that it only made sense to buy in bulk. Bhodi would import bricks of China White from his home country, and we'd buy half a kilo from him directly while another friend of ours put up money for the other half. This was the uncut stuff, straight from the factory. It was even imprinted with a little tiger logo. Normally dealers would step on it and resell it, but since Lynn and I were using it all personally, we could just chip away small but potent amounts. We only bought the bricks a couple of times: twenty grand worth would get us by for more than half a year. What a bargain.

Strangely, Jim's and Pam's fates did nothing to deter me. I rationalized that Pam had been too overcome with depression to think clearly, and that's the only reason she overdosed. And if Jim died from heroin, which wasn't proven, it was likely because he was mixing it with liquor. Why would anyone drink when they're on heroin? It's not only dangerous; it's redundant. I thought I was being so fucking smart. From my perspective, Jim and Pam were rare exceptions. What happened to them couldn't possibly happen to us. We knew tons of people who were doing heroin, and none of our friends were overdosing.

Then our friends started overdosing.

One of the people who taught us how to shoot up was Jimmy Kardashian, a distant relative of, yes, *those* Kardashians. His branch of the family made their money in waste management, but he was the black sheep, so they made him drive a garbage truck to earn his allowance. Jimmy was also a personal assistant to Danny Hutton from Three Dog Night, so we knew him through the music scene. He was a funny and entertaining guy, but he was also a terrible junkie.

One day Jimmy passed out at our house and we couldn't wake him up. We had some friends over who knew basic junkie first aid. Common "wisdom" was that if someone ODed, you were supposed to throw ice on their balls. It's actually a really bad idea: it can send the person into shock and make things worse. But we grabbed the ice trays out of the freezer, dragged Jimmy into the bathtub, and tried to drop the temperature of his testicles. When that didn't work, we dragged him into the driveway and stuck a garden hose down his pants. Anything to avoid calling 911. We knew he wasn't dead, but his skin was turning a sickly shade of green. We were screaming and slapping him as the hose soaked him through. He finally came around. I gave him a dry pair of pants and said, "You're outta here." One of our friends gave him a lift home and we never hung out with him again. Jimmy hadn't done anything wrong, other than remind us of our own mortality, but we couldn't face him after that. He died of another overdose about a year later.

Another new friend that heroin brought into my life was someone who had served as one of my biggest inspirations: Paul Butterfield. A mutual friend introduced us, knowing that we had music and heroin in common. Paul didn't want to talk about music, though. He just wanted to score. I didn't usually sell drugs because it was a needless risk, but I sold him some of our China White supply because hey, it's Paul Butterfield! He kept calling for more and more, and he kept stiffing me on the payments. I didn't care so much about the money. It was just so insulting. And disappointing. This was the guy who had shaped my sound, and as a result shaped my entire life. Without Paul Butterfield, who knows if there would've been a Robby Krieger? But he didn't care about the Doors, and soon I stopped caring that he was Paul Butterfield. He wasn't an electric blues god anymore. He was just another pathetic junkie welching on his debts. I stopped taking his calls. And he, too, later died of an overdose.

I only sort of overdosed once. I had a friend in town from New York and we chased a few dragons together before deciding to head over to Jock Ellis's house. Jock was a trombonist who played with Zappa and also played on some of my jazz albums. We were sitting around a table with some guys who were passing a joint. I didn't realize it was hashish, so I took a giant puff. A moment later I felt myself sliding out of my chair, and then suddenly time jumped forward and the guys were shaking me awake. Jock was laughing because he thought I was a lightweight who couldn't handle a little hash. It probably wouldn't have been as comical to him if he'd known my system was already full of opiates.

Just because Lynn and I never properly ODed doesn't mean we were never in danger of killing ourselves. On more than one occasion I hit an artery instead of a vein and sent my heart rate skyrocketing. You can die from doing that, even if it's not technically an "overdose." My body was healthy enough to get through it, but it's like playing Russian roulette with your circulatory system.

Bhodi, meanwhile, was arrested while flying back to his home country. He and his traveling companion were dressed like flashy pimps, with something like a hundred grand in cash in their suitcases. His well-connected father made sure he didn't do any time, but he was never able to come back to the States. The friend he was traveling with spent some time in jail, got out, and dated Bhodi's sister for a while. I know Bhodi's dad didn't like that. And I know Bhodi's friend ended up murdered. I can't prove that those two facts are related, but I'm not interested in investigating any further.

I had my own problems with the law. When the Robby Krieger Band flew to a small island off the coast of Italy for a show, I loaded up several syringes with my usual dose and packed them in my carry-on bag. I managed to dodge the drug-sniffing dogs and stroll through customs without any issues, but I went to take a piss before leaving the airport and stupidly left my bag unattended outside the bathroom. When I came out, it was gone. I asked an airport cop if anyone had found a bag, and he ordered me to go with him to the security office. As he led me to an isolated back room, I realized how dumb it was for me to have asked a cop to help me find my heroin. My mind raced to come up with stories and excuses. We walked into the office. Some other cops opened my bag and gestured indignantly at my syringes.

Without missing a beat, I said, "Oh, thank you so much! You found my insulin!"

They paused for a moment, confused. *"Diabetico?"*

"Yeah, yeah! *Diabetico!* Thank you!"

And they actually let me go.

I will never understand how trained security officers could see cloudy, brown liquid in a syringe and be fooled into thinking it was insulin. I wonder if part of me wanted to get caught. Maybe I subconsciously knew I was lying to myself about how bad things were getting and figured if I got myself busted I'd be forced to reckon with it all. But the authorities kept letting me off the hook.

One time I was buzzing along Mulholland Drive in a rented Corvette, right after scoring. My Porsche was in the shop, so I was excited to see how the Corvette stacked up. I was flooring it and squealing around all the curves, just begging to be pulled over. My subconscious wish was soon granted. As I shoved the dope under my seat, the cop hopped out of his cruiser and pulled a gun on me.

"WHAT THE FUCK ARE YOU DOING?!"

My hands automatically went up. "Sorry, man! I just rented this car and I wanted to see how it would do on Mulholland."

"I DON'T GIVE A SHIT! I'M TAKING THIS CAR! I'M TOWING IT DOWN TO THE STATION!"

I wish I could tell you what I said to calm him down, but all I remember is that gun pointed at my head. I don't know if it was my race or my apparent wealth or my natural charm that relaxed his trigger finger, but somehow I walked away with only a ticket.

Another time I was busted with coke, not heroin. I was speeding up Benedict Canyon Drive and I had the radio turned up loud so I didn't hear any sirens or notice the cops behind me. They thought I was refusing to pull over, so I unwittingly ended up in a brief high-speed chase. When I finally realized what was going on and stopped the car, the cops were understandably pissed. They threw me in the back of a squad car and searched my vehicle.

Moments later, in a booming, oh-so-pleased-with-himself voice, a cop called out loudly, "Mr. Krieger! Is this your cocaine?"

There was no talking my way out of it this time. The cops were so delighted to have a reason to fuck with me. One of them opened the door of the squad car, farted into it, and then locked me in with the aroma. Later, another officer did the same thing. I'll take a fart over a gun pointed at my head any day, but they were making it clear that there would be no mercy when it came to the charges. They took me down to the station and started the booking process. I had been through this before as a kid, but I didn't have my dad to bail me out this time. Cocaine was a much bigger deal than pot, and I almost went to jail for pot. What was I about to face?

The cops who brought me in huddled with some of the other

cops at the station. Someone there had apparently figured out my musical background.

Moments later, in a polite and friendly voice, a cop said, "Mr. Krieger...could we have your autograph?"

I signed stuff and shook hands and they sent me home. No charges. No court date. No record. (They kept the coke, though.)

The reason I had coke was because Lynn and I had reached a new level of idiocy: speedballs. At first we would do a little coke and then do a little heroin to balance it out. But eventually every junkie wonders what would happen if you put the chocolate and the peanut butter together. What happens is you love it, and you do lots of it really fast. With plain heroin you usually take one or two shots a day. With speedballs you take one shot after another after another after another until you run out and then you go out and score more and then repeat for days on end. The danger of an overdose or a heart attack goes through the roof, as does the danger of getting behind the wheel of a car without realizing you haven't slept for four days straight. My grip on reality had become frighteningly loose. Little itchy bugs kept appearing on my skin and I didn't realize they were hallucinations until I went to a doctor to ask about them and he kicked me out of his office. Things were getting out of control, even from a junkie perspective.

You can usually spot a speedballer by looking at their bathroom ceiling. Whenever you shoot up you draw a little blood into the syringe to make sure you've hit a vein. When you're done you need to clear out any leftover blood residue so it doesn't coagulate in the needle. Since speedballers are too lazy to make their way to a sink and dispose of the blood sanitarily, they just squirt it out of the syringe in a random direction. The drops of blood end up on the walls, floor, and ceiling, which speedballers are rarely motivated to clean. The tiny, telltale red speckles become a permanent part of the decor. Next time you're in a cheap motel or the bathroom of a fast-food restaurant in a bad neighborhood, look up. See if any junkies have left their mark. I had noticed bloodstained bathroom ceilings at our friend Danny Sugerman's house and Paul Butterfield's house. Now my ceilings were stained, too.

It was no longer possible to deny that Lynn and I were hopelessly addicted. When I was touring with my solo band, I needed drugs just to make it through a show. When we had a meeting about making a Doors movie, I nodded off in the middle of it. When we invited a bunch of friends over to the house for my birthday party, Lynn and I locked ourselves in the bathroom with our dealer soon after everyone arrived, and by the time we came out it was after midnight and everyone had left. Once when Ray, John, and I were doing a radio interview, the DJ made a reference to Jim Morrison being a heroin addict and I snapped back and denied it far more loudly and forcefully than anyone would've expected from the usually quiet Robby Krieger. As the words left my mouth I was overwhelmed by what felt like a panic attack. I had never experienced anything like it before. Could've been withdrawal, could've been my own cognitive dissonance collapsing in on itself. I abruptly stopped talking and walked out of the interview. I rushed to the bathroom, where another fix made it all go away.

The greatest tragedy was that the same way I realized something was wrong with my mom, my son, Waylon, realized something was wrong with me. When his fifth-grade teacher invited me to career day at school, Waylon begged me not to go. He was already picking up on his parents' odd behavior and was already aware of how potentially embarrassing we could be. But Lynn and I went anyway. As I played "Love Me Two Times" on guitar for the kids, Lynn nodded off in the chair next to me and started slowly slumping forward. When the song ended, the applause from the class jolted her awake just before she fell over completely. Waylon's classmates didn't seem to notice—they thought his dad was pretty cool. But Waylon was humiliated all the same.

As Waylon wondered why his parents were always locking themselves in their bedroom for hours on end, he learned to fend for himself. He became an expert at microwaving TV dinners. I wish I could say the neglect was the worst part, but the drugs would also fuel raucous fights, like the time Lynn chased me around the house with a barbell and used it to smash through a door. I barely remember that incident, but Waylon can still picture it all too clearly. There was so much I wish he hadn't seen. I'm still haunted by the idea of my son watching in terror as I gouged holes in my arm with a pair of tweezers to fend off invisible bugs.

One day I went to a band meeting at Paul Rothchild's house, only to discover that there was no band meeting. It was an intervention. John, the band member I had always been closest to, saw my path of self-destruction mirroring Jim's and took the initiative to round up Ray; my brother, Ronny; a few of my friends; and even my accountant, who had noticed all my troublingly sizable cash withdrawals. Unlike with Jim's intervention, John had recruited an official addiction specialist to guide the discussion. I felt trapped, and I was angry that they had lied to get me there. But I knew they were right. It's embarrassing to think about how I was once on the other side of an intervention with Jim, and how much of his behavior we had all put up with before we addressed it, and how I had apparently pushed people to a similar limit. But recognizing that my friends cared about me enough to organize something like that was a healthy kick in the head.

When I went home and told Lynn what happened, she was a little insulted that they hadn't tricked her into an intervention, too. Either way, Lynn and I agreed we needed to stop. Even before the intervention we already knew the speedballs were out of control, so that was the first thing to go. The cocaine withdrawal symptoms weren't so bad, so once we committed to quitting that, we were able to stick to it. Of course, it helped that we still had heroin to fall back on.

After Bhodi was arrested, we were getting most of our stuff from a guy connected with the Russian Mob who looked just like Boris Yeltsin. He was importing stuff from Afghanistan that had a grayish tinge to it—who knows what it was cut with? Later we were getting brown tar from Mexico through a dealer known as Joe the Junkie, who looked exactly like what you're picturing. China White was more of an "up" high that actually gave you energy, while the Afghan Gray made you sleepy. The Mexican Brown was barely enough to keep you from getting sick.

It took another couple of years before we gathered the willpower to quit drugs entirely. Joe the Junkie had turned me on to his supplier, a group of Hells Angels who lived somewhere out in Simi Valley. I drove way the fuck out to this isolated little house, carrying a bag full of cash. A troop of Angels greeted me with suspicious snarls and I handed over the bag to a guy who looked like an angry refrigerator with a beard. I stood there sweating as they counted the money. It was thousands of dollars. They could've just kept it and given me nothing. Not like I could call the Better Business Bureau and report them. What if I had miscounted the cash by accident? Was I about to get beaten with a monkey wrench and dragged behind a motorcycle because of a math error? I knew I shouldn't have dropped out of UCLA!

They handed me a brick of shitty dope and I left unharmed. But that was the final wake-up call. Lynn and I agreed to use the Hells Angels heroin to taper off gradually, and against all odds we actually stuck to it. After the drugs were gone we had a doctor prescribe us methadone, and we spent twenty days feeling generally awful. But we kicked it. We were done. Clean. The whole process was so brutal and unpleasant that no one in their right mind would ever want to repeat it. It was the perfect incentive for staying straight. We couldn't imagine ever doing heroin again.

Then we did heroin again.

We made it a long time without relapsing, but in the nineties Lynn went in for surgery and the doctors prescribed her some opioid painkillers. Sometimes those are even harder to quit than dope. When her prescription ran out she suggested getting more heroin, and I needed shamefully little convincing. We sunk back into our old habit for about a month but quickly realized how stupid we were being. We submitted to another twenty days of methadone misery and we finally, officially, put heroin behind us for good.

At least for now.

They say once an addict, always an addict, so it's always possible that something will send Lynn or me over the edge again. But once our heads were clear, we wondered why we ever did it in the first place. And even though we dodged some bullets, there were still ugly long-term effects. I'm pretty sure it fucked me up creatively. I can still write music, but lyrically I'm always blocked. I used to think all those great jazz artists who found heroin before me were aided by the drug. Now I wonder how much better their music might've been without it.

The harsher consequence, though, was passing my addiction down to my son. Waylon was around ten years old when our dark experiment began and he was in his late teens before it ended. You'd think he would've seen me all fucked up and sworn off drugs forever, just as I should've sworn off drugs after seeing what happened to my mom. But it doesn't seem to work that way. One of my biggest regrets in life is not being a better role model or a more responsible dad. At the same time, when Waylon fell into his own addiction, I was able to understand and help in a way most parents couldn't. It's not the normal or ideal way of bonding with your child, but it brought us closer than ever.

When Lynn and I relapsed, we weren't even enjoying ourselves. The reason we were able to quit again so quickly was because it became obvious we'd never be able to match that first high again. It was the same lesson I had already learned with acid years before. And it was a window into what likely drove me to addiction in the first place. I loved playing and collaborating with new musicians in the seventies and eighties, but it was repeatedly made obvious that I would never again achieve what we did with the Doors. Accepting that fact drove me deeper and deeper into an unacknowledged depression and left me wide open to any chemical that could lighten the emotional load. While I should've been basking in appreciation for what we had created, I was only able to focus on the darkness of never experiencing it again. Once you've been a part of something like the Doors, one way or another, you'll forever be chasing that first high.

WAYLON

Everyone Lynn and I knew seemed to be getting married. Ray, John, Bill Siddons, Bruce Botnick... by the end of 1970, they all had wives, and Lynn was sick of being a "girlfriend." I resisted as long as I could, but I did love her, after all. There was no grand proposal, just a long conversation and a practical decision. We went ring shopping at Frances Klein, a posh antique jewelry store in Beverly Hills, and she picked out a vintage platinum band with a ruby and a diamond encircled by a figure eight of smaller pavé diamonds. She treasured it until thirty years later, when she was clapping her hands at a concert and the setting came loose, sending all the stones flying. I hope whoever was sweeping up that night kept their eyes open.

We picked the day after Christmas 1970 to get married, but with everything closed for the holidays, we had to drive down to Gardena — a distinctly unromantic city south of the airport — to find a courthouse willing to do the ceremony. My brother, Ronny, and his wife, Sue, came along to be our witnesses. We were so unprepared that we had to borrow cash from my brother to pay for all the fees, since the court didn't accept credit cards. We all smoked some weed before the ceremony and couldn't stop giggling. The justice of the peace had these big, thick glasses and was taking the whole thing so seriously, which made us all laugh even harder.

"DO YOU, SIR, TAKE THIS WOMAN..."

We were cracking up so much we could barely get out the words "I do." Afterward we invited Ronny and Sue out to a celebratory dinner, but since it was so last-minute they had already made other plans, so Lynn and I just went home, fed our cat, and went to bed. We didn't take a single photo of the whole event.

The modesty of it all was by design. It seemed like the people we knew who had grand, lavish weddings ended up divorced pretty quickly, while the ones who got hitched casually or quietly had marriages that lasted. I was the best man and Lynn was the maid of honor when John married Julia at a famous yoga temple in Pacific Palisades, where lush gardens surrounded a man-made lake. It was a beautiful and well-attended event. And they split up two years later. Ray and Dorothy, on the other hand, eloped at city hall with Jim and Pam as their only witnesses. I didn't even know they had gotten married until Jim mentioned it onstage the next night, and they stayed together for the rest of Ray's life. I've always felt that the more of a show you put on about your relationship, the more you have something to prove. Lynn and I agreed we didn't need anything flashy, and we're still together, so my theory has panned out pretty well so far.

Other than the tax break, one of the reasons marriage made sense to me was because we were ready to have kids. A couple of years earlier, we weren't ready. And Lynn got pregnant.

We had only been dating for a little while and I was constantly touring. Having a baby would've torn us apart. *Roe v. Wade* was still several years away, but just because abortion wasn't legal didn't mean women weren't getting them. Several of our friends had

worked with a guy named Dr. Leon. He was a little pricey compared to other black-market options, but he was highly recommended, and—having heard horror stories from friends who literally
had their abortions in back alleys—this wasn't something we
wanted to be cheap about.

Dr. Leon met us at a neutral location near our house. He was a
balding, overweight man who was probably in his seventies, and he
had a tall, well-built assistant with him. They put a blindfold on
Lynn so she couldn't see where they were going, and they had her
slump down in the back of their car so the cops wouldn't get
suspicious.

They drove off. All I could do was wait and worry, so in an
attempt to distract myself, I went to the movies and fidgeted
uncomfortably through a matinee showing of *Barbarella*.

Lynn was taken to some sort of apartment complex and given a
shot that knocked her out completely. She has no memory of where
she was, what it looked like, whether she went to another location,
or anything about the procedure. The next thing she knew she was
in the car on the way to meet me at the prearranged drop-off spot.
Lynn had a few cramps but physically she was otherwise fine. As we
parted ways with Dr. Leon, he attempted an awkward compliment
with the most awkward phrasing: "She has a wonderful skin."

When we were finally married and ready to have kids, it didn't
happen easily. Four months into her first intentional pregnancy,
Lynn started bleeding and cramping. I was on the road with the
Doors, so Lynn made a doctor's appointment and called my mom
for a ride to the hospital. My mom was a ball of nerves when she
picked up Lynn because she had borrowed my dad's Maserati,
which he usually never let her drive. And this was before my mom
stopped taking pills, so she was also spaced out on codeine. Lynn,
who was already freaked out about her condition, had to hold her
breath as my mom stalled and bucked and sideswiped several cars

during the drive. Lynn claims it was the scariest car ride of her life (and between her experiences with me and Jim that's really saying something).

Lynn had miscarried. She underwent a D&C, which is a procedure that clears away the tissue left inside and which knocked her back even more than the illegal abortion. They discovered that Lynn has Rh-negative blood, which caused her body to attack the fetus like it was a foreign invader. The loss of the pregnancy was traumatic for both of us after four months of anticipation, but all we could do was accept it and move on. The doctors gave her a shot to correct the blood issue, and she took some time to recover physically and emotionally.

She got pregnant again while we were living in England and I was working with the Butts Band. This time we were more guarded about our excitement. When we got back to the States, we checked in regularly with the doctors, we did all the Lamaze classes, and everything went well. Except for the actual delivery. Lynn was a couple of weeks late, so they scheduled an appointment to induce labor. (I couldn't shake the feeling that the doctor was trying to squeeze us in between golf games.) Once she was induced, everything happened so fast. Lamaze went right out the window. The pain from her contractions was far more intense due to the induction, so they gave her a saddle block—an IV anesthetic so named because it completely numbs the area that would come into contact with the saddle of a horse. Even with that, Lynn was still screaming in agony. We didn't understand why until much later: the saddle block IV had fallen out. She was experiencing peak pain with zero relief. The baby shot out—it's a boy! But then Lynn's blood pressure dropped and her temperature spiked to a dangerous level. I was suddenly rushed out of the room. I don't know what exactly happened, but her body was likely reacting to the trauma of such a painful birth. The doctors had to knock her out with drugs so they could work on her. I envisioned all kinds of worst-case scenarios.

We found out later that she had come disturbingly close to a serious complication that could've killed her. But she made it through. And after she woke up, she was finally able to hold our beautiful newborn son.

We named him Waylon because I'd always liked how the name sounded on Waylon Jennings, and we gave him the middle name Sonnenuhr after our favorite type of German wine. I played him lots of reggae on guitar since we had just gotten back from the UK and Jamaica, and of course I played him the same *Peter and the Wolf* score that my dad used to play for me.

I even went a little overboard and created a *Peter and the Wolf* of my own: an original musical storybook called *A Cat's Tale*. It's about three cats that find a hole in their litter box, which leads them into a *Wizard of Oz*–type adventure. They cross paths with a crazy soldier, a king, a turtle, a duck, and an army of mice, and the cats join forces with all of them to defeat a two-headed monster called the Grongus. I spent over a year recording it with Bruce Botnick, and I was able to recruit some amazing vocal talent. Cartoon superstar Mel Blanc did several of the voices, June Foray (who voiced Rocky the Flying Squirrel, Cindy-Lou Who, Granny from *Looney Tunes*, and a zillion other famous characters) played one of the cats, and the crazy soldier was voiced by Frank Nelson, who you may know from his work with Jack Benny, his appearances on *The Great Gildersleeve* radio show, or his catchphrase: "EEE-Yeeeeeesssssss?"

We had violins and cellos and saxophones and backup singers. Mike Stull from the Butts Band and Bonnie Bramlett from Delaney & Bonnie sang leads, Grant Johnson from the Psychedelic Rangers came in to play piano, Lynn voiced one of the cats, and I, of course, played guitar. I took it to Elektra with the hope that they'd help me release it as an album and produce an animated movie to go along with it, but they thought I was insane.

After all that effort, Waylon didn't really seem to care much about my musical gift to him. He was only about three years old at the time, and while the silly voices were fun, the songs were too sophisticated for a child that young. I shelved the whole thing, figuring I'd play it for him again when he was a little older. But I basically forgot it existed until he was too old for a children's album.

I should've known not to put so much stock in grand gestures. I wanted to share my music with Waylon, but I needed to let him find music of his own. Instead of bonding by teaching him guitar, we bonded as I taught him to surf and took him on ski trips. Later, when he became a teenager, he discovered his own sounds and his own favorite musical styles, and he learned guitar with no urging from me. He started putting his own bands together and ended up playing in a group called Bloodline, with Joe Bonamassa and the sons of Miles Davis, Sammy Hagar, and Berry Oakley. And as an adult he joined me on the road, playing guitar and later handling vocals for the Robby Krieger Band.

When it came to marriage and kids, I always felt like I wasn't prepared. And I was right: I ended up married to the best partner a person could ask for, and I've spent my golden years traveling the world with my son and playing music by his side.

Nothing could've prepared me for that.

THE SOFT PARADE

We walked out of the brand-new Elektra Studios for some fresh air while we were recording *The Soft Parade* and some guy walked up and punched Ray right in the face. It was a pretty solid hit. Knocked off Ray's glasses. We asked the guy why he did it, as if he might give us an answer that made sense. He was clearly mentally disturbed, but from what I could gather he was angry because he thought we had written a song about him. At least he was a fan.

It wasn't the only punch thrown during those recording sessions. Jim showed up at the studio one day with a bloody nose and a big smile on his face. His brother-in-law was with him; the two of them had been out drinking. The brother-in-law apologetically explained, "He kept telling me to hit him, so I did!"

Jim's drinking was at its peak when we were putting together *The Soft Parade*. We were used to alcohol affecting his behavior, but now it was affecting his creative output. He wasn't writing, and he had run out of old material. It meant I had to step up to fill in the songwriting gaps. Which was fine by me. But it threw off the balance that made our other records work so well.

Paul Rothchild, meanwhile, had earned the nickname Little Hitler for his rigid, torturous producing style. His perfectionist drive had been validated by the success of *Waiting for the Sun,* so we were again subjected to endless takes and infinite tweaks, and again Jim drank to cope with the drudgery. One of the reasons Paul was even more obsessive on *The Soft Parade* compared with our other albums was likely because his cocaine dealer always happened to be hanging around the studio. And he wasn't there to give input on microphone placement.

When Paul suggested bringing in an orchestra to fill out some of the songs, I wasn't a fan of the idea. But writing such complex and grandiose arrangements turned out to be a stimulating challenge, and when you're in the studio listening live to all those strings and horns, the power of it just washes over you. Still, it felt like we were copying the Beatles. Or worse: copying the Stones when they were copying the Beatles. We may have had a bunch of fancy instruments, but we didn't have George Martin. One day George Harrison dropped by the studio, and I'm sure he took note of our copycat orchestra, but he was polite enough not to comment on it.

The Stones also happened to be in town. They were working on the song "Gimme Shelter" at Elektra Studios around the same time, and I got to drop in on the session when Mick Jagger and Merry Clayton recorded their famous vocal duet. It was obvious they had a hit on their hands. I later learned they had pulled Merry out of bed at the last minute for the session; I remember wondering at the time why she was recording with curlers in her hair. Curtis Amy, who played the sax solo on "Touch Me," was dating Merry at the time and was there with me to watch her sing. He and Merry got married about a year or two later. Must've been some magic going around Elektra Studios to bring the Stones, the Beatles, the Doors, and Merry and Curtis together.

The Soft Parade marked a break with tradition when Jim suggested we credit ourselves as individual songwriters instead of sharing credit as a group. This has allegedly been traced back to an argument Jim and I had about the lyric "Can't you see me growing, get your guns" in "Tell All the People." But I was never so precious about my words that I'd argue fiercely against Jim wanting to change them. And if I tried, do you think I'd win? Whenever Jim wanted to change a lyric, he just did it. He was the poet. I was the guitarist. He was the guy who declared we want the world and we want it now and no one here gets out alive and we got the numbers gonna win yeah we're taking over. And on the title track for *The Soft Parade*, he wrote the line "Better bring your gun." Would he really cower at one little line about revolution? The songwriting credit change, as far as I could tell, was more about Jim recognizing how little he had contributed, and feeling uncomfortable about people assuming the lyrics always came from him.

A perfect example of Jim suggesting an easy lyric change was when he came up with the title for "Touch Me." When I originally wrote it, the title was "Hit Me," since it was inspired by blackjack. In the *Feast of Friends* documentary, there's footage of me trying to teach the band a card game called five fifty-five, but they weren't quite getting the rules, so I ended up taking all their money. It planted the idea in my head that the motions of a card game — people upping the stakes and refusing to show their hand — would be a good metaphor for a contentious relationship, and the lyrics flowed from there. Jim worried that people wouldn't get the symbolism and would take the phrase "Hit me" literally. By swapping out a single word, he changed the whole song for the better and undeniably helped "Touch Me" become a hit.

"Touch Me" always confuses musicians because the intro leading into the vocals runs for seven bars when traditionally it would run for eight, or at least some other even number. Every time I cover the song with a new group of musicians, they invariably get it wrong, and I have to spend half an hour training them to fight their instinct to play that eighth bar. And then I have to explain that when the same part comes around a second time, we play it for only six bars for some reason. The ending of the song also tends to confuse people because buried in the mix you can hear us (along with Paul Rothchild and his cocaine dealer) chant the old slogan for Ajax laundry detergent: "Stronger than dirt!" Fans still puzzle over the deeper meaning of it, but it was as simple as someone pointing out that the final four notes of the song lined up with the Ajax jingle perfectly, and we thought it'd be funny to throw it in there. Never let it be said that the Doors didn't have a sense of humor. Or that Robby Krieger took his lyrics too seriously.

In December '68, after *The Soft Parade* was finished but not yet released, we played a show at the Forum in Los Angeles. We had enough money to hire a live orchestra to really showcase our new material, and we had enough pull to dictate who our supporting acts would be. Ray insisted on having a guy named Lui Tsun-Yuen open the show, playing traditional Chinese music on an instrument called a pipa. Predictably, this did not go over well with eighteen thousand Doors fans. We thought it would be cool to have Jerry Lee Lewis, one of our early rock 'n' roll heroes, play the direct support slot. His guitarist came up to me before the show and asked to borrow a guitar — "Any ol' Fender rock-a-day guitar will do!" All I had were Gibsons, which he politely accepted. We didn't realize that Jerry Lee had renounced rock as the devil's music, so the crowd was treated to a set of mostly country tunes instead. It went over even worse than the Chinese pipa music. As the crowd booed him, Jerry Lee said, "For those of you out there who love country music, God bless ya. And for everybody else, I hope you have a heart attack!"

After that lovely warm-up, we went onstage and played a bunch of new songs that the crowd didn't even know, flush with strings and horns instead of the raw Doors sound they were expecting. All things considered, we were received well. But we probably should've thought our plans through a little better.

The following month, we flew to New York for our first-ever show at Madison Square Garden, and we again hired a string and horn section to present our new songs in their fully realized form. Back when I graduated high school, my parents let me take my first-ever trip to New York with Bill Wolff and my friend Scott, who played kazoo in the Back Bay Chamber Pot Terriers and supplied us all with boo at Menlo. We tramped around the Village and saw some blues acts at Café Wha?, but we spent the lion's share of our time getting stoned in our hotel room and stuffing our faces with delicious local pastries known as Devil Dogs. A mere five years later I was back in New York, playing to a crowd of twenty thousand people at the city's biggest arena.

Despite Madison Square Garden's size and reputation, it wasn't originally intended to host rock concerts. Their PA system was built to announce sports. We had our own PA, but it was hardly powerful enough for a venue that size. The sound was slapping back from the rear walls, and Jim had to sing with no monitors. If you're not familiar with musical equipment, find someone you know who is a trained singer and ask them what it would be like to headline Madison Square Garden with no monitors and you'll likely arrive at a new appreciation for Jim Morrison. The crowd forgave the technical limitations and seemed to enjoy the set, even though the sound of our grand, dulcet orchestra was pumped at them through the same loudspeakers that blasted the end-of-period horn at hockey games.

The Soft Parade was dismissed as indulgent by a lot of critics and fans due to the fanciful instrumentation, but the strings and horns only appear on half the songs. If we had rearranged the sequence of the tracks, I wonder if it would've been as distracting. For the fiftieth anniversary of the album, we released a remixed, orchestra-less version of some of the songs, but the problem is, they were specifically written to accommodate the orchestral arrangement, so they sounded too empty. I added a few guitar parts to fill things out, but I'll always wonder how different the album would've been if we'd just written it as a four-piece. I don't regret going out on a limb and trying something new, though. It was an experiment, and experiments teach you very valuable lessons. In this case, the lesson was clear: Never try to copy the Beatles.

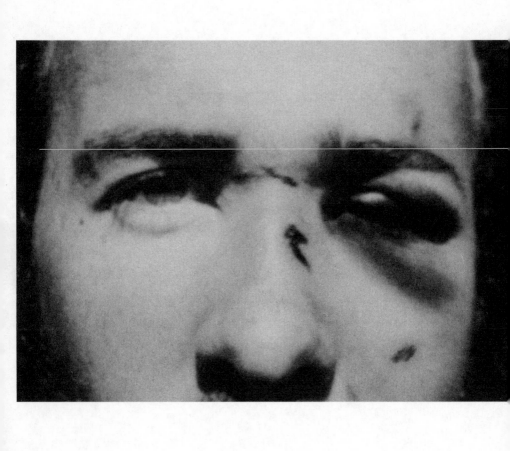

THE BLACK EYE

Fortune-tellers usually don't predict doom and gloom in your future—it's bad for business. When the Doors played a show in Santa Barbara in the summer of '68, my friend Bob Cranson from UCSB dragged me, John, and our friends Sharon and Donna to see a palm reader while we were in town. I scoffed at the idea, but Bob swore that Miss Clara had the Gift. Miss Clara was a small, elderly woman with a thick German accent who did readings out of her modest living room. One by one, she read our auras and traced the lines on our hands. She made vague promises of health, happiness, and success for John, Bob, and Sharon. She told me I'd live a great life and that I'd invent some new form of "musical language." I'm still waiting for that to happen. It was interesting that she pegged me as a musician, but that was easy enough to explain. She might've been too old to recognize us from the Doors, but she probably noticed the calluses on my fret hand or the long thumbnail on my picking hand.

When it came to our friend Donna, though, Miss Clara's mood shifted. She spoke with more gravity. Almost pity. She said, "You will have a very unfortunate life. It will be very difficult. But you will live through it, and you will be okay."

"Oh, thanks a lot!" Donna sarcastically replied.

We didn't give Miss Clara's words much weight. But we would recall them vividly about six months later.

+ + +

Donna and Sharon were fixtures at the Whisky a Go Go. I don't think they were officially employed there, but Donna was a tall, sexy brunette and Sharon was a short, cute blonde, and the club saw an obvious benefit to keeping them around. We got to know them well during our residency, and later they both ended up living with me at my place on Topanga Beach. We occasionally shared the same bed but I was still with Happy at the time, so believe it or not, it was purely platonic (the sixties, man). When Lynn and I started dating, though, she wasn't too fond of the perceived competition.

After I'd had a particularly bad fight with Lynn, Donna talked me into taking a fishing trip to Mexico with her and her new boyfriend, Milton. The idea of skipping town for a while and clearing my head about Lynn was appealing, and we had just finished recording *The Soft Parade* so a little rest and relaxation sounded good, too. We could've easily driven a few hours down to Baja, or we could've stayed right where we were: we lived on the California coast—there was an ocean full of fish in walking distance. But for some reason Donna wanted to make the drive to Guaymas, a small port city on the Mexican mainland over eight hundred miles away.

The only problem was that I had to be back in L.A. a few days later to appear on *The Smothers Brothers Comedy Hour*. We figured out that if we drove in shifts through the night the whole way there and the whole way back, we'd end up with one full day of fishing. It was an insane plan. When I look back, I'm left wondering if Donna was scheming to make either Lynn or Milton jealous, but either way, I was an idiot to agree to the trip. I provided the fishing gear, Milton provided his brand-new Dodge van, and Donna took the first driving shift.

Milton's van was a big, boxy thing, and the wind tossed it all over the road as we made our way to the border. Once we crossed into Mexico, the speed limits vanished and I took over the driving, getting us up to a hundred miles per hour for a while and then backing down to eighty after the engine ran too hot.

Night fell. Donna went to sleep in the back seat while Milton and I chatted up front to stay awake. On either side of us the two-lane highway sloped off into a pitch-black desert. There were no streetlights. There were hardly any other cars. Our visibility was limited to the scope of our headlights, which, for a couple of hours, illuminated nothing but a long, straight, empty stretch of boring blacktop, which slowly lulled us into complacency.

And then the road curved.

I hit the brakes and yanked the wheel to the left, but it was too late. We skidded off a small cliff and my aborted turn sent the van into a roll. The headlights reflected off the upside-down desert sand. It seemed like we hung in the air for an unnatural period of time, during which my brain concluded, "You're not going to survive this."

We slammed into the ground.

Blackness.

+   +   +

I awoke to some local villagers pulling us from the wreck. Apparently similar accidents happened often in that particular spot. I could see from the trail in the sand that we had rolled pretty far. My knee ached, and I had some cuts and bruises, but it didn't seem like any bones were broken. Milton had fucked up his foot but seemed relatively fine overall. We were grateful that we had worn our seat belts, even though we weren't required to do so by law.

Donna, though, had been lying down in the back with no seat belt on. Her wails filled the otherwise silent night air.

An ambulance arrived surprisingly fast. I hadn't processed just how rough the road was on the way down, but every time the ambulance hit a bump, Donna would scream in pain. Milton and I yelled at the driver to slow down, but at the same time we all wanted to get Donna help as quickly as possible.

We arrived at a small Mexican hospital that was dingy and cramped and had low lighting, like something out of a horror movie. This wasn't a place equipped for serious emergencies. We got them to give Donna something for her pain, and when she fell asleep, we loaded her back into the ambulance and had them drive us across the border to a hospital in Tucson, Arizona. They patched Milton and me up and went to work fixing whatever was wrong with Donna. I contacted my uncle Sonny—the dermatologist whose Arizona address I had used for my draft physical—and since he was a doctor he was able to refer us to some specialists who could hopefully offer Donna some help.

When Lynn heard about what had happened, she and Sharon made the drive all the way out to Tucson to check on us. Whatever Lynn and I had been arguing about before I left suddenly didn't seem so important anymore. Making that drive showed me how much Lynn cared, and who she really was. If there's a silver lining to the whole incident it's that my relationship with Lynn deepened significantly that night.

The doctors kept an eye on Donna while the rest of us returned to L.A. I barely made it back in time for the *Smothers Brothers* appearance. I walked into the studio with a bulging black eye and played down the seriousness of the accident when the rest of the band asked me about it. The makeup people wanted to cover up my shiner, but I resisted. When they pushed, Jim stepped in and said,

"He doesn't have to wear makeup if he doesn't want to." They backed off.

Thankfully we only had to mime our songs; Jim's vocals were the only element that weren't prerecorded (and you can tell because he forgot to come in on the second chorus of "Touch Me"). But I still had to stand there and pretend to play, and pretend like I hadn't recently almost died. The truth is, though, I never really dwelled on how bad things might've gone for me. My bigger concern was Donna.

Her lower spinal cord had been injured. They attempted to repair it with surgery, but it didn't work. She was paralyzed from the waist down. She would never walk again without help.

As she struggled to piece her life back together, I struggled with survivor's guilt. Why her and not me? Both of us had been driving recklessly, but I was the one behind the wheel at the time. Could I have done something differently? Was this my fault?

My dad recommended a psychiatrist to help Donna through her adjustment, and to help me with my guilt. The shrink did his best to remind me that the whole thing was an accident; I wasn't drunk or high — it could've happened to anyone. He told me, "In a situation like this, there's enough guilt to go around for twenty people," and he said I shouldn't blame myself. It's easy enough to say, but much harder to internalize. I stopped going after a few sessions.

Whether I was responsible or not, I told Donna I'd always take care of her. Thankfully the Doors were successful enough that I was in a position to offer her more than just comforting words, and I started sending her regular checks. But her friends convinced her not to trust my generosity, and to sue me. That hurt. I was trying my best to make things right, but here was an official legal action reminding me that I'd never be able to give her back what had been taken from her, no matter how much money I might have. In the end, Max Fink got the lawsuit thrown out. But I had told Donna I'd take care of her, and I meant it. I was lucky enough to have the money to be able to help her, and she was unlucky enough to be in the back seat that night. I try to balance things out where I can.

I bought her a house in the Valley and a specially designed Volvo for her to get around in, and I sent her a healthy monthly stipend for other living expenses. I even convinced the Doors to dedicate the proceeds from two of our shows to her, which netted her six figures. Jim ribbed me about it at the time: "Why do *we* have to give her money? Why don't *you* do it?" It was a dark joke meant to lighten a heavy situation. All four of us had befriended Donna in the Whisky days. John even dated her for a while. It was the least we could do.

She bounced back pretty well at first. I visited her often when she was still in the hospital. There was a group of Vietnam vets in her wing, paralyzed from war injuries. Some of the quadriplegic patients called themselves the Quad Squad and entertained themselves by ramming into one another with their motorized wheelchairs. Donna had all the male patients wrapped around her finger. She later fell in love with one of her physical therapists, got married, moved to Australia, and had a couple of kids. It was almost a happy ending, but unfortunately the marriage didn't last, and she ended up moving back to the Valley.

We kept in touch, but her embarrassment over the lawsuit and other personal issues in her life made things awkward. Two or three times I arranged to meet her and her lawyer at her house to discuss details about future monthly payments, but when I got there she'd make a polite excuse for why she couldn't see me. Whatever her reasons, I didn't want to make things worse, so I took the hint and stopped trying to force a friendship. After not hearing from her for a long time, her financial manager told me she had died. He had been accepting checks from me for a full two years after she passed away before he got around to mentioning it. I never found out the exact cause of her death or whether it was related to the accident. She was only in her mid-fifties. I just hope at least some of the money her manager collected went to her kids.

To this day, Doors fans will approach me and ask about my black eye on the *Smothers Brothers* show. It's the single most common question I get, even though everyone seems to think they're the first one to ever ask me about it.

I usually say Jim and I got in a fight before the show. Sometimes I'll say we were attacked by rednecks who didn't like our long hair; other times I'll say Jim and I were drunkenly battling each other. Sometimes I'll say I hit my eye on a desk. Part of the reason I do that is just to be mischievous. I used to love it when Jim gave conflicting stories to the press to keep people guessing about us, and I like carrying on that tradition. But part of it is that it's just easier to offer a phony answer than to constantly relive one of the most difficult experiences of my entire life.

My black eye should serve as a reminder that no matter how much a person thinks they know about the Doors, there's always more to the story.

Much more.

THE WINGS OF MADNESS

When Baudelaire contracted syphilis, he wrote, "Today I felt pass over me / A breath of wind from the wings of madness." When Jim Morrison contracted syphilis, he was eager to feel that same breath of wind. Most people would be scared, or at least upset, if they contracted a potentially lethal STD, but Jim was excited to feel closer to all those disease-ridden nineteenth-century poets and painters and philosophers he idolized. He confided in me that he was going to let the disease go untreated so he could experience what it was really like to go insane. I pleaded with him to reconsider. His little biological experiment could have easily killed him, like it did some of the famous names now buried beside him at Père Lachaise cemetery. He got pretty seriously ill, but he stuck to his guns for a while. Until the pain of urinating got to be too much and he finally went to a doctor.

You couldn't tell Jim Morrison what to do. And if you tried he would make you regret it. He was forever rebelling against his navy officer father. Anyone who attempted to step into a role of authority over him became the target of his unresolved rage. So what could we do when we saw his rebellion manifest itself as alcoholism? Jim's drinking had ramped up gradually since the beginning of the band, but in the wake of the Miami Incident it was isolating him from the rest of us and making it hard to be his bandmate, let alone his friend. It was one self-destructive binge after another, and the worse it got, the more obvious it was that the booze could kill him just as easily as an untreated case of syphilis.

Today, if you have a friend who has an addiction, you can call up the people close to them and say, "We need to do an intervention," and everyone will know what you're talking about. Interventions didn't exist in the sixties. Nobody was allowed to judge anybody for how much they drank or how many drugs they took. It wasn't cool. You might make a concerned comment, or you might yell in frustration if it got really bad, but beyond that you were helpless. If a rock star has an issue with addiction today, there's a multibillion-dollar rehabilitation industry dedicated to helping them get clean. But back then if you told someone they needed to go to "rehab," they wouldn't even have known what you were abbreviating.

Thankfully my dad was an early adopter of psychotherapy, so when he saw what we were going through with Jim, he volunteered to help us out. There was a much stronger stigma attached to seeing a shrink back then, but my dad had been doing it unashamedly for years due to a history of panic attacks, and he really believed in the process. He didn't use the term "intervention," but he recommended that we all sit down with Jim as a group to compassionately confront him about his drinking and get him to agree to seek professional help. He offered to host the meeting at his house and be our guide through the whole thing.

Jim had recently gotten too wasted at some party or another . . . I've since lost track of the incident that pushed us to have the intervention in the first place. But he was in Post-Embarrassment Humble Apology Mode, so we caught him at a very receptive moment.

We didn't have to trick him or surprise him; we just told him we wanted to talk, and he agreed. I picked him up and drove him to my parents' house.

Sure, my dad was an establishment stiff from a dusty, older generation, but Jim held him in high regard. Jim's dad had fiercely tried to dissuade him from pursuing music, but my dad was known to occasionally pick up hitchhikers on Sunset so he could casually brag about how his son was in the Doors. John's parents were older and unhip, but my dad had a collection of boogie-woogie records. Ray's parents were nuts, but my parents had let Jim crash at our house, had let the Doors practice in their living room, and had even recommended the lawyer who was keeping Jim out of jail in Miami. I think Jim envied the relatively healthy environment I had grown up in, compared with his own rootless childhood, which always had him moving from one military town to another. My dad was the exact opposite of Jim's dad in terms of being caring and supportive. When my dad spoke to Jim out of genuine concern, Jim listened.

We told Jim he wasn't looking good. We told him we were worried about him. He didn't argue. He didn't fight back. My dad told Jim about his personal experience with psychotherapy and how it had helped him. After a while, he and Jim even went into another room to talk privately. Jim didn't want to fuck up the band. Not consciously, anyway. He recognized that he had a problem, and he wanted to be better. Jim agreed to stop drinking.

It lasted for maybe one or two weeks. He also agreed to see a shrink. That lasted for maybe one or two sessions. No matter how deeply Jim may have wanted to change, addiction doesn't just go away. I wasn't naive enough to think that one little talk would change everything forever. But we had hope. He came to the meeting. He listened. He tried to follow up. All of that was far beyond what I had expected.

We tried hiring bodyguards for Jim who were tasked with keeping him sober, but Jim would end up convincing them to drink with him. We tried funding film projects for Jim in hopes that it would keep his idle hands busy, but Jim would end up getting drunk with the crew. We tried nagging. We tried the intervention. But Jim kept drinking. And eventually we ran out of things to try.

THE TRIAL

In 1969, for some reason people started hijacking planes to Cuba several times a month. New laws were passed, and airline personnel were on edge. Toward the end of the year, while awaiting trial for the Miami Incident, Jim and his friend Tom Baker caused another incident, this time on a flight from L.A. to Phoenix. They were on their way to see the Rolling Stones play, but they got drunk on the plane and harassed the cabin crew. The airline might have brushed it off in the past, but because of all the new anti-hijacking legislation, Jim and Tom were taken into custody when they landed. There was bail and fines and Max Fink had to go to Phoenix and deal with all of it. The trial and legal mess would play out over the following seven months, running parallel to the trial and legal mess in Miami.

Tom Baker was a New York actor who played the lead in Andy Warhol's *I, a Man* and transitioned from being a member of Andy's entourage to being a member of Jim's entourage. From what I understand, Tom was actually the one mostly responsible for the trouble on the Phoenix flight, but I honestly never researched the details of that episode too deeply. I didn't bother to ask Jim about it and he never volunteered the story. I had come to accept that this was life in the Doors.

The established narrative among Doors historians is that the Miami trial caused a divide between Jim and the rest of the band. But if anything, the trial gave us a reason to be sympathetic toward Jim, and in fact helped heal the divide that had been growing since *Waiting for the Sun.* We felt bad for him. We weren't happy about being pulled off the radio or having our shows canceled, but after the initial wave of bad press, the whole thing actually made us look cool, and it was easy enough to bounce back. Records made more money than touring back then, so if all we cared about was lost revenue, we were better off with the extra time to write new songs, and John wanted to take time off from playing live anyway. It wasn't an ideal situation, but it didn't turn us against each other. Jim was being railroaded by a bunch of asshole politicians trying to further their careers. Phoenix may have been his fault, but Miami wasn't, and we knew that.

Jim and Max Fink outside the Miami courthouse

Anita Bryant (who would later become one of the nation's biggest anti-gay crusaders) and Jackie Gleason (who was an even worse drunk than Jim) headlined a Catholic-backed and Nixon-endorsed Rally for Decency in Miami to publicly decry the lewd acts of Jim Morrison. I remember seeing some young kids on TV pretending to be outraged by the Doors. It was all so fake. Even if Jim had exposed himself, none of them were at the show to see it. They were just using us to push a fundamentalist agenda, and they didn't care who they hurt in the process.

It was a year and a half of motions and filings and adjournments and everything else before we actually ended up in a courtroom. In September of 1970, Ray, John, and I flew to Miami to testify. Max Fink was handling Jim's defense. He didn't prep us much in terms of what to say. All we had to do was tell the truth: nothing happened. (Although I did downplay Jim's drunkenness a little.) Most of the questions were answerable with a simple yes or no. The only real highlight was when the prosecution was trying to suggest that Jim had simulated oral copulation on me and Jim was explaining that he only kneeled down to admire my guitar playing.

The prosecutor said, "You have seen Robby Krieger do that solo thousands of times, haven't you?"

"Could be," replied Jim.

"But you got down on your knees to study the intricate finger work?"

"Well, he gets better all the time."

The jury seemed to be entertained. It was probably the most fun case they could've been assigned to.

The lawyers played a recording of the Miami concert, which was musically a mess but hardly lewd enough to justify throwing someone in jail. I was glad they didn't have some of Jim's worse rants on tape. They had over a hundred photos from that night and not one of them showed Jim doing the thing they had accused him of doing.

I got the sense that even the prosecutor didn't really believe in the case and was just going through the motions.

Between court dates, Jim put on a brave face and talked about how he was striking a blow for First Amendment rights. But underneath he was afraid. He was facing several years behind bars, and even if he ended up with a shorter sentence, they'd be sending him to Raiford Prison — the facility that would later house Ted Bundy. Jim had grown up in Florida; he knew Raiford's reputation. No matter how solid his case was, he knew things could still go very wrong for him.

I was in denial. How could any rational jury find him guilty? But this was The System, and sometimes The System isn't rational. And it was also Florida, where nothing ever makes sense. Jim was found guilty of indecent exposure, even though he hadn't exposed himself, and he was found not guilty of drunkenness, even though he had been unmistakably drunk.

Six months. Hard labor.

As shocked as we were, we still didn't think it was the end of the world. Jim was able to post bond and remain free while his appeal was pending, and — still in denial — we took it for granted that he'd eventually be cleared, or that they'd at least knock his sentence down to something much lighter. But he died before his appeal went through, so we never found out.

Forty years later, and without technically apologizing for anything, the governor of Florida arranged for Jim to receive a posthumous pardon. I suppose if it's a choice between pardoning him or letting the conviction stand, I choose the pardon, but we all felt like it was far too little, far too late. The Miami Incident began with politicians using Jim Morrison to show how righteous they were, and it ended with politicians using Jim Morrison to show how gracious they were. And that, unfortunately, is how The System works.

Live at the Hollywood Bowl

ONE FROGGY EVENING

When we played Madison Square Garden, our bassist kept laughing at us onstage. We had hired Harvey Brooks, who played bass on *The Soft Parade* (as well as on Dylan's *Highway 61 Revisited*), to join us along with our fancy orchestra. During the ride out of "Wild Child," Jim stood nose to nose with Harvey and seductively repeated the line "Your cool face... Your cool face..." while staring deep into Harvey's eyes. Harvey nearly lost it. Later on during the set, Jim, Ray, John, and I were disagreeing over what song to play next, and Harvey cracked up again. He found it hilarious that we were leaving the audience hanging to have an impromptu debate in the middle of headlining the world's most famous arena.

We almost never used set lists. When we did, we rarely stuck to them. It kept us from getting bored with our own music because we weren't repeating the same songs every night. And it forced us to read the crowd and tailor our show to each individual audience. We sometimes planned out the first couple of songs, and we knew we'd end things with "Light My Fire" or "The End," but between those we went with whatever felt right. One of us would call out a song or offer up a musical cue, and the rest of us would go with it. Other times we'd gather around the drum riser for a quick discussion. If Jim was too drunk, or if one of us was feeling stubborn, it could derail our momentum. But on nights when we were all operating on the same wavelength, it gave the show a spontaneous, unpredictable energy.

When we were booked at the Hollywood Bowl in 1968, though, we made a very official set list, and we practiced it daily during the week leading up to the show. Practice was as unusual as set lists for us. During the Whisky days we were playing multiple sets every night, and after that we were always touring or recording, so we never had a chance to get rusty. But the Hollywood Bowl was going to be a big deal. We were going to bring in a mobile studio to record a live album, and we were going to bring in a full camera crew to create a concert film. If we screwed up musically, or if we had to resort to one of our momentum-killing drum riser conferences, it would be embarrassingly documented for all eternity, so we resolved to stick faithfully to our set list, and we rehearsed until we had every song down perfectly.

And that was the problem.

+ + +

I had never actually seen a concert at the Hollywood Bowl before we played there. For most of its history, the Bowl was a place to see opera and classical and jazz. Even during the sixties, rock bands were a relative rarity. My first view of the famous band shell was while walking onto the stage under it before our soundcheck, and gazing out over the thousands of empty seats that would soon be filled with our fans. Just as with *The Ed Sullivan Show*, it was our turn to make our mark on that prestigious stage after the Beatles and the Stones before us.

We were determined to rip the place up. We had signed a sponsorship deal with the Acoustic Amplifier Company—a small local manufacturer—and we told them to bring down as many amps as they could. They stacked thirty-six speaker cabinets on the stage. Enough for them to hear us all the way down at the Whisky.

But as I plugged in my guitar, Decibel Meter Guy appeared. I don't know what his official title was, but he held up a little device that measured volume, and then he informed us that the Hollywood Bowl had a decibel limit, and we were way over it. He walked around the venue holding up his decibel meter, checking and rechecking as we gradually and reluctantly turned down our volume knobs. By the time we made Decibel Meter Guy happy, I was using only one amp out of the eight that were supposed to be dedicated to my guitar, and its volume knob was at two instead of ten. When you play guitar at a volume that low—especially with a solid-state amp like the ones Acoustic made—the signal doesn't break up to give you any distortion. It sounds too clean. All those massive, powerful speakers...and I would've been better off if I had stuck a microphone up against my suitcase-size Fender Twin Reverb.

Since we had already loaded all the cabinets onto the stage, we just left them there. People still marvel at photos of the mighty wall of amps we had on display at the Hollywood Bowl show, but only a few were actually functioning. Still: they looked pretty cool.

I've always been dissatisfied with my guitar sound at the Bowl show, but after all these years no one has ever come up to me and complained about it, so maybe I'm being too picky. Acoustic made great amps for keyboards and bass, but I didn't realize how different my guitar would sound through a solid-state amp compared with a tube amp until we had already signed our sponsorship deal. Vince Treanor later hollowed out an Acoustic cabinet and filled it with JBL speakers and a quality power amp so we could appear onstage with Acoustic gear while still sounding good. The company used a picture from our Bowl show on the cover of their 1968 catalog, and they apparently credit me with getting them off the ground since I was one of their highest profile early adopters. Happy to help, guys!

Despite the wet blanket of Decibel Meter Guy, we were still poised for a historic night. Bruce Botnick had a mobile studio in a sound truck behind the stage. Paul Ferrara was directing several camera operators positioned around the venue to immortalize the evening on 16mm film. We were thoroughly rehearsed and ready. But you know what they say about best-laid plans.

Before the show, we all went to dinner with Mick Jagger. Nice guy. But of course he spent most of his time talking to Jim. He seemed to take a liking to Pam, and there was some flirting going back and forth. Jim, of course, wasn't happy about it but couldn't say anything without coming off as uncool. When we walked out onstage, Mick and Pam were seated next to each other, right up front. It's intimidating enough to have Mick Jagger staring up at you while you're trying to perform; you don't need the added worry of him going home with your girl at the end of the night.

Jim also took some acid right before we went on. Some interpret this as his way of sabotaging the show, but I really believe he wanted to do a good job that night. He had been rehearsing just as intently as the rest of us, and he was just as excited as we were about planting our flag on the Hollywood Bowl's stage. He probably thought the acid would help, not hurt. But he must've taken too much. Or not enough. Either way, he mainly stayed glued to his mic stand, rather than jumping all over the place as usual. We were bathed in blinding, bright lights for the sake of the cameras, and Jim kept asking for them to be turned down. Ray kept reminding Jim that they couldn't lower the lights because they were filming, Jim would seem to understand, and then later he'd ask for the lights to be turned down again.

You can tell Jim was nervous at the show because he was smoking onstage. He rarely smoked, and it was usually when he was nervous. I would always chuckle when he did it because he always looked like a teenager holding his first cigarette. But I found those little bits of awkward vanity to be among his more endearing traits.

One element of playing the Bowl we hadn't considered was that the venue wasn't designed for rock 'n' roll. It was designed for well-mannered people to sit down and quietly relax while watching a philharmonic orchestra. We had played plenty of shows to seated crowds, but at the Bowl, a good portion of the chairs are confined to separate little boxes, preventing people from standing and sweating and undulating together. Being unable to feed off the crowd's energy was yet another reason Jim likely felt more inhibited than usual.

Between the preexisting nerves and the boxed-in seats and the blinding lights and the acid and Mick and Pam and Decibel Meter Guy and the multiple unblinking eyes of the camera crew, Jim was frozen. He became a little more animated toward the end of the set, but after all that preparation and all that buildup, the result was one of his mellowest performances. And of course that's the one we got on film.

There's a classic Warner Brothers cartoon in which a construction worker discovers a frog that can sing and dance and do acrobatic maneuvers like a seasoned vaudevillian. The construction worker runs all over town, trying to tell people how amazing the frog is, but whenever he puts the frog in front of anyone else, it doesn't sing or dance or do much of anything. It just sits there with its eyes half shut and croaks out a defiant *"BurrrrrAAAppp."*

Jim Morrison is the Warner Brothers frog.

We played hundreds of shows with Jim, and those who were there for the good ones will testify to his brilliance. When he was enveloped in the darkness of an auditorium he was the most explosive showman anyone's ever seen. His voice pierced the air. His body flew about the stage as if it were possessed. Fans were induced into fits of madness and wanton destruction. Chaos reigned. But when he stepped onto the stage at the Hollywood Bowl, and the bright lights hit him, and the cameras started rolling...

"*BurrrrrAAAppp.*"

It kills me that we don't have more footage of Jim at his best. Why didn't we think to shoot any of our Fillmore shows?! We had a riot in Chicago two months before we played the Bowl and a riot in Cleveland a month after; why didn't we have cameras rolling there?! We brought the audio equipment on the road to record our *Absolutely Live* album; why didn't we bring a film crew, too?! If we were touring with Jim today, there would be thousands of smartphones capturing every single moment from every conceivable angle in ultra-high definition. But as painful as it is to not have any video evidence of our greatest moments, those moments wouldn't have existed in the same form if people had tried to capture them. I can at least be glad that the few lucky crowds who got to experience Jim did so to the fullest, and as one, without the distraction of a bunch of little screens.

It's not that the Hollywood Bowl show was awful. All that practice paid off: John and Ray played great, and Jim's voice sounded good. It just wasn't one of the shows that made people fall in love with the Doors. We shelved the live album and concert film for years, hoping to capture something better. But the Hollywood Bowl was the best we got, and it will represent our live show forever. As much as Jim was the languid frog, the rest of us will always be that sweaty, frazzled construction worker, running around town and going slowly insane while swearing to everyone that the frog *just* put on the most incredible performance ever when no one was looking. Honest!

Val Kilmer and Oliver Stone

ENOUGH TO BASE A MOVIE ON

For the record: the Doors never did peyote in the desert.

It just never happened. The four of us never did any psychedelics as a group, in fact. I only did peyote once, after Jim died, at Paul Ferrara's ranch in New Mexico. I dropped acid with Jim and John many times, but separately, and Ray had sworn off acid by the time I met him.

Yet so many people believe our desert peyote trip actually happened. When *Family Guy* or *Wayne's World 2* or anyone else wants to parody the Doors, they reference us hallucinating in Death Valley. People don't realize they're not referencing our lives. They're referencing a movie very loosely based on our lives.

Oliver Stone invented the scene of us doing peyote for his 1991 film *The Doors*. It was a beautifully shot and edited scene, which is probably why it sticks in everyone's minds. It was meant to illustrate Jim's inspiration for the Oedipal section of "The End." I guess the whole band wandering through pristine sand dunes at sunset is more cinematic than Jim mumbling facedown on the floor of a motel room.

Also for the record:

✦ Jim never climbed onto a car outside the Whisky and screamed about being the Lizard King to a gathered crowd on the Sunset Strip. He didn't walk around reciting his own poetry out loud like some kind of asshole.

✦ I never heard anything about Jim locking Pam in a closet and setting it on fire, and as far as I know, there's no real evidence that it ever happened.

✦ Jim didn't throw a TV across the room during the *Soft Parade* sessions because he was mad about a commercial. He accidentally knocked a TV off a small stool years earlier when we were recording our debut album because he was dancing around on acid. Bruce Botnick still has the TV. He says it still works.

✦ I barely ever saw Jim hanging out with Patricia Kennealy, and if he ever married her in some sort of Wiccan blood ritual, he never spoke a word about it to anyone I ever knew. Jim and Lynn once went to some sort of Ouija board séance thing with Alice Cooper, but they left early because Jim thought it was stupid. For a guy who always mocked astrology and spirituality and transcendental meditation, I can't imagine him taking a Wiccan wedding even remotely seriously.

✦ Jim and Pam didn't invite their respective lovers to Thanksgiving and get in a big fight about it. They almost never fought in front of us, actually. I only remember celebrating one Thanksgiving at their house, but no one pulled a knife on anyone, and no one stomped a roasted duck into the ground. It was actually a very pleasant evening.

I get it: You can't show reality in a movie because reality is boring. You have to invent drama and combine characters, you have to compress years into hours, and you have to blend fact and fiction for the sake of telling a compelling story. But even though the audience knows that going in, they still come out feeling like they've witnessed the truth.

❖   ❖   ❖

John Travolta once came to my house dressed like Jim. Leather pants and all. Ray and Danny Sugerman (who had cowritten the Doors biography *No One Here Gets Out Alive*) were running around town with him in the early eighties, trying to get a Doors movie set up. John was a really nice guy and it was cool to see how much he wanted the part, but I wasn't sure if the guy from *Saturday Night Fever* could really sell himself as Jim Morrison.

Ray and Danny spent years talking to production companies and financiers, but they weren't having much luck. George Paige, the producer of our *Dance on Fire* video collection, finally got us all in a room with some serious investors, and it looked like the project might move ahead. I nodded off during the meeting due to a combination of heroin and boredom, but I perked back up at the end when Ray announced, "Oh, and by the way, I'm directing." The room fell silent. We never heard from those investors again.

Oliver Stone had been a Doors fan since his days in Vietnam, and we all loved his film *Platoon,* which won the Oscar for Best Picture and Best Director. I was always a little hesitant about the idea of a Doors movie, but when bigger studios got involved and Oliver signed on as director, I was excited. Ray, John, and I each met with Oliver individually. He was an excitable guy who spoke a mile a minute and had all kinds of ambitious ideas. Exactly what you'd expect from a big shot film auteur. My meeting with him went fine. John's meeting with him went fine. Ray, however, was jealous that he had been passed over as director, so he got drunk before his meeting and he and Oliver reportedly got into an ugly shouting match. Two hardheaded visionaries with oversize egos—it was easy to see why they wouldn't get along. After that, Ray refused to participate in the movie in any way, and Oliver told him his participation was no longer welcome. It was the one thing they agreed on.

Tons of names were thrown around for the role of Jim, and I was incredulous when I learned that Val Kilmer had landed it. I was at Oliver's office when Val introduced himself. I didn't know who he was, but I knew he didn't look anything like Jim Morrison. When he played me a video of himself performing some Doors songs with a backing band, though, I was instantly on board. He not only had the voice but also captured Jim's movements and subtle mannerisms in a way that was almost spooky. He ended up providing the vocals for about 90 percent of the concert and studio scenes, rather than lip-synching over Jim, and once or twice even I was fooled when I heard the playback. On set we had to refer to him as Jim, and he stayed in character even when the cameras weren't rolling. There were a couple of times when he was shooting a concert scene and they'd call "Cut" and our eyes would meet, and...for a brief moment...

I was played by Frank Whaley. I liked his performance in Oliver's previous film, *Born on the Fourth of July*, but it's hard for me to say how accurately he captured me on-screen in *The Doors* because I have no idea how I appear to others from the outside. He was a cool guy, though, and he was eager to learn more about my guitar technique. I gave him a bunch of lessons and he faked it pretty well.

Kevin Dillon played John, and my friend Bruce Gary from the Knack did most of his drum coaching. John gave Kevin a few pointers but I wish he'd been more involved or maybe even stood in as a stunt drummer because John has a flourishing, visual drumming technique that's hard to replicate. But I'm probably the only person who cares about a detail that small. Kyle MacLachlan's portrayal of Ray bore little resemblance to the real Ray, but that's because the real Ray refused to meet with Kyle. Meg Ryan captured Pam's goofy, sweet side very well but didn't dig into the shrewd, focused part of Pam's personality. Part of that is because Pam wasn't around for Meg to talk to, but most of it was the way her character was written. Jim is shown as a womanizer in the movie, but Pam was just as much, if not more, of a man-izer. It definitely went both ways.

I have no critiques of the actors, only of the script they were given. The movie didn't explore the relationship between the band members, or show how our songs really came together. Ray was written as a foil for Jim, but they didn't incorporate his father figure vibe. John was written as a petty whiner; they didn't show how much of a go-getter he used to be. I was also written as a whiner who kept refusing to take acid with Jim, when in reality no one ever had to twist my arm. In the desert scene, my character says that he's afraid of his dad, and Jim suggests that I kill him. My dad was pretty bummed when he saw that. I had to explain that it was Oliver making stuff up, not an actual quote.

The script did the biggest disservice to Jim. He came across as a pretentious, obnoxious, stupid drunk who was a dick to everyone around him. I'm not saying he wasn't a drunk, and I'm not saying he couldn't be obnoxious at times. But he wasn't blitzed twenty-four hours a day with a bottle of Jack in his hand, screaming about death. He was funny, and shy, and when he was out of line he knew it, and he was sorry. He had a way of making everyone who met him feel like he was their best friend. I don't know how you show that on screen; maybe it's too complicated. But while the movie gained us a lot of renewed attention, it also turned off a lot of potential fans who saw Jim as a one-dimensional drunken boor.

But I knew what we were getting into. I knew that once Hollywood got ahold of our story it wouldn't be "our" story anymore, so I tried to just go along for the ride. Even though I have issues with the final product, being on set for the actual production process was fun. You can see my blink-and-you'll-miss-it cameo when I walk by the band backstage at the London Fog (which didn't have a backstage) while they're talking to an unnamed manager (who didn't exist) and his assistant (who is played by Paul Rothchild). John has a cameo, too, as the studio engineer who records Jim's poetry. He managed to negotiate for a speaking part since he was trying to get his acting career going at the time.

I signed on as a consultant and was mostly brought in to help them get the live concert scenes right. Oliver had his own specific vision but he listened to my input, and he and his crew did a commendable job of capturing the look and feel of the Whisky, and the New Haven and Miami shows. But again, the power of cinema can mess with your mind. For years I thought Patricia Kennealy was backstage with Jim in New Haven, because that's who he's with in the movie, even though they didn't meet until much later. And for years I thought we only played a couple of songs in Miami before the stage collapsed, because that's how it is in the movie, but later on when I heard a recording from the actual show I was reminded that we played almost a full set.

Other moments in which accuracy was a low priority:

✦ We didn't play a single show in the city of San Francisco during the year 1968, much less an outdoor show at night where the crowd danced naked around a bonfire. The only outdoor shows we ever played in Northern California took place during the day. I don't remember any bonfires at our shows back then. And why did Oliver think everyone was freely dancing naked at our concerts all the time when Jim had gotten in trouble for nothing more than a *rumor* that he showed his cock?

✦ Jim didn't meet Pam while stalking her to her house in the Venice Canals. She came to see us at the London Fog. And she lived in Orange County.

✦ Jim didn't pressure me into taking acid before our Miami show. I quit doing acid long before then, and as far as I know, Jim didn't do any acid that night either.

✦ Jim couldn't have gone to Ray's daughter's birthday party because Dorothy didn't get pregnant until after Jim died. Also: Ray has a son, not a daughter.

Jim very rarely levitated in public

Again, I get it. It's a movie. I was able to put that stuff aside when I saw the finished film. But Ray took every inaccuracy as a personal slight, and ranted to anyone who would listen about how horrible the movie was for altering history. Ironically, though, when Ray published his memoirs a few years later he took major liberties with the truth and overdramatized nearly every single story he told. He brutally railed against Oliver Stone in his book for distorting the story of the Doors while committing the exact same sin on the adjoining pages. Maybe he would've done a decent job of directing after all.

Oliver didn't tell the story of the Doors; he told his own original story based on his personal interpretation of what the Doors were in his mind. He may have gone overboard with his use of dramatic license, but his job wasn't to document: it was to entertain. And if you put aside historical accuracy and judge *The Doors* as a rock 'n' roll movie…it's a pretty great one. As far as I'm concerned, Val Kilmer deserved an Oscar for how well he embodied Jim. The concert scenes were all superbly shot. It's a film with compelling visuals, an epic scale, and a gripping pace. It's got sex, drugs, poetry, death, and a pretty decent soundtrack. Could've been worse. Could've been boring.

The only problem is that history and memory are so easily warped. We all remember things differently. We all color in the missing details of the past in our own way. We're all influenced by what we see on the page or on a screen, even if it runs contrary to our own recollection of events. Ray's autobiography contains so many exaggerations I could barely get through it. John's autobiography is more reliable but still has some inaccuracies, and still editorializes from his individual perspective. Outside authors and music journalists and Jim's former friends and lovers (and even friends of his former friends and lovers) have all published their own narratives with their own agendas. Oliver Stone's movie is laughable as a historical artifact, but parts of it have seeped into the official record. Even the many documentaries about the Doors get some of the basic facts wrong, or spend too much time focusing on trivial things. Jim, as I've mentioned, used to toy with the press for his own amusement, and I have occasionally done the same, so it's not hard to find publications in which the Doors contradict each other, or even contradict themselves. Ask two fans who were standing right next to each other at the same Doors show what they saw and they will have wildly different interpretations of the night. And everyone's account is simultaneously true and false.

I'm doing my best here to tell all these stories as accurately as I can. I've fact-checked myself and consulted with others along the way, and I've put a lot of mental effort into untangling my reality from the versions of reality presented by others. But my memory is as inherently flawed as anyone else's. I have my own biases and perspectives. My brain is old, and always getting older. And I'm vulnerable to the sticky influence of all the mass media retellings of my own life. Not to mention that most of what I'm describing happened while my whole generation was drifting through a haze of weed and pills and acid, and we didn't bother to take notes, let alone film everything on our phones.

There is no one correct, conclusive, definitive version of the history of the Doors. And there never will be. William Blake and Aldous Huxley warned us of that from the beginning. Even if you somehow managed to clear away all the dramatizations and the misrememberings and the legends and the lies and cleanse the doors of perception, our band's story would still appear as it is:

Infinite.

Celebrating the fiftieth anniversary of Morrison Hotel *with Miley Cyrus on vocals and Henry Diltz snapping photos*

MORRISON HOTEL

Toward the end of the *Soft Parade* sessions, we rebelled against ourselves. We all had dinner at a Mexican restaurant near the studio, and we kept ordering round after round of margaritas and Bohemia. We went back to the studio and drunkenly played a bunch of rock 'n' roll covers and blues improvisations. It was noisy and sloppy and not meant for anyone else to hear. A subconscious scream to ditch all the overproduction and get back to making music the old-fashioned way.

If there was a silver lining to the Miami Incident, it was that our canceled shows left us with nothing but time to write. Jim and I went back to collaborating the way we had in the early days. He had words, I had riffs, and we both finally had the chance to sit down and combine them. It wasn't exactly the same as it was back in my parents' living room, since the trial and our personal lives and Jim's filmmaking ambitions were new distractions, but it was at least reminiscent of a more pure era.

We had given up on the backward pianos and the string sections and the Moog and all the experimentation, and Paul and Bruce had gotten much better about dialing in drum sounds quickly. And Paul loosened up a bit — a bit — when it came to insisting on extra takes. We just got in the studio and jammed, and the songs came together organically.

"Roadhouse Blues" was a perfect example. All we knew was we wanted to write something bluesy. I was fooling around with a riff, and Jim asked me to play it again while he threw some words over it. We had invited John Sebastian from the Lovin' Spoonful to come in and play harmonica with us — credited as G. Puglese, his father's (misspelled) birth name, since his label prohibited him from playing on other bands' albums — and he added some amazing improvisations of his own. Bit by bit we all added parts that worked and discarded parts that didn't, and by the end of the session one of our greatest hits had taken shape almost on its own.

On our first album I overdubbed the bass lines for "Soul Kitchen," "Twentieth Century Fox," and "Back Door Man" but we otherwise always had the help of talented session bassists to thicken up our sound. When we needed a bassist for *Morrison Hotel,* we grabbed the first guy we could find in the hallway, but he happened to be blues-rock pioneer Lonnie Mack. We all knew Lonnie by reputation: he was an amazing guitarist with a promising career, but he fell on some hard times and became disillusioned with the music industry. Fritz Richmond (Elektra's assistant engineer and former jug player for Jim Kweskin and the Jug Band) ran into Lonnie on the street, where he was trying to make a living by selling Bibles out of the trunk of his car. Fritz offered Lonnie a job at Elektra Studios taking care of random day-to-day tasks. Lonnie wasn't expecting to play on an album the day we grabbed him in the hallway, but he came in and, with hardly any direction, laid down the perfect bass line for "Roadhouse Blues." When I open up the chorus on the A and Jim bellows "Let it rollllllll...," Lonnie's bass comes at you like a steamroller. Lonnie took pride in being a guitarist and thought bass was beneath him, so for years I'd kid him by introducing him to people by saying, "This is Lonnie Mack, a great bass player."

"I'm no goddamn bass player! I'm a fuckin' guitar player!" It took him a while to finally appreciate the joke and laugh along.

At the beginning of my guitar solo on "Roadhouse Blues," you can hear Jim exclaim, "Do it, Robby, do it!" But after the record came out Lonnie insisted to everyone that Jim actually said, "Do it, Lonnie, do it!" Lonnie always appeared to be convinced he was telling the truth, but now I wonder if maybe he was trying to get me back for always trying to define him as a lowly bass player.

Other songs came together just as naturally. The riff for "The Spy" was a slow-motion adaptation of Danny Kalb's "Hello Baby Blues." One of the most popular tracks on the album started with me jamming a G chord and occasionally hitting the low E string on a guitar with out-of-phase pickups, which gave it a funky *wah-wah* sound. Ray, John, and session bassist Harvey Brooks helped me flesh it out and record it, and when Jim showed up he liked what we had done and paired the music with fragments of a couple of poems from his old notebooks—mainly one called "Abortion Stories." Paul balked at the title for being too controversial for 1969, so Jim spat out a nonsense title that had nothing to do with the lyrics and from then on the song was known as "Peace Frog."

"Indian Summer" was one of the earliest songs I ever wrote, and was actually the first song we ever recorded together as the Doors. It was intended for our debut album but it didn't make the cut because it was eclipsed by the similar Indian vibe of "The End." I wrote the music for it during our Whisky residency, inspired by my Indian music class at UCLA. The teacher was a young Indian woman, and I—the guy who fell asleep every night listening to Ravi Shankar—was her star pupil. Near the end of the semester I gathered up the nerve to ask her on a date. We went out only once, to check out an Indian music store. We never even kissed. Most likely she didn't even realize it was a date. If she ever found out that she was the inspiration for that song, I hope she didn't think I was creepy for writing all the lyrics about love: those were Jim's.

The song "L'America" ended up on *L.A. Woman* but was written and recorded during the *Morrison Hotel* sessions. I modeled the riff off Dave "Snaker" Ray's version of Lead Belly's "Fannin Street." We submitted it for the soundtrack of a Michelangelo Antonioni film called *Zabriskie Point,* and Antonioni actually came down to the studio to hear it personally. The producer (or whoever he was with) said something like, "And this is the song we're going to use in the film."

Antonioni's face darkened and he angrily professed, "Only Antonioni will decide what song will be in the film!"

Ray and I shared a look: we knew right then that the song was not going to be in the film. We never heard from Antonioni again, and the movie ended up bombing. Probably due to the lack of Doors music.

Ray came up with the name for the album and the cover concept when he happened to drive by the actual Morrison Hotel in downtown L.A. It was a flophouse charging $2.50 a night for rooms, which was dirt cheap even back then. When we went down there with photographer Henry Diltz to shoot the cover, the desk clerk wouldn't let us take any photos in the lobby. We resigned ourselves to posing outside on the sidewalk, but when the desk clerk left his post, Henry told us to run inside and pose by the window and he quickly knocked out a few shots before the clerk came back. We had our album cover.

Fifty years later, to celebrate the anniversary of *Morrison Hotel*'s release, we held a small concert, a documentary screening, and a photo exhibition in the building next to the former hotel. The Robby Krieger Band played a set of Doors songs, with actor Dennis Quaid sitting in on vocals for a few of them. The cops came in to warn us of a noise ordinance and—just like the old days—they shut us down before our set was finished. We also had the former hotel's window repainted with the original Morrison Hotel lettering, and throughout the course of the day over three thousand people stood in a line that wrapped around the block so they could—just like the old days—rush in and out of the lobby for a quick photo.

When you're in the midst of creating something, you hope people will like it, but you have no way of knowing what it will turn into. When Jim told me to keep jamming that simple guitar riff, I didn't know it would become "Roadhouse Blues." When Henry Diltz clicked his shutter that day, we didn't know he had captured an iconic album cover that fans would be so excited to re-create half a century later.

After we originally shot the cover for *Morrison Hotel,* we went looking for other places to shoot and stumbled upon a dive bar called the Hard Rock Cafe. "Hard rock" wasn't a commonly used phrase back then—the name likely had nothing to do with rock 'n' roll, but we liked the musical connotation. Unlike the hotel clerk, the bar owner let us shoot all the photos we wanted, as long as we kept ordering drinks, which wasn't a problem. Henry proceeded to get some more great images that ended up on the back cover and inner sleeve of the album. The camera drew the attention of the barflies and bums outside, and we made some new friends. One guy asked Jim for some money, and Jim asked him if he'd do something to earn it.

"Can you sing?"

"I can whistle. I have the loudest whistle in the world."

"Okay, let's hear it."

He fucking WHISTLED, man. We were all holding our ears. He wasn't exaggerating: it was the loudest whistle in the world. Jim asked him, "How do you do that?"

"Jesus does it for me."

We all dug deep and gave him probably the most money anyone's ever made from a single whistle.

A few years later, when John and I were living in England, we discovered a popular local diner with a bold yellow and red sign outside that read Hard Rock Cafe. We learned that the owners' inspiration for their restaurant's name was the back cover photo from *Morrison Hotel*. We thought it was funny. When we moved back to the States we assumed we'd never hear about the Hard Rock Cafe again. But you never know what something is going to turn into.

Sue and Ronny

BLUE JACARANDAS

My brother, Ronny, started dating a girl named Sue around the same time I started dating Lynn, and when they served as witnesses at our wedding, Sue signed the marriage license with the last name Krieger. That was how we learned they had eloped not long before we did. Sue was as antisocial as Ronny was, which is probably why they gravitated toward each other. She had some minor emotional issues that caused her to occasionally melt down over small inconveniences, but she was a wonderful sister-in-law overall, and she cared deeply about my brother.

When Ronny finally gave up on his dream of becoming a golf pro, he and Sue started their own gardening business, and then later, in the early eighties, I bought them a ranch in Santa Clarita, where they could make some money boarding and breeding horses. Plants and animals seemed to calm them, but depression was still a constant in Ronny's life.

My dad, always the cheerleader for psychiatry, constantly pressed Ronny over the years to seek help. Ronny was never interested, but my dad finally insisted when Ronny's mental issues manifested as stomach pains. He was diagnosed with manic depression. The doctors treated him, gave him some medication, and he seemed better. For a while.

A disturbing pattern developed. Sue would call me or my dad to tell us that Ronny had gone missing. This wasn't like when Jim would get drunk and bail on a recording session only to turn up the following afternoon. Ronny would disappear for days, or even weeks, and become one of the nameless, wandering, vacant-eyed homeless people you see on the streets of any major city. My dad or Sue would drive around and find him, or the cops would pick him up. Usually down by the beach. We'd take him to a mental hospital and have him temporarily committed. They would put him on meds and he would normalize. They'd send him home and things would be fine. Then, after a while, he would go off his meds and the cycle would start over from the beginning.

The first couple of times we found him wandering, my dad and I had to physically wrestle him to get him into the car, but he eventually got as used to the routine as we did, and he would submit in silence. When he was on his meds, he would be fine for months, sometimes even years. We'd all start to feel optimistic. And then Sue would call again.

I visited Ronny in the hospital once or twice and it was easy to understand why he didn't want to be there. It was dark, and eerily quiet. Most of the patients were too sedated to move. He was kept in a room with a little window in the door for the orderlies to peer through to check on him. I asked him why he kept disappearing. He said, "I was going through some really weird things. I'll tell you someday, but you wouldn't believe it if I did." He never told me. My twin intuition made me think he had seen aliens, or God. Either way, once he was back on his meds he would realize that the whole thing had been a delusion.

But part of him still wondered: *Was it...?*

When he was out of the hospital he wouldn't want to talk about his time inside or his illness. The humiliation of the whole thing probably further weakened his already fragile mental state. Every time the cycle repeated, he ended up a little bit worse than before. There seemed to be no way to reverse it.

And then, when Ronny and I were only in our mid-forties, Sue called one final time.

They found Ronny's body floating in the ocean not far from my old place on Topanga Beach. We don't know if he fell in, if he walked in willingly, or if he was pushed. I never believed he'd do something like that intentionally, but, as I've been forced to learn more than once in my life, you can't predict the actions of an imbalanced mind.

There are companies that specialize in scattering people's ashes at sea. They ferry you out to the legally required three-mile distance from shore and oversee the whole process. Sue told us that an ocean burial had been Ronny's wish, so my parents and I went with her down to San Pedro harbor and boarded one of those special ash-spreading boats to say goodbye. We each said a few words; I told Ronny I hoped to see him in the next life. My dad poured the ashes over the side and said, "Well, this is what you wanted." I never dug into what exactly he meant. But the tone was one of frustration. He always felt that Ronny should've sought out psychiatric help sooner, and that he didn't do enough to help himself. But if Ronny had the capacity to help himself, we wouldn't have been on that boat.

Ronny's descent mostly played out during the years I was on heroin, so his death didn't hit me as hard as it should have. I was numb to normal human emotions. And it was probably one of the reasons I kept myself numb for a while after. I didn't want to face the feeling of powerlessness brought on by not being able to help him. I didn't want to face the guilt of not being a better brother and not defending him when he was picked on as a kid. People tell me I shouldn't blame myself, but I do, and I probably always will. I left him vulnerable to bullying. I kept talking about how great acid was. I was off living my dream with my band while his dreams were being dashed. I was too wrapped up in drugs to give him the attention he needed when things got bad. Maybe it's irrational to think any of that stuff matters in the face of an incurable chemical imbalance, but still: I wish I had been there for him.

When Ronny and Sue had their gardening business, they planted a jacaranda tree in my yard that still grows there today. Most of the time it just blends into the background of my landscaping. But every now and then it will catch my eye, the breeze will blow through its purple flowers, and I'll take a moment to remember my brother. One of its seedpods must've been shed at just the right time under just the right conditions because right around the time Ronny passed away, a second jacaranda tree sprouted out of the ground close by. It has since grown up to be roughly the same size and shape as the first one. A pair of nonidentical twins. Standing together, always.

Robbie and Ronnie

Jim's final show—New Orleans, December 1970

IMMORAL IN NATURE

When the Doors headlined a rock festival in Toronto in the fall of '69, Alice Cooper famously threw a live chicken into the audience, and the crowd tore it to pieces. The Doors never did anything that terrible, but everywhere we went that year, we were the band the cops had their eyes on.

After the Miami Incident, it was hard for us to get gigs in the States. The few promoters who were willing to book us were denied permits by their local governments. And even when we were able to book a show it wasn't guaranteed to happen. On the day we were supposed to play Salt Lake City, the venue chose to cancel the show and refund all the ticket money because a member of their board of directors had flown out to see us in Boston the night before and thought we were "uncontrollable." Even though we had a $10,000 penalty written into our contract guaranteeing a clean show. In Philadelphia, a local official tried to revoke our show's license citing some law from 1879 that allowed the cancellation of an event that may be "immoral in nature." The promoter had to fight it for a month, all the way up to the morning of the show when the license was finally reinstated. In Las Vegas, the county sheriff also tried to deny our show's license, calling Jim a "sickening entertainer." He considered us too tasteless. For Vegas!

When they couldn't block us, they made sure there was a heavy police presence at the venue to keep us in line. It was made clear in the press, in our contracts, and in their glares that if we stepped out of bounds in the slightest, there would be dire consequences. Part of me had always hoped for Jim to be more controlled, but the authoritarian vibe sucked the life out of him, and out of our performances as a whole. Be careful what you wish for.

We explored options outside the country and booked a massive show for forty-eight thousand people at the Plaza Monumental bullfighting ring in Mexico City, but we were still met with government hassles. Our permits got all fucked up and we ended up playing a series of shows at a fancy club for rich people instead. We tried to arrange a free concert in a park while we were there so the poor and working-class people could see us as well, but again the government stood in our way. Meanwhile, the president's son was zipping us around in a limo, offering us groupies and fistfuls of cocaine. The uncontrollable, immoral, sickening Doors all had our girl-friends and wives with us, so we politely declined and opted to spend our time at the archaeological museum instead.

Not every show after Miami was a bummer. When we weren't being dogged by the cops, Jim still rolled around and jumped into the crowd, and the audience still rushed the stage here and there. Overall Jim took the opportunity to focus more on singing than theatrics, and our sets from that era were some of our tightest. We taped several shows for our *Absolutely Live* album that year and the recordings speak for themselves.

People always say Jim had gotten sick of being a rock star after the Miami Incident. He was sick of certain aspects of it, for sure. He was sick of the expectations from audiences and critics. He was sick of the scrutiny from law enforcement. But he wasn't sick of performing. Some of our shows in '69 and '70 were our longest. On multiple occasions the venue staff would turn on the house lights or cut the power because we had extended our set past the agreed-upon time, and Jim had to demand that they let us continue. We were banned from the Cobo Arena in Detroit not because of profanity or indecency, but because we kept playing for an hour after their union curfew due to audience demand and Jim's insistence. Those aren't the actions of a guy who didn't want to be onstage anymore.

Some people theorize that Jim gained weight and grew a beard around that time to purposefully sabotage his image. But the weight was an inevitable by-product of his heavy drinking. They call it a beer gut for a reason. If you look at pictures of Jim as a kid, he was always a little pudgy, or at least had a round face. When we started the Doors, he was doing a bunch of acid, which messes with your appetite, and he was a broke college student on a limited food budget. That's when he got all skinny and his perfectly sculpted cheekbones emerged. After the first couple of albums, he replaced appetite-suppressing acid with calorie-heavy alcohol, and once he had money he could also afford to eat well. At restaurants he'd often order three entrées at once. He wouldn't gobble them all down; he just liked having options. A waitress once balked at his order:

"You're ordering three dinners?"

"Darling, I'm a millionaire. I can order whatever I want."

The beard wasn't meant to hide him from the spotlight; it was to hide his double chin. He grew it around the time he started hanging out with Frank, Paul, and Babe. They all had beards, so he joined the gang. I can't fault Jim for being a follower, though: John and I also cultivated scraggly facial hair right after Jim did.

Jim stopped being able to fit into his leather trousers and would more often be seen in what we privately called his Engineer Bill pants. They were blue-and-white-striped slacks, reminiscent of the outfit worn by our favorite train-conducting children's TV host from the fifties. The pants and the beard and the gut weren't a good look, but to say they were a conscious rejection of his rock star image is reading too much into it. After all, no one ever accused Elvis of shunning stardom when he started wearing more forgiving fabrics.

Our performance at the Isle of Wight Festival in the summer of 1970 is also held up as evidence that Jim was losing interest in the Doors. It was a subdued performance and Jim barely moved—that much is true. But a little context: he had just flown directly from his trial in Miami to play the show, and he was expected to fly immediately back to Miami afterward, so his court case was likely weighing on him more at that show than at any other, and the jet lag probably didn't help. He also knew the festival was being professionally filmed, which always seemed to make him self-conscious. He met with the lighting guys beforehand and insisted on only dim red lights. I don't know if he was trying to piss off the filmmakers or if he was embarrassed about his appearance, but either way, he knew he was probably ruining their footage. He wasn't phoning it in entirely, though. Physically it wasn't much of a performance, but vocally it was one of his best.

Everyone wanted something different from Jim. If he got wasted and went crazy onstage, people would complain that he didn't sing the songs well. If he stayed sober and focused on his vocals, people would complain that he was boring. But if he consciously tried to find a middle ground, he'd be putting on an act rather than just being himself. Jim had good shows and bad shows before Miami, and he had good shows and bad shows after Miami. John focused on the negative and pushed for us to stop touring until Jim sorted himself out. Ray focused on the positive and pushed for us to keep going. I, as usual, was caught in the middle. The guys both made compelling points, but we had three months off after Isle of Wight while the trial concluded, and we had fun writing and recording the *L.A. Woman* album during the break. Jim was still drinking, of course, but beyond our failed intervention I didn't see the need for any drastic measures. We played a show in Dallas in December 1970 and it was fine. It wasn't flashy or crazy or historic, but Jim sang well and we got to play some of our *L.A. Woman* songs publicly for the first time. In a way, it was nice to finally play some shows where the focus was on our music rather than our antics.

But then came New Orleans. It wasn't that bad of a show at first, but as it went on, Jim deteriorated before our eyes. I've read all kinds of accounts of the show, but I seem to have blocked most of it out of my mind. All I really remember is the end of the set, when Jim sat down on the drum riser and slumped forward as if he was barely able to stay awake. Ray wrote in his autobiography that he saw Jim's essence leave his body through his crown chakra and vanish into the night air...or something. I just saw a guy who had probably taken a bunch of barbiturates. Either way, Ray and I finally agreed with John that we should stop touring. We may have disagreed about the significance of some of Jim's post-Miami performances, but the New Orleans show removed any doubt: he needed some time off. In the dressing room afterward, I asked Jim what was wrong. He tried to slur out one of his classic apologies and I immediately knew we weren't going to have any sort of productive conversation, so I left him alone.

John and I went down to Bourbon Street later that night. We hopped from bar to bar, had a few drinks, and soaked in some authentic New Orleans jazz. The evening had been a disappointment, but I was trying to put it behind me. We'd figure something out. We'd do better next time. I didn't realize we had just played our last show with Jim Morrison.

Me with the Ramones at the Hollywood Palladium, 1992

THE NEW CREATURES

I had never heard of slam dancing until I went to see the punk band Fear at the Troubadour in 1979. I always knew the Troubadour as a folk venue, so Fear was definitely a change of pace. I sat in the balcony and marveled at the way the lead singer, Lee Ving, drove the crowd into a violent frenzy. He reminded me of Jim. I wasn't the biggest punk fan, but when Ray went on to produce the band X, I saw them a few times, and I even recorded some parts for one of their later-era albums. I loved the Clash when I saw them on their first U.S. tour (even though I was originally only there to see their opening act, Bo Diddley), and I joined the Ramones onstage at the Hollywood Palladium in the nineties for their cover of our song "Take It as It Comes." The actual musicianship of punk rock was too simplistic for my taste, but I dug the vibe and the energy. At least it was better than disco.

By the late seventies music had changed. The world had changed. I started to believe the Doors would soon be forgotten completely. We'd had our day. The kids had moved on to a new sound. That's usually how it goes.

Ray started a band called Nite City with a singer named Noah James who was a hard-drinking wild man, just like Jim. The only flaw was that Noah didn't have the redeeming quality of being a genius. Ray declared with all the confidence in the world that Nite City would be the next Doors, and would soon become the top band in the country. They lasted about two years.

Around that same time, I was touring and recording as a jazz fusion solo artist and it was like being thrown back to the earliest days of the Doors. Touring in vans. Playing small clubs. Barely breaking even. I usually worked a Doors song or two into the set as a reward for the fans who turned out and politely sat through my jazzy noodling, but I was determined to embark on something entirely new. In the late seventies I started a new wave band called Red Shift that had songs like "Hyena People" and "Sexorsize," and in the mid-eighties I tried my hand at producing electronic dance music under the name Robby's Hobby with synth-heavy songs like "The Oil Slut" and "Nasti Kinki." It would be fair to describe some of those experiments as ill-advised. But I didn't want to be like Ray, attempting to recapture a moment in time and a creative chemistry that could never possibly be recaptured. I wanted to make something different and original, even if it didn't have the mass appeal of my previous band. I'm proud of a lot of the music I produced after the Doors ended—one of my solo albums was even nominated for a Grammy—but I was acutely aware that if I wanted to make lots of money and play to thousands of screaming fans every night, jazz fusion was not the way to go.

John ventured the furthest from the Doors by leaving music behind entirely and studying acting. I went to see him in a few plays, and he actually wasn't bad. Although once he invited me to some sort of weird, interpretive modern dance performance, and it was tough for me to come up with supportive compliments afterward. John even managed to get a few small TV and film roles. He was a waiter on *One Day at a Time,* he was a motorcycle salesman on *Coach,* and he was Luke Perry's AA sponsor on an episode of *Beverly Hills, 90210.* His most prominent speaking part was as a berserk punk drummer named Toad in a low-budget screwball comedy called *Get Crazy* (which also featured Lee Ving of Fear, by the way). John plays drums in the movie while the singer of his band is freaking out on psychedelics. Talk about range! In all seriousness, though, it's easy to poke fun at the early struggles of any acting career, but I really admired John for going so far out of his comfort zone.

We were three guys trying to redefine ourselves. Being a member of the Doors wasn't something we were ashamed of, but it became a shadow over our heads. I had written my only number one song when I was barely twenty years old, and I felt pressure to top myself every time I tried to write another one. Compared to the alternatives, runaway success is a good problem to have, but it seemed like the path in front of us was destined to be all downhill. We were only in our thirties but it felt like we had already lived a full lifetime. Where do you go from there?

As the seventies gave way to the eighties, the release of the *American Prayer* album and *Apocalypse Now* subtly reminded the world of the Doors' existence. Then there was the book.

No One Here Gets Out Alive started with Jerry Hopkins, a *Rolling Stone* writer who had previously written about us, and who had accompanied us on our trip to Mexico in '69 for a feature article. He was a respected journalist and biographer who put together a thoroughly researched manuscript about Jim's life. But every publisher rejected it. Danny Sugerman joined up with Jerry to make the book more appetizing.

Danny was a nerdy teenage kid who kept showing up at our office until he talked his way into a job answering our fan mail. He hadn't even graduated high school by the time Jim died. He went on to manage Nite City and he worked closely with Ray to keep the Doors alive in people's minds. He was probably one of the biggest Doors fans who ever lived, and Jim was likely the most important and influential figure in his life. But Danny wasn't there. He wasn't around when the band formed. He wasn't in the studio. He wasn't on tour. When we met him he wasn't even old enough to get into some of the clubs we were playing. But he claimed to be an insider and he punched up Hopkins's manuscript by exaggerating some stories and completely inventing others. I could go page by page and catalog all the falsehoods in the book...we never played a bar mitzvah...we never went to Disneyland as a band...I didn't whisper in Jim's ear at the New Haven show...but those aren't worth getting upset about. I could forgive Danny for taking a little creative license and even putting a few words in my mouth. But there were a few parts where it seemed like he was also putting words in Jim's mouth, and that, for me, is where he crossed a line.

What made things more complicated was that Jerry and Danny had some uncredited help. On more than one occasion Bill Siddons would arrive at Danny's house on Doors business to discover Ray sitting behind a typewriter, embellishing the manuscript even further.

Their plan worked. *No One Here Gets Out Alive* instantly topped the *New York Times* best-seller list. There was a big release party at the Whisky, where I got to tell Timothy Leary about the time Jim and I dropped acid and sat onstage next to him during his lecture at the Santa Monica Civic Auditorium. I don't remember seeing a manuscript until I had an actual copy of the published book in my hands, at which point it was too late for me to fix any inaccuracies or effectively complain. But even with all the massaged stories, I have to admit it's still one of the better books out there about our history. The problem is that it defined us, and it still defines us, even though most people have heard by now that it was heavily sensationalized.

Meanwhile, Ray made it his mission to talk to everyone with a microphone, notepad, or camera about the legend of the Doors. College radio, high school newspapers, anyone who would listen. Anytime the press wanted an interview, Ray was the one who gave it to them, and he made sure they never went home without something juicy. He didn't see the harm in spicing up stories about Jim in the name of arousing public interest in the band. And he got the most mileage out of spreading his favorite rumor, the one that had given *No One Here Gets Out Alive* its cliff-hanger ending: Maybe Jim's not dead.

The source of so many Doors myths can be traced back to Ray, and he went so deep with it that he convinced himself of some of his bullshit. He and I have visited Jim's grave together several times, and after one of our visits we were in the car on the way back to the hotel and Ray said, "He's not in there, man. I can tell."

"Come on, Ray. Jesus Christ."

More than almost anyone else on the planet, I understood what Ray was going through. Ray, John, and I all dealt with Jim's death in our own way. While John and I tried to push away from the Doors, Ray tried to cling tighter, as though he could will Jim back to life if he just wished hard enough. It wasn't logical, but there's no logic in grief. John and I were grieving, too, though. And while we were trying to escape the Doors' shadow, Ray kept making it loom larger.

There was no forum for John and me to rebut Ray's stories. What were we supposed to do: tweet at him? Unless we were going to chase down every college radio DJ he talked to and publicly smear our bandmate, we had to accept that Ray had become the official mouthpiece of the Doors, and that everything he said was corroborated by our *New York Times* best-selling biography.

Our *Greatest Hits* album came out soon after the book, and *Rolling Stone* put Jim on the cover the following year. In the mid-eighties, several of our songs were used in an episode of *Miami Vice* and on the soundtrack to *Platoon*. The teen vampire movie *The Lost Boys* opened and closed with Echo & the Bunnymen's cover of "People Are Strange." Dance music and synth pop had taken over the charts, and suddenly our songs were helping to fill a rock 'n' roll void. Whether we approved of his methods or not, Ray's mythmaking had met the moment. A new generation was discovering our legend. More importantly: they were discovering our music.

But there was a price to be paid. John and I originally assumed that Ray's promotional efforts were motivated by money, but I came to realize much later that his incentives weren't financial. He truly believed in the Doors, and he couldn't stand to let us fade into obscurity. I eventually came around to give Ray credit for what he had done, even if he didn't do it as artfully as I might've liked. But John always held it against him. The wedge that slowly grew between Ray and John as a result would brew all kinds of ugliness, and would exist for the remainder of Ray's life. I'd like to think our music is strong enough to survive on its own, but without Ray fanning the fire during the years when John and I had given up, would we have maintained relevance? Or would we be some little-known band that only snobby vinyl collectors know about? Regardless of how noble Ray's intentions may or may not have been, John and I have been sentenced to spend the rest of our days untangling fact from fiction when it comes to our band's history. Long after we're gone, I'm sure some myths will always persist. But thanks to those myths, so will the Doors.

THE OTHER TRIAL

Ray was the reason we turned down Woodstock: "It's gonna be a bust, man. It's too far from New York. No one's gonna drive all the way out there and hang out in the middle of a field for three days!" Seemed logical. We didn't think we had missed much until the *Woodstock* movie came out the following year, at which point we all gave Ray a ton of shit. To his credit, he readily admitted that he had fucked up.

John actually went out to see Woodstock as a spectator, but I think I'm the only member of the Doors to ever play at any of the Woodstock events. It was the infamous 1999 version, with all the fires and assaults and overpriced bottled water. I played early in the day and left before all the rioting, so I personally had a great time. The band Creed invited me to play "Roadhouse Blues" with them. When their singer, Scott Stapp, sang "Well, I woke up this morning…" and held the microphone out to the crowd, a hundred thousand voices replied:

"AND I GOT MYSELF A BEER!!!"

There was a lot wrapped up in that moment. It was the closing of a thirty-year gap between Woodstock and the Doors. But what struck me even more was that it wasn't a crowd that had come to see the Doors. It was Creed's crowd. I was an unannounced guest. Yet they sang Jim's lyrics at the top of their lungs, as if "Roadhouse Blues" was the song they had been waiting to hear all day.

We had seen an uptick in album sales and media coverage during the nineties after the Doors movie came out, but for a long time it was hard to truly gauge where we stood among music fans. The internet was still in its infancy and nobody had heard the phrase "social media" yet. If I hadn't personally sat down with Eddie Vedder at the Rock & Roll Hall of Fame ceremony, I don't know if I would've ever known how much the Doors had influenced him. And if we hadn't ended up in a studio with Creed, Jane's Addiction, Days of the New, Smash Mouth, and Stone Temple Pilots, I might not have realized that Eddie wasn't an anomaly.

Creed had extended the Woodstock invitation after they laid down tracks alongside all the aforementioned artists for *Stoned Immaculate,* an album of Doors covers recorded by popular bands of the late nineties with some musical backing from Ray, John, and me. We couldn't believe all these younger artists had been so inspired by our songs. So many bands jumped at the chance to work with us that even the outtakes were impressive: Chrissie Hynde's version of "Touch Me" and Marilyn Manson's industrial spin on "Five to One" had to get cut due to red tape with their labels. I have to admit I was a little out of touch when it came to a couple of the newer groups, but when Aerosmith contributed a cover of "Love Me Two Times," I genuinely couldn't believe it. Aerosmith? Doing a song I wrote? How far did this thing go?

Around the time we were finishing the album, we filmed a show called *Storytellers* for VH1 on which bands—as the title indicates—tell stories about their songs and then play them. We brought in a bunch of the singers who were featured on *Stoned Immaculate,* and Ray, John, and I ran through some of our greatest hits. But before the taping, John and Ray nearly came to blows.

John had released his autobiography in the early nineties and said some things in it that Ray didn't like. Ray released his autobiography in the late nineties and said some things in it that John *really* didn't like. John had given me and Ray copies of his manuscript before it was published so we could request changes if we thought he had written anything embarrassing or offensive, but Ray hadn't extended John and me the same courtesy. (If he had, I might've objected to him calling it *Light My Fire;* shouldn't I have first dibs on that book title?) From what I understand, John had avoided reading Ray's book at first, but by the time we got together to practice for *Storytellers,* John had finally gone through it, and he had more than a few objections to how he was portrayed. When John arrived at our first rehearsal, Ray greeted him cheerfully in the parking lot, but John was clearly angry. Ray put his arm around John and said something like, "Let's let bygones be bygones," but John shoved Ray off of him and put up his dukes like he was the Notre Dame mascot. Were they actually going to physically fight?!

John said something to Ray along the lines of "Fuck you" and headed into the practice studio. All we could do was follow him inside and start rehearsing. The tension was palpable, but—just like when we sat down to practice for the Rock & Roll Hall of Fame ceremony—the music took over and reconnected us. We managed to put on a tight, energetic performance for the TV taping, and I doubt any of the singers or audience members had a clue that John and Ray had been at such odds with each other only days before. If there's one thing the Doors have always been good at, it's playing under tension.

It would've been a happy ending, if that's where it had ended.

But while the taping temporarily smoothed things over, the following several years would tear us even further apart. *Storytellers* would be the last time the three of us ever shared a stage.

+   +   +

I only met Jim's father once. In court. He was in his mid-eighties at the time and we spoke only briefly, but he came across as a nice guy. Aside from the fact that he was suing me for several million dollars.

John had recruited Jim's family and Pam's family to join him in a lawsuit against Ray and me in 2003. Due to Jim's and Pam's lack of detailed estate planning, the Morrison and Courson families had ultimately agreed to evenly split Jim's estate, including his ownership share of the Doors. It was easy for John to call the families to arms because Ray's big mouth had gotten him into trouble with pretty much everyone over the years. First it was Ray's ego coming to the surface when we were the Doors without Jim, then it was Ray unilaterally ending the band in England, then it was Ray embellishing Jim's legend in the press, then it was Ray fostering the Jim's Not Dead rumors in the wake of *No One Here Gets Out Alive,* then it was Ray's autobiography making sensational claims, and in between were other minor skirmishes that got under people's skin. Ray was a super smart guy with a wonderful heart, and I loved him like a brother, but he was hopeless when it came to interpersonal politics. It was going to blow up in his face eventually.

Here's the timeline of the explosion:

1968

General Motors offered the Doors $75,000 to use "Light My Fire" in a commercial for their new car, the Buick Opel. This was unusual. Commercials rarely used rock 'n' roll music back then. The car looked cool and was fuel efficient, and we couldn't see any reason not to accept the offer. We had already provided music for a Ford Motor Company training film; why would we view this any differently?

Normally we made all band decisions unanimously, but Jim had gone missing. I've since heard that he was maybe off in Europe or something, but all I know is he wasn't around, and no one knew how to get ahold of him. We had no reason to think he'd have a problem with the offer, so we accepted.

When Jim got back from wherever he was, he was upset about the Buick deal. The story most people like to retell is that he was livid about the idea of our music appearing in a commercial because it sullied our art. But in reality he was mainly upset about us making a decision without consulting him. Jim didn't write "Light My Fire." It wasn't about protecting the sanctity of his poetry. It was that he took the business part of the band seriously, and he always wanted us to be four equal partners. It was a legitimate complaint. But, for the record, his rage against commercialization was barely noticeable next to his rage about being excluded from a band vote.

There was, though, a little hypocrisy involved. Jim was mad at us for making a unanimous decision without him, but he often made one-man decisions that had a unanimous effect on the band. Showing up at shows wasted. Skipping recording sessions. It would be easy to make a list. After all, the only reason we agreed to the commercial without him was because he had *disappeared* without telling us where he was going. He wasn't gone for a few hours, or a few days. It was at least a week or two. If being consulted on band business was such a priority, he could've at least left us a contact number. We would've called him!

In the end, the deal was canceled and the commercial never aired (although Buick still ran print ads with the tagline "Light your fire"). It was never as big of an issue as Doors historians make it out to be. We all got over it quickly and moved on with our lives.

1984

Ray, John, and I licensed "Riders on the Storm" to a Pirelli tires commercial that aired only in the UK. I don't remember much about the particulars of the offer or the ad or anything. Our songs were being licensed for lots of movies and TV shows in the mid-eighties, so it didn't really stand out in any way. It was a unanimous vote, and it was, again, not a big deal at the time.

2000

Ray and John seethed at each other during our rehearsals for *Storytellers*, but the music carried the day. Ray and I had occasionally been writing and demoing some new songs together around that time, and since the TV taping had gone so well, we invited John to join us. He came over with some bongos and we laid down some rough musical ideas. (I'm sorry to report to die-hard Doors fans that those tapes are currently misplaced.) It was just one session, but I hoped playing together would continue to have a healing effect.

2001

General Motors once again approached the Doors, this time offering a staggering $15 million to use "Break On Through" in a Cadillac commercial. By this point, Jim's brave stance against the Buick ad and corporate America had become a key pillar of Doors mythology. We embraced it, because whether or not it was entirely true, it was a philosophy we could support. Plenty of other commercial offers had come in over the years and it was easy enough to turn them down on principle. But this was *fifteen million dollars.* So the three of us had a meeting.

Ray, frankly, needed the money. He wasn't on the verge of home-lessness or anything; he had just made some bad financial decisions and had invested in some musical projects that never took off, and the extra cash would've helped him out. I wasn't originally in favor of doing the Cadillac ad: I liked the idea of holding out and not licensing our music to commercials. But Ray needed help, and that took precedence over any lofty ideals I had about artistic purity. Not only was Ray the one who started the band that made John and me rich in the first place; he was my friend. I would've done the exact same thing for John if he'd been the one in need. I'm not going to be the guy who tells his friend he can't have several million dollars for a song he helped write.

John didn't mind being that guy. He said we couldn't do the commercial because Jim wouldn't want it that way and the band had to protect its integrity. He probably sincerely believed that, but I suspect at least part of him was also glad to have a chance to stick it to Ray.

Either way, John didn't want to do it, so we said no. And again, we all moved on.

2002

It was clear that the bad blood between John and Ray would always be an issue, but it was also clear that — when we really wanted to — we had the ability to push the past aside and play well together. After years of shrinking away from the Doors, I was finally re-embracing our music. More and more Doors songs gradually crept onto the Robby Krieger Band's set list. I sat in with a couple of Doors tribute bands and the crowds went nuts when I stepped onstage. *Stoned Immaculate* and *Storytellers* and Woodstock and recording with Ray and John again opened me up to the idea of doing some sort of reunion.

The manager of the Robby Krieger Band, Tom Vitorino, was the one who originally set up the *Storytellers* episode, and after it aired he fielded an offer for an official Doors reunion as part of a festival tour put together by Harley-Davidson to celebrate their one hundredth anniversary. I was in. Ray was in. And so was John. At first.

John reconsidered due to his long-running battle with tinnitus, but he signed off on Ray and me performing as the Doors for the Harley gigs and said he might join us for shows in the future. Of course we said we'd always keep his spot reserved for him.

"You guys go be the Doors." Those were his words.

We contacted Stewart Copeland from the Police to take John's place. We were all fans of his drumming, and I had met him back in the late eighties, when his brother Miles put out an album of mine called *No Habla*. Finding a new singer had been a historically traumatic undertaking, but *Stoned Immaculate* and *Storytellers* had basically served as an unintentional audition process. Ian Astbury of the Cult had performed on both and was definitely one of the standouts. He had the right look, the right vibe, and a powerful voice. Danny Sugerman was a friend of Ian's and had been lobbying to connect him with the Doors for a long time already. The Cult was on hiatus, and the Doors were about to go off hiatus, so Danny's idea finally made sense.

We did a quick, four-song set at the House of Blues for a press event, and we played our first official Doors "reunion" shows at the L.A. and Toronto stops of Harley-Davidson's 100th Anniversary Open Road Tour. We had a great time. The fan response and the press coverage were positive beyond our expectations. Everyone seemed happy, from what I could tell.

2003

Soon after the Harley shows, we booked a tour that kicked off with a gig at the Palms in Las Vegas, and we promoted it with an appearance on *The Tonight Show with Jay Leno*. Just before the Palms show, John called me and demanded we change the band name and no longer appear as the Doors. It seemed abrupt to me since our plans to continue touring as the Doors were announced in the press months earlier, before we had even set foot on the Harley stage. I chalked it up to a genuine misunderstanding, and Ray and I brainstormed alternate names. We told John we would call ourselves the Doors of the 21st Century from then on. John and I mutually agreed that it was a mouthful, but he said it would be sufficient, so the promotional materials for all our future shows touted our band's new, unwieldy name.

John rounded up Jim's family and Pam's family and filed a lawsuit anyway.

The heart of the complaint was that even though we were billing ourselves as the Doors of the 21st Century, some of the promotional materials displayed "of the 21st Century" in a smaller font size, effectively advertising us as the Doors, and we weren't the Doors. John had joined the Robby Krieger Band onstage at a couple of European festivals in the nineties and the promoters announced us as the Doors without our permission. We were both upset about it, but we were also both aware that things like that aren't always under the band's control. No matter what Ray and Ian and Stewart and I called ourselves, "THE DOORS" would always be the featured phrase on the poster. Even if we toured as Four Guys Who Are Absolutely Not The Doors, guess which two words would be the biggest in the ads? We adjusted our logo, we agreed to change the name, we made sure not to use John's image, we prominently displayed Ian's and Stewart's names in the ads and posters to try to eliminate confusion. Were we really going to go to court over font size?

Making a distinction between the original band name and the new band name was important to John because he felt we weren't "The Doors" without Jim. Which is understandable. But Ray and I just didn't think it was that big of a deal. We assumed most of our fans understood that Jim wouldn't be appearing live with us, no matter what we called ourselves. And besides, back in the seventies, John, Ray, and I toured as "The Doors" for over a year after Jim died. We put out two albums together without Jim as "The Doors." When we reunited for Jim's *American Prayer* poetry album, the cover read, "Music by the Doors." When we released *Stoned Immaculate,* there was a list of artists on the cover followed by "and the Doors." When we did *Storytellers,* we were introduced as "The Doors." But now, even though he originally said it was okay to play as the Doors, John had decided we weren't the Doors, even though we weren't even touring as the Doors.

John claimed publicly that he was defending the integrity of the band, and that's why he was able to get the Morrison and Courson families on his side. Admiral Morrison was nice to me when I met him, but the fact is, he had practically disowned his son when he found out Jim wanted to be a rock singer. Was he suddenly in it to defend artistic integrity? It's probably worth mentioning that a few years earlier Jim's parents were very much in favor of doing that Cadillac commercial.

Meanwhile, we had to replace Stewart.

While most fans were distracted by the inevitable debate over whether Ian was the right replacement for Jim, it became clear to us that Stewart wasn't the right replacement for John. John was known for his laid-back style. Stewart was known for playing right on top of the beat. He once told me that Sting used to ask him to take downers before Police shows so he would slow down. His technique made our songs feel too rushed, and he also inserted new fills, which made our songs feel too busy. We simply weren't musically compatible. But how do you fire Stewart Copeland? He's Stewart Copeland!

Around the time of the Vegas gig, Stewart developed a medical issue and told us he'd need time off from touring to recuperate. Ray and I figured this was a safe excuse to replace him, because after thirty years of waiting to play again we didn't want to wait even longer. We brought in Ty Dennis, former drummer of the Motels and regular drummer of the Robby Krieger Band, who already knew most of the songs and had a better sense of John's feel. We thought it was a mutually amicable parting of ways, but Stewart decided to sue us, too. He claimed we owed him the money he would've earned if he had kept touring, even though keeping him on would've meant canceling tour dates anyway. We settled out of court; it wasn't worth fighting about. But since Stewart was mad at us, John was able to recruit him to bolster the claim that we were abusing the band's name.

Out of all the arguments in John's case, the one I understood the least was his claim that he wasn't invited to join the reunion. Of course we invited him. We practically begged him! Multiple times. He turned us down. He said he'd join us in the future. We told him he was always welcome, and we meant it. Even on the witness stand in court, Ray said John was always welcome to play with us no matter what. And years later, even after he sued us, I still kept inviting him. Never for a moment would we have preferred another drummer over John, no matter how strained our personal relationships might have become. It's his music, too.

I was optimistic that we'd eventually figure out a fair way to settle things, but once lawyers are involved, everything gets ugly. Fast.

At the beginning of it all, Jac Holzman offered to mediate the dispute for us, which made sense to me. He was a smart guy who we all respected, and he had an equal relationship with all of us, so he could be impartial and compassionate. But John refused. He wanted to go to court. So we went.

2004–2005

Ray and I kept touring as the lawsuit dragged on and as the lawyers argued about font sizes. We figured we had a good shot at winning, or at least coming to some reasonable compromise. But we made a crucial mistake.

Our lawyers convinced us to countersue John. It's a standard tactic: you sue us, we sue you, you drop your suit, we drop ours. They figured the best angle was to attack John for blocking the Cadillac commercial and other advertising opportunities, adding up to an exaggerated claim of $40 million. We had left all that stuff in the past, but—legally speaking—if the lawyers made it look like he had cost us forty million bucks, we could cancel out the few million he was asking for and we could all just walk away. Ray and I weren't wild about the idea, but our lawyers assured us this was how the game was played, and we assumed they knew best.

It was a fiasco. John didn't see it as a legal move: he thought we were trying to personally destroy him. He wailed at me in between trial sessions, "How can you do this to me?! Forty million? I'll be broke!" I tried to explain that it was a legal strategy and he'd never actually have to pay out that money, but it didn't calm him down. His lawyer asked Ray on the stand to justify the amount we were asking for, and Ray responded with a clumsy joke about how he was just looking for enough to send his son to college. The joke didn't land, and the countersuit fueled John's fire. Instead of dropping his original suit, he created a whole new narrative for the public and the press. The story was no longer a dispute about the technicalities of how we advertised our new band name. It was now "My greedy bandmates sued me so they could sell Jim Morrison's poetry to corporations! All they care about is money, and I am the lone, principled warrior who is defending the legacy and integrity of the Doors!"

John had painted himself into a corner with his original case. Now he was repainting the whole room to get himself out. The focus shifted to the age-old debate about Art vs. Commerce, and Ray and I were on the less romantic side. Journalists became eager to demonize us. Fans turned against us. John was able to get a whole bunch of high-profile musicians to write letters in support of his case. When people pointed out that John had previously agreed to use one of our songs in a Pirelli tires commercial, he had some response about later hearing Jim's voice in his head, regretting the ad deeply, and donating his share of the money to charity. Oddly, I don't remember him mentioning that at the time.

And our lawyers weren't done screwing up: they accused John of being a terrorist.

I forget what their "evidence" was—something about one of the environmental organizations John supported, I think. Our lawyers explained later that it was an attempt to basically paint John as an unstable radical who was incapable of making sound business decisions, which is why they also used an article he wrote about music and money or something as an excuse to call him a Communist. Whatever their strategy or rationale was, we had no idea they were going to smear John's character like that on the stand. This was only a few years after 9/11, when "terrorist" was an even more charged word than usual. We scolded our lawyers after the proceeding, but the damage was already done. And again John was able to bring this up in the press and make us look like dicks. To be fair, he has every right to be angry about that one. We didn't know they were going to say that shit, John. I'm sorry.

Despite all the missteps and mudslinging and font measurements...we won! Sort of. The jury determined that there had been breaches on both sides, but they found for Ray and me on most of the counts and decided that nobody owed anyone any real money. That was pretty much the best outcome we could've hoped for. Ray and I went back to touring, and we were even writing and recording new material with Ian. Then we got a call that said the judge had overturned the jury's verdict.

Judges can do that?

I still don't quite understand it, but the judge declared the jury to be an "advisory jury." I don't know why we made all those poor people sit in that jury box for months and months to listen to us bitch at each other if the judge was just going to decide things on his own, but that's The System for you. There were papers and filings and appeals, but at the end of the day Ray and I basically handed over half of what we had made during our reunion tour to John and the Morrisons and the Coursons. We continued touring under the name Riders on the Storm, and then later as Manzarek-Krieger.

Seems like we all could've saved ourselves a lot of trouble if John had just given us a list of acceptable band names from the beginning, instead of saying, "You guys go be the Doors."

+ + +

So whose side would Jim have been on?

Regardless of what our original Buick argument was really about, and regardless of how different the world is now, John is probably right to assume that Jim would've turned down the Cadillac commercial. But I haven't spoken to Jim since 1971. Sometimes people change.

I honestly don't know where Jim would've stood on the idea of a partial reunion, but either way, the last thing he would've done was spend two years and millions of dollars on lawyers to drag his friends through the legal system. If there was one thing Jim was sick of toward the end of his life, it was courtrooms.

What was it all for? Led Zeppelin ended up happily taking Cadillac's money and doing their commercial (even though the tagline "Break through" no longer matched the music). Did Led Zeppelin lose any credibility over it? Would anyone even remember the ad if we hadn't made such a stink about it? How much free publicity has John given Cadillac in all his media appearances since the trial? How much am I giving them right now? At the end of the day, feuding publicly with each other for so many years and forcing our fans to choose sides over such a petty dispute did far more damage to our legacy than any fucking car commercial.

Don't get me wrong: I love the fact that we've walked away from all the money General Motors has offered us over the years, and I think it's pretty cool that we've (mostly) refused to put our music in commercials. And I'm glad John feels so strongly about protecting what we built together. If it hadn't been part of a legal strategy to defend against John's original lawsuit, we never, ever would have thought to bring up the Cadillac commercial in court. But at the same time, it's hard for me to feel high and mighty about taking some principled stance against music licensing when nearly every major artist I can think of has sold a song to a commercial by now. I don't judge them for it. We did an ad for the round rubber things that go on the bottom of a car; we just didn't do an ad for the car itself. John may not have wanted Cadillac to use "Break On Through," but he signed off on the exact same song being used in a *Rock Band* video game, an episode of *So You Think You Can Dance*, and a trailer for the animated kids' movie *Minions*. After a while the boundaries of artistic integrity start to get pretty fuzzy.

We all went through an emotional adjustment when the Doors first ended. John became a different person. I think my heroin addiction was also scary for him, and we became more distant as a result. He had more grudges with Ray than with me, but he probably harbored a lot of anger toward me for not coming down off the fence and siding with him more strongly on a number of issues over the years.

And yet when John and I saw each other in the hallways of the courthouse, we were usually very friendly toward each other. We chatted. It was abnormally normal. He has since published a book all about the trial, which, aside from a few complimentary passages, largely paints Ray and me as villains, and he has given tons of interviews bad-mouthing us as greedy monsters. And yet he and I are still in touch. We've appeared at events together and we've even played publicly together a few times. I'm not happy about everything that's happened between us, but I try to focus on our history. The Psychedelic Rangers. Meditation classes. Living together in Laurel Canyon. England and Jamaica and organizing my intervention. I still call him a friend. I hope he still refers to me the same way.

When the Doors were inducted into the Rock & Roll Hall of Fame, Creedence Clearwater Revival was honored on the same night, but they had so much unresolved bitterness from their own legal issues that they refused to take the stage together. I don't ever want the Doors to be like that. It's harder to let go than it is to let anger fester, but I feel like we owe it to our fans to get along as best we can, no matter what we've been through. Whatever happened in the past, whatever happens in the future, I still see us as all for one. Just like it was from the beginning. That is the element of our legacy I try my best to protect.

+ + +

In February of 2007, hundreds of fans gathered on Hollywood Boulevard to watch Johnny Grant, the honorary mayor of Hollywood, unveil a brass-lined, coral-pink terrazzo star on the Hollywood Walk of Fame dedicated to the Doors. Legendary radio DJ

Jim Ladd praised us in an introductory speech, and Ray and I each said a few words to the cheering crowd, as did Jim's nephew, Dylan. We celebrated afterward with our friends and families at a private party thrown for us at the Hollywood Roosevelt Hotel across the street. Our star ended up in a pretty prime spot, right next to Julie Andrews, and right in front of (where else?) the Hard Rock Cafe.

John claimed he couldn't make the ceremony because he was obligated to do a radio interview. I'm sure it was a very important and very real radio interview that totally existed and couldn't have possibly been rescheduled. But it's a bummer that the divide between us ran so deep that he couldn't even enjoy a beautiful moment like that.

I was always the peacemaker in the band, but it was more than just my personality that allowed me to remain on good terms with John. No matter what he said or did, or how hurt or angry he made me, John was the one who got me into the Doors. I will never forget that. I just wish John hadn't forgotten the same thing about Ray.

Lynn and Poppy

L.A. WOMAN

I had to learn the hard way why you should never keep wild, exotic cats as house pets. We weren't well educated about animal welfare back in the late sixties, and the laws restricting the exotic pet trade were practically nonexistent, so Lynn and I didn't realize how bad of an idea it was to buy a leopard cat. It's basically what it sounds like: a leopard-like animal the size of a house cat, native to Southeast Asia. We got it while we were still living at my place on Topanga Beach, but it escaped and was never seen again. Later on we had a margay, which is kind of like the South American version of a leopard cat, but we were too ignorant to know it required a very specialized diet, and unfortunately it got sick and had to be put to sleep. This is why people should never keep wild, exotic cats as house pets.

One of the weird things about having an exotic cat is that you end up socializing with other people who have exotic cats. We got to know Gardner McKay, a TV actor from an old show called *Adventures in Paradise,* who kept two cheetahs in his yard. We knew a guy named Shorty who was in the business of smuggling big cats into the U.S. from Mexico. My friend Sharon who used to live with me at my house on the beach introduced us to another guy who owned a cougar. We were at his house one night when the cougar grabbed Sharon's purse and wouldn't let it go. She had no choice but to let the cougar keep it. Another perfect illustration of why people should never keep wild, exotic cats as house pets.

In between losing our leopard cat and finally learning our lesson with the margay, Lynn and I stopped into a sketchy exotic pet shop near the airport. It was full of huge snakes, colorful birds, and even a couple of monkeys, and we came home with a pet bobcat. Lynn named her Poppy, after the flower, and she was adorable at first. She lived with us at our house in Benedict Canyon, and for the first two years she even slept in our bed. Then she got big. And territorial. One day, out of nowhere, she slashed at my legs and shredded my jeans with her powerful claws. On another occasion, she got outside, and when Lynn chased her down, Poppy sank her fangs into Lynn's arm and sent her to the hospital. My brother and his wife were pet sitting one night and they made themselves a leg of lamb for dinner. Poppy, likely sick of her usual diet of chicken necks, lay in wait like the hunter she was genetically programmed to be. When the perfect moment presented itself, she snatched the lamb right out of their hands. They tried to get it back from her, but after one serious snarl, they decided to make alternate dinner plans.

We couldn't trust Poppy around guests, so we fenced in our patio and kept her outside when people came over. She would pace back and forth and scowl through the window, conspiring to rip the intruders' faces off. Her aggressive behavior got so out of control we eventually had to give her away to a guy who owned a ranch up in Ventura. He specialized in retraining pet wildcats to properly hunt so he could release them back into nature. But unfortunately Poppy kept attacking him, and he had to put her to sleep.

Please learn from our stupidity and ignorance: People should never keep wild, exotic cats as house pets.

+ + +

Poppy's memory lives on in the song "Hyacinth House." I have heard so many elaborate interpretations of that song, invoking everything from the Greek myth of Hyacinthus to Oscar Wilde's pet term for his lovers to the Miami Incident to heroin addiction to Jim's ex-girlfriend Mary. But it was really just a lyrical portrait of one particular night at my house in Benedict Canyon.

Jim, John, and some other friends had come over to the house for dinner. I was fiddling around on my guitar and recording it on my Revox two-track tape recorder to see if we could capture anything interesting. In about ten minutes Jim had written the words, and in another ten minutes I had written most of the music.

The title and first line came from the red hyacinths growing on the hillside in our backyard, visible through the bay window in our living room. Jim wrote the line "to please the lions" while watching Poppy pace on the patio. The line "I see the bathroom is clear" was inspired by Babe walking out of the bathroom after occupying it for an embarrassingly long period of time. "Why did you throw the jack of hearts away?" was a reference to a card game we were playing.

The only line I can't definitively trace to a source is "I need a brand-new friend." It might be worth noting, though, that the song was written on the same night that Jim took his final (and unsuccessful) shot at starting things back up with Lynn. He was having trouble with Pam at the time. Maybe Lynn was supposed to be his "new friend," or maybe he needed a new friend after Lynn's rejection. But I'm just speculating.

The songs that would eventually constitute our *L.A. Woman* album were almost all written like that, in a relaxed, collaborative way. We wrote more as a group for that album than we had for any other. The title track was distilled from jam sessions, with all of us contributing equally. Jim started with a handful of lines and added lyrics as he went while John kept it interesting with time changes and Ray and I harmonized on the melody and traded solos. "Riders on the Storm" was also a communal effort, written while we were fooling around with the song "(Ghost) Riders in the Sky." I dialed in a low tremolo sound on my guitar, emulating the way the Ventures used to play that song. John laid down a smooth jazz groove the way only John can. Ray created yet another genius hypnotic bass line with his left hand and yet another all-time-classic keyboard intro with his right. Jim's "killer on the road" lyrics came from the plot of his film *HWY*, since it was at the forefront of his mind at the time. They had shot a scene in which he made an actual prank phone call to the poet Michael McClure. (You can hear the audio in the rough cut of the film that exists today, or on the *American Prayer* album.) Jim told Michael that he had been hitchhiking in the desert and murdered the driver who had picked him up. Most of us wouldn't be able to get away with a joke like that for long. I don't know what it says about Jim that Michael had no trouble believing him.

"Love Her Madly" was the only song on *L.A. Woman* that I

wrote on my own, but of course Jim, Ray, and John gave it deeper dimensions when we workshopped it together. Lynn's temper was the inspiration for that one. Whenever we fought she'd walk out the door and slam the shit out of it. The madder she was, the louder the slam, so I came up with the line "Don't you love her as she's walking out the door?" She was a little embarrassed when she heard the song, but she still loved it. I adapted the title from the way Duke Ellington used to end his shows by saying "We love you madly!" to the audience. The line "Tell me what you say" was a nod to Ray Charles. "A deep blue dream" was an invocation of water—again, the four elements. As for "seven horses seem / to be on the mark"... heaven knows. It rhymed and it fit John's rhythmic punctuations. Don't ask me why seven. Jim always encouraged me to write things that would confuse people. And he loved the line about the horses.

We were so excited to play our new material for Paul Rothchild, but he wasn't impressed. He famously said that "Riders on the Storm" sounded like "cocktail music." (Later, when "Riders" became an FM hit, he tried to alter history by claiming it was "Love Her Madly" that he had described as cocktail music, but what sense does that make? It was Ray's tinkling keyboard intro that had brought on the insult.) I couldn't believe he responded so negatively to songs we were so positive about. He had always been able to find promise in even our weakest material, but for the first time he gave up on us before we began.

Part of it was losing Janis. She had died only a month before we met with Paul, and his emotions were still raw. I don't remember what exactly prompted it, but when he saw Jim on a similar path of self-destruction, he said, "I will not go through this again!" Mostly, though, I think Paul thought the Doors were on their way down. Our previous two albums had been a struggle and the Miami trial had taken a toll on our ability to tour, so it was a sensible calculation for him to decide to flee our sinking ship.

Paul shrugged in my direction and said, "Robby, why don't you produce it? You're into this stuff." I don't know why he singled me out—maybe because I seemed the most enthusiastic about the new songs. I was probably the most technically minded in our group, but only enough to run a two-track Revox, not a professional mixing console. Even if I had the required expertise, I knew the other guys weren't going to sit back and let me make all the decisions, so instead we decided to coproduce the album as a band with Bruce Botnick.

Our entire approach to recording changed, and it made all the difference. Instead of working at Sunset Sound or Elektra Studios, we created a recording studio at the Doors office. Bruce put the mixing board upstairs by the offices and ran the cables downstairs into our rehearsal room. We recorded everything live, with Jim singing all the vocals in the bathroom. Since we weren't being charged by the hour, we never had to watch the clock, and we could record anytime we wanted, day or night. Without Paul there to insist on a zillion takes, we could just play until something felt good and move on, and Jim never had enough downtime to get too wasted. We brought in Elvis's bass player Jerry Scheff, and we hired a rhythm guitarist named Marc Benno so I could record my lead parts live and not have to waste time overdubbing them later. The whole album came together in weeks instead of months. And since Jim was always at the office anyway, he almost never missed a session. There were even a few days when Jim showed up before the rest of us. I can't believe it took us six records to figure out that recipe.

"Been Down So Long," "Cars Hiss by My Window," and "Crawling King Snake" were all done in one day. Jim, as always, was pestering us to do more blues. Blues, blues, blues, blues, blues. He was like a broken blues record. So we put Blues Day on the calendar to placate him. One full day of blues and nothing but the blues. Jim's one chance to get it all out of his system. He was practically giddy with anticipation. And then—out of *all* the days we worked on *L.A. Woman*—it was the one day Jim didn't show up. We'd normally be pissed at him for missing a recording session, but we couldn't help but laugh at the fact that he had ditched us on the day he had campaigned so hard for.

We made Blues Day happen the next day instead, and it was incredibly productive. We channeled Jimmy Reed, Muddy Waters, Freddie King, and John Lee Hooker, and by the end of the session we had three solid album tracks and then some. On some of the Blues Day outtakes, you can hear Jim experimenting with the "Mr. Mojo Risin'" motif that he'd later incorporate into "L.A. Woman." I remember him being so excited to explain to us that "Mr. Mojo Risin'" was an anagram of his name, which was unusual: Jim very rarely went out of his way to explain his lyrics to us. He liked to keep everyone guessing, including his bandmates.

One of the Blues Day outtakes was a song called "Paris Blues," and it became a source of intrigue for hard-core Doors fans for years. It wasn't good enough to make the album and we didn't put it out later because the master tapes and my personal cassette dub were lost. The only copy that survived was Ray's cassette dub, but one day he left it inside a tape recorder and his then-infant son, Pablo, started playing with the buttons. At several points on the tape the music abruptly cuts out and all you can hear is Pablo making gurgling noises. Even without Pablo's remixing, though, it's just not that great of a tune. There's a reason it was considered an outtake, and there's a reason we were never too concerned about the masters going missing. Pablo was probably trying to do us all a favor.

Even though we moved quickly on *L.A. Woman,* we still put effort into production value. Ray played a Hammond organ on "Changeling," "Hyacinth House," and "The WASP." We had previously bought the Hammond for him as a Christmas gift, but he didn't think it would look good in his house so it just stayed at the studio (and eventually vanished, unfortunately). At least he used it on a couple of songs. For "L.A. Woman," I used my trusty bottleneck and an Oberheim ring modulator to create the motor sound at the beginning. People still ask us what kind of motorcycle we used in the studio. And the final touch was the rain effect on "Riders," which was Jim's idea, and which came from a sound effects record that Elektra had released years earlier.

Jac Holzman convinced us to release "Love Her Madly" as the first single even though I was against it. One of the interesting side effects of our four-way writing and royalty split was that ego and money didn't enter into the decisions over which songs became singles. Why fight to feature my own song when we're all credited and paid the same either way? Without any ulterior motives, we could be objective about what was best for the band. We thought "Changeling" represented the album and the attitude of our live show better than "Love Her Madly," which reminded us too much of the commercial pop vibe of "Hello, I Love You." And we loved "L.A. Woman" but didn't want to deal with editing down another song for radio like we had with "Light My Fire." Ultimately we listened to Jac, and as usual, he was right.

Several of the songs on *L.A. Woman* would go on to rank among our greatest hits, but we only ever got to play a few of them live, at our last couple of shows. In my opinion it's probably our second-best record, right after our self-titled album. It showed that we still had something to offer. If Jim hadn't died, we most likely would've continued on in a similar blues-rock direction. We had discovered a writing and recording process that worked well for us, and we had rediscovered a sound that inspired us. We were finally having fun making music again.

And then one day while we were mixing the record Jim came in, handed us all copies of his latest poetry book, and said he was moving to Paris. We pointed out that the record wasn't fully mixed yet. He said he trusted us to finish it without him. There was no one last drink. There was no one last meal. A few days later he was just gone.

IN TRIBUTE

There was, for a very short time in the early eighties, a low-budget rock opera based on Jim Morrison's life playing at Gazzarri's on the Sunset Strip. It was produced by Jim's sister and brother-in-law (the one who showed up at the *Soft Parade* sessions after punching Jim). They happened to be holding auditions for the role of Jim one night while I was playing with my jazz band a block away at the Roxy, and a bunch of the actors decided to come to my show. I heard about the auditions only a few minutes before I went on. Someone even told me a couple of the actors had gotten into a fight in the parking lot. So there I am onstage, when suddenly a gaggle of Jim Morrisons walk in and push their way to the front.

I started a chant with the crowd: "Clones go home! Clones go home!"

I knew that Jim had an impact on people, and I knew that his image and words had power. But it never once crossed my mind while he was alive that years later, people would try to literally become him.

The lead role in the rock opera went to a lifelong Doors fan

SET THE NIGHT ON FIRE

named Dave Brock, who then went on to form one of the first (and best) Doors tribute bands, Wild Child. I didn't understand what a tribute band was back then. My only point of reference was the Elvis impersonators who performed in seedy lounges and served as officiants at Vegas wedding chapels. But suddenly in the eighties and nineties, a bunch of Doors tribute acts popped up. Some are named after our songs, like Crystal Ship, Strange Days, and the Unknown Soldiers. Others reference our band name, like the Doors Alive, Unlocking the Doors, the Bootleg Doors, and the Dirty Doors. And then there are more obscurely named ones, like Of Perception, the Ghost of Jim Morrison, and Mr. Mojo Risin'.

At first I recoiled at the idea of bands imitating us. Elvis impersonators had become such a punch line I worried that tribute bands would turn our legacy into a joke. And it was at a time when I was trying to branch out into other styles of music and establish my own identity separate from the Doors. But through his persistence, Dave Brock eventually convinced me to sit in with Wild Child and play a few songs. And it was a blast. The crowd went crazy, and it showed me how much our music still meant to people. I've sat in with Wild Child a number of times over the years, and I've also played with the Soft Parade in New York, and Peace Frog in L.A. The keyboardist for the Soft Parade actually subbed in last-minute when the keyboardist for the Robby Krieger Band was sick. The drummer for Peace Frog became the Robby Krieger Band's drum tech. And the guitarist for Wild Child became the guitar tech for Manzarek-Krieger (and even filled in for me live when I ended up with a spinal infection before our shows in Mexico and Bolivia). My affinity for tribute bands grew so much that when the Robby Krieger Band toured Europe, I brought Wild Child with me as an opening act. After a while I started thinking, *Why should they have all the fun?*, which led to me playing more Doors songs live with my band, and eventually helped convince me of the value of a reunion.

When Ian Astbury stepped down from singing with Ray and me, we replaced him with Miljenko Matijevic from Steelheart and then Brett Scallions from Fuel, but eventually we brought on Dave Brock to front Manzarek-Krieger. We resisted for so long because we didn't want the stigma of becoming our own tribute band. But we couldn't deny that Dave had the voice for it, and he knew the songs inside and out. Ironically, the one place Dave couldn't do a straight-up Jim Morrison impression was onstage with actual members of the Doors. He kept Jim's spirit alive, but he brought his own personality to the gig. And he was a good golf partner to have on our off days.

The crazy part is that Dave has probably made more money with Wild Child over the years than the Doors ever did when we were touring in the sixties. Tribute bands have become so embraced that they're able to travel the world and command serious guarantees. The only downside for Doors tribute acts is that they have to convince someone to dress up like Robby Krieger. When I was sitting in with the Soft Parade, I kept getting distracted by my personal clone, who was forced to duplicate the worst hair in rock 'n' roll.

Not all clones are created equal, though. Just as the Doors have often attracted unstable fans, they've attracted more than a few unstable imitators. One poor guy fell to his death from the window of his New York apartment while drunkenly mimicking Jim's antics. Like Jim, he was only twenty-seven years old. And a guy calling himself Cliff Morrison claimed to be Jim's illegitimate son, and started a band called Lizard Sun (sun...son...get it?). He was promoted by Jim's rock opera–producing brother-in-law, and my son, Waylon, even played guitar with him for a while, until we all got a little uncomfortable with how much Cliff was using his alleged connection to the Doors to market himself. When DNA testing finally became available, Cliff took a test. And failed. But that hasn't stopped him from continuing to claim he's Jim's offspring.

(I actually have a theory that Jim was shooting blanks. All that sex with all those partners for all those years? I'm surprised there aren't a dozen other Cliffs out there.) Cliff kept trying to get me and the other Doors to legitimize him as Jim's son, even without the DNA. I tried to reason with him and told him to drop the "Morrison" and just make music under his own name. He didn't listen, so I finally had to tell him to stop calling me. Then in 2010 he held up a gas station at gunpoint and led police on a high-speed chase until they spun his car out and Tasered him to get him into custody. He went to jail for a few years, but he's out now, and still making music while claiming to be a Morrison. And still calling me.

I've lost count of how many people have either consciously or unconsciously attempted to imitate Jim. Whether it's Val Kilmer in *The Doors* or Jimmy Fallon in his hilarious parody of our *Ed Sullivan* appearance or Weird Al perfectly capturing our songwriting style for a song about Craigslist or one of the singers from the dozens of Doors tribute acts out there, it's incredible how many people want to embody Jim Morrison. Even though sometimes the impersonations can be comical, and even though, yes, you can now hire a Jim Morrison impersonator to marry you at a Vegas wedding chapel, I don't worry about the tackiness tarnishing his memory anymore. Every time someone squeezes themselves into an uncomfortable pair of leather pants and a blousy pirate shirt and sensually rubs a microphone stand while summoning a syrupy baritone, it's a testament to the power of his legacy.

It's funny, though: no one ever dresses like the fat Jim . . .

OTHER VOICES AND FULL CIRCLE

Of all the mysteries surrounding the Doors, the one that maybe confounds people the most is why we thought we could still be a band after Jim died. It seems so ridiculous now, but there was some logic to it.

When Jim moved to Paris, none of us thought the band was over. We knew Jim needed a break, we knew he might be away for a while, but we had no reason to think he wouldn't be back and that we wouldn't pick up where we left off. He even called the office from abroad and spoke to John on the phone. He asked how *L.A. Woman* was doing and said he'd be back in a few months. Some people say he was done being a rock star, or that he was running away from the Miami charges, or that he just wanted to live a quiet life as a poet. I don't buy it. The bottom line is that Jim loved to perform. Even in Paris, when he was supposed to be getting away from it all, he couldn't resist jamming with a local bar band. He had his demons. But the stage was where he exorcised them.

So while Jim was away we proceeded as if he would be back any minute. We jammed together and did some writing so whenever

Jim was ready we'd have a jump on our next album. We had no intention of moving forward without him. We were just making the most of our time while we waited around.

Jim, as everyone knows, didn't come back as planned. After taking some time to process that emotionally, we were left with some heavy, intimidating questions about who we were and where we were going.

Could we still write a Doors album without Jim?

Well, we pretty much already had. After months of jam sessions we had amassed plenty of material, so we assembled it and set to work on what would become *Other Voices*. We needed some lyrics, but I had been coming up with those since the beginning, so it wasn't new territory for me. Ray and John were excited to try their hand at it as well. Ray ended up writing the words for the album's first single—a song called "Tightrope Ride," about what it was like being in a band with Jim—and John wrote the lyrics to "Ships with Sails," which was one of my favorite songs of the post-Jim era. It was a new dynamic, but it wasn't that odd for the three of us to write and record together without Jim. When Jim didn't show up to record "When the Music's Over" after his naked acid trip, the three of us covered for him. When Jim was out of song ideas and drinking heavily during the *Soft Parade* sessions, I wrote more songs to make up for it. When Jim didn't show up for rehearsal at my parents' house because he was in a Blythe jailhouse, we quickly came to understand that he might not always be around. He had been preparing us to cope with his absence from the beginning.

Besides, we needed a mission. Without a new album to work on we would've just moped around and wallowed in our grief. I was only twenty-five years old at the time. Not only had I just lost a dear friend and irreplaceable writing partner; I was facing the idea that our band was over and my career was over and my life may as well have been over. If we hadn't stayed busy, the weight of all that would've crushed us.

And we were actually having fun! We recorded *Other Voices* with the same setup we had used for *L.A. Woman,* working with Bruce Botnick at the Doors office. We brought in an amazing Cuban conga player named Francisco Aguabella to add some layers of percussion, and we brought in Emil Richards (the vibraphonist we had jammed with at the Maharishi's Tahoe retreat) to play marimba. Jerry Scheff from *L.A. Woman* and Ray Neapolitan from *Morrison Hotel* came in to play bass, as did Jack Conrad, who was working with Helen Reddy and who we later recruited to tour with us full-time. We leaned more into our jazz influences since we didn't have Jim there to insist on the blues. It was exciting to experiment with new sounds and styles, and we genuinely liked the songs we had come up with. Looking back, it's not our strongest work (to put it politely), but it didn't feel forced or unnatural. We were moving forward, and it felt good.

We wrestled with the idea of bringing in a replacement singer, though. We felt like it was still too soon. For a minute we even considered doing an all-instrumental album, but then decided that would be an overcorrection. We figured it'd be best if we took on the vocal duties ourselves. Out of the three of us, Ray was the natural choice for a lead vocalist since he had sung in his previous band and had the right personality for it. But if I'm being honest, I never really liked Ray's voice. Not that I liked my own voice any better. Sure, I had done all those Dylan covers in college, but once I was in a band with Jim, I understood what a real singer could be, and I was not in the same league, or even playing the same game. Ray and I took turns with vocals and harmonized as much as we could. Neither of us sounded great on our own, but when we sang together, it at least helped to cover up our individual weaknesses.

Jac Holzman gave us mountains of encouragement. He probably knew how much we needed it. We always liked Jac, but it wasn't until much later that we truly appreciated him. No other label owner would've put up with even half of what Jac did. Columbia dropped us after one run-in with Jim on acid. Would they have covered for us after Jim took a fire extinguisher to a recording studio? Would they have stood by us after New Haven? After Miami? Jac threw us parties to celebrate our accomplishments and looked the other way when Jim ruined them by getting too wasted. Jim even used to hit on Jac's girlfriend; how many label heads would've let that slide? Even if there was some other label out there that could've made it through all of that, how many of them would've offered the Doors a multi-record deal once Jim Morrison was out of the picture?

For Jac, it wasn't all about money. There are more successful bands that have been dropped by their labels for less than what we put him through. During one of our contract renegotiations, our lawyer at the time, Abe Somer, approached Jac with a pretty bold proposal. The label had originally paid us $5,000 to own a chunk of our publishing rights, which was pretty common back then. Publishing is potentially worth a lot of money if, say, for instance, a certain blind Puerto Rican guitarist decides to cover one of your songs, or in the unlikely event that a luxury car brand wants to give you fifteen million bucks to use your music in a commercial. But we, like most bands making their first record, said, "Wow! Five thousand dollars! Thanks!," and signed it away. Abe made a case to Jac that he should give us 100 percent of our publishing. He didn't think Jac would actually go for it; he was using it as a negotiation tactic to make Jac compromise on other deal points. But Jac just said, "Okay," and handed it over, because he thought it sounded fair. It's almost impossible to imagine another record label being run that way. In fact, it's almost impossible to imagine *any* business in *any* other industry being run that way.

Jac believed in us from the beginning and he looked after us to the end. He wasn't naive enough to think a Morrison-less Doors album (let alone multiple albums) would break any sales records, but he stood by us like he always had. His undying support was — for better or worse — one of the big reasons we had the guts to press forward.

When it came to playing live, we thought back to Amsterdam, where Jim had missed the show but the crowd still embraced us. Maybe they'd welcome us the same way now? There was only one way to find out, so we set out on tour for the first time in almost a year. To our relief, the audiences were enthusiastic and open-minded, and the critics gave us far more credit than we expected. The shows were smaller, but it wasn't like we were playing to half-empty bars. In L.A., we filled the Hollywood Palladium. In New York, we played to a packed house at Carnegie Hall. As we stood on the boards of one of the most prestigious stages in the world, it seemed like people still wanted to see us.

Carnegie Hall, November 1971

Nowadays people discuss the post-Jim Doors with the attitude, "What were they thinking?" But at the time it made sense to write songs. It made sense to record. Our label was behind us all the way. Our critics gave us kudos. Our fans still turned up and enjoyed themselves. We were having fun. Why not keep it going?

When we put out our next album, *Full Circle,* we actually scored a minor hit with "The Mosquito." It was inspired by a trip Lynn and I took to a town in Baja, Mexico, called Mulegé. It's an isolated oasis on the Sea of Cortez where you can pull all kinds of sport fish out of the water. Lynn and I stayed at a quaint little resort and reeled in some sierras, dorados, yellowtail, and bonefish. At night, the resort staff would cook up our catch and some local musicians would come down from the nearby hills to serenade us. They were like mariachis, but they wore ragged clothes instead of the traditional fancy outfits. They had a song about a mosquito that I wanted to learn, but when I got home I couldn't quite remember it (and to this day I've never been able to track it down), so I wrote my own mariachi-sounding tune with simple Spanish lyrics about a mosquito. It was popular with Doors fans in Spanish-speaking countries, and for some reason in Austria and the Netherlands, where it charted in the top twenty. French singer Joe Dassin recorded a cover that charted even higher in France and Finland. Not too many Doors fans in America are familiar with "The Mosquito" today, but in other parts of the world it's one of our most covered songs after "Light My Fire."

The other tracks on *Full Circle* were...not as popular. "The Piano Bird," which was John's song, was probably my favorite after "The Mosquito." And I was proud of my tongue-in-cheek lyrics to "Verdilac," which is a (misspelled) Russian term for a vampire that feeds only on the blood of its loved ones. The rest of the songs I could do without—and the fans and critics didn't like them any more than I did.

We kept touring through 1972 and our shows still drew several thousand people each night. We returned to Florida for the first time since the Miami Incident and there was a two-mile-long traffic jam leading to the venue. In Indianapolis and Boston we played past the venue curfews when the crowds demanded we be allowed to finish our encores. Amsterdam once again saw us without Jim and once again thoroughly enjoyed themselves. And we wrapped it all up with another Hollywood Bowl performance (although this time as the support act for Frank Zappa).

It all imploded at the end of the year when we went to England to find a new singer. But we could have kept going. Touring and recording as the Doors without Jim Morrison wasn't ideal, but it also wasn't as insane as it might seem today. Still, it was destined to end. After the initial grace period, our egos were clashing, our new albums were selling dismally, our critics had lost patience with us, and our individual visions of where the band was headed musically were incompatible. The only thing we had going for us in the end was that our fans were still there to support us, for which we'll always be deeply grateful. As much as we were mourning Jim, so were they. Watching Ray, John, and me roll through town one more time was maybe a communal way of saying farewell.

But at the same time, it's like that old joke:

How do you get to Carnegie Hall?

Lose enough popularity that you can't fill Madison Square Garden anymore.

Lynn and Julia

THE KING

One night while we were working on *Other Voices,* Lynn and John's wife, Julia, were out on the town and driving through West Hollywood when a monstrous Mercedes-Benz 600 started honking at them and chasing them dangerously through traffic. When they halted at a stoplight, the Mercedes pulled up on their right. The driver was Elvis Presley.

This was 1971 Elvis, with dyed black hair and his trademark sunglasses with "EP" carved into the bridge and lightning bolts along the side. He asked the girls what they were up to. Julia, who was normally a smooth talker, clammed up completely. Lynn made an awkward attempt at playing it cool by asking, "Where's the gala event?" In the brief period before the light turned green, Elvis invited the girls to a party at his hotel suite at the Century Plaza Hotel (the same hotel where, twenty-two years later, the Doors would be inducted into the Rock & Roll Hall of Fame).

Not surprisingly, Lynn and Julia were the only people at the "party" aside from Elvis and the Memphis Mafia. They were all friendly, but they were all carrying an alarming number of guns. There were guns on the nightstand, guns on the bathroom counter, guns everywhere. It couldn't have possibly been legal. But it was Elvis: he made his own rules.

The girls told Elvis and the guys about their husbands in the Doors, but it hardly deterred the Memphis Mafia from hitting on them. Elvis said he was a fan of Jim's, particularly his voice on our version of Junior Parker's "Mystery Train," which Elvis had also covered. Elvis took a liking to Julia, so they moved into the bedroom and left Lynn behind with his gun-toting, medallion-wearing, drooling entourage. Lynn called us at the Doors office to tell us to come down and meet Elvis, but we were busy working. In retrospect, we really should've taken a break and accepted the invite. The world could've probably waited an extra day to hear *Other Voices*. I never got another chance to meet the King. If Jim had still been alive, I'm sure he would've made us drop everything and head over to the hotel. Although if we had gone over there, it might've gotten awkward if John realized what Elvis and Julia had been up to.

After spending a significant chunk of time dodging the clumsy come-on attempts of the Memphis Mafia, Lynn finally ran out of patience and pounded on the bedroom door to tell Julia it was time to go. Elvis invited them both to fly with him to Tahoe, where he had a two-week run of shows booked. Julia wanted to go and was mad when Lynn turned down the offer. Julia and John's relationship was obviously already strained at that point, but they were technically still married. She couldn't just fly off to Tahoe on her own without Lynn as her cover story. Elvis was disappointed, but don't feel too bad for him: he picked up the phone right in front of them and invited actress Peggy Lipton to travel with him instead.

When Lynn and Julia came to the studio and shared the family-friendly version of their night with Elvis, our session bassist Jerry Scheff was jealous. He had been touring and recording with Elvis for over two years at that point. He had never gotten that much one-on-one time with him.

THIS IS THE END

The first time Jim died I was shocked and upset, but by the second or third time I got used to it. We had gotten pretty calloused to rumors about the demise of famous musicians since we were living through the "Paul is dead" era. It was a time when a silly urban legend had everyone spinning their Beatles albums backward to listen for cryptic clues about the alleged secret passing of Paul McCartney. We'd hear similar conspiracy theories from various sources that Jim had died, but they were usually easy to disprove by turning and seeing him next to us, or at most by making a quick phone call.

But Bill Siddons had been making phone calls all night. And no one was answering.

Bill had gotten a call at around four in the morning from our British label rep, who said multiple French media outlets were trying to confirm a story about the death of Jim Morrison. Bill called Pam in Paris to find out what was going on, but she wasn't picking up. He called her every half hour until around noon, when she finally answered. It wasn't a rumor this time.

Bill called the rest of us to explain what was happening, and then drove straight to the airport and hopped on the next available flight to Paris. After years of people crying wolf, part of me didn't think it was true, but most of me knew it was.

Things were a bit of a blur after that. Bill called from Paris to tell us that Jim had been buried in a sealed coffin. It made no sense at the time, but I've come to assume Pam did that to avoid an autopsy that would reveal heroin in his system. We were pissed that Bill hadn't personally seen the body. What had we sent him over there for?! But it's not like we had given him specific instructions about what to do if he arrived to find a casket that had already been bolted shut. As young as we all were, Bill was two or three years younger, and there's no textbook to prepare you for that kind of situation.

I didn't cry. I was sad, but I was also in shock. Which seems naive in retrospect. The warnings had been staring us in the face for so long. My dad warned us. Paul Rothchild warned us. Jimi and Janis warned us. Jim himself warned us. It's not that we couldn't believe it; it's that we didn't want to believe it. We always joked that Jim would outlive us all and be like one of those drunken Irish poets who go on to be a hundred years old. It was what we had to tell ourselves to emotionally deal with him dancing on the edge all the time.

I'm almost ashamed to say that my immediate reaction was relief. But it's the truth. When you first step off a roller coaster, you don't reminisce about what the ride meant to you. You just gasp for breath. We had been on a six-year roller coaster ride with Jim. It was full of double loops and corkscrew turns and drops that suspended the laws of gravity. We needed a moment for our heart rates to return to normal.

Another unexpected reaction was one of happiness. Not because I was glad he was dead, but because you usually feel happy when a friend gets what they want. Jim had fulfilled his prophecy of following Jimi and Janis to the grave. He had achieved his goal. The context was different when my brother and my parents died: they all wanted to live. Jim's death was a tragedy to everyone else, but I don't know if he would see it that way. But what did he know? He was only twenty-seven.

When the magnitude of it finally sank in, a mixture of more understandable emotions came to the surface. Sorrow that he was gone. Anger that he had been so irresponsible. Fear of never finding another creative partner on the same level. Guilt that we hadn't done more to help him.

I know we tried an intervention, but I wish we had tried another one. But if we had done a hundred interventions, we would've wished we had done a hundred and one. There was a spiral of what-ifs. What if we had taken a firmer stance on his drinking? What if we had stopped touring sooner? What if Miami hadn't happened? What if he hadn't left for Paris? Everyone who knew Jim went through some version of that spiral, and it affected us all differently. You try to tell yourself it was inevitable, but then you tell yourself that's just an excuse, and the spiral continues.

I've always wondered if Jim had a medical condition he never told anyone about. He and I went to the same doctor for a while, and the doctor once made some offhand comment to me that alluded to something being seriously physically wrong with Jim, as if it was common knowledge. I didn't pay it much mind at the time, and the exact wording has since disappeared completely from my memory, but my curiosity about what the doctor might have meant still gnaws at me. Most people chalk up Jim's death to a heroin over-dose, but the official medical report said it was a heart attack. Maybe it wasn't drugs after all. Maybe Jim knew his time on this planet was short. Maybe that's why he had no fear of death. Maybe that's why he lived the way he did, taking everything to extremes, putting himself in danger, not caring about money or the future.

It's just a theory. But the last thing Jim's death needs is more fucking theories.

If I can put one specific theory to bed, it's the idea that he's still alive somewhere. If Jim had faked his death, he would've popped up on a stage somewhere by now to sing the blues. In terms of how he died, I know there are a ton of theories flying around out there, but I've never bothered to research any of them too deeply.

Was it heroin? Could've been. People will tell you that Jim was never the "type" who would do heroin, but neither was I — until I did heroin. Jim was experimental and reckless. He was the guy who gulped down a brick of hash on a whim in Amsterdam and sent himself to the hospital. Who knows what he got up to in Paris? Pam was definitely into heroin; maybe he finally got curious. It was popular in Paris at the time; maybe he was trying to absorb the local culture. It wasn't behavior his friends would've predicted, but it's not impossible. In fact, I lean toward it being very possible. Mixing booze and heroin would be the simplest explanation for his sudden exit. But I wasn't there, so I can't say for sure.

Was it a heart attack? Could've been. It's rare for a twenty-seven-year-old to have a heart attack, but it's not unheard of. Jim was definitely sick for a while before he left. He had a nasty, lingering cough that was bad enough for us to push him to see a doctor. Maybe there was some undiagnosed respiratory issue. He was in France for a few months; I have no idea if he got better or worse.

The details don't really matter, but I understand the obsession. Jim's death is a hard thing for some fans to accept. Pam couldn't accept it, and it dragged her into a black hole of depression that she never crawled out of. John couldn't accept it, and he wrestled with his rage toward Jim for years. Ray couldn't accept it, so he convinced himself that Jim was still alive. I couldn't accept it, so I ended up chasing the dragon. Poring over conspiracy theories is a way for people who miss Jim to cope with his loss. But eventually — even though it's much easier said than done — we all have to move on.

Did Jim die in his bathtub? Did he mistake heroin for cocaine and take too much by accident? Was his body moved to the apartment from a nightclub bathroom? Did Pam lie to the cops? Was the coffin empty? Was the CIA involved? I wasn't there. I haven't investigated. I don't know what's credible.

I just know my friend is gone.

+   +   +

I had never seen a cemetery like Père Lachaise. I don't even think another cemetery like it exists. I'd heard it was beautiful, but the experience of walking the cobblestoned, tree-lined pathways among weathered mausoleums and monuments bearing so many distinguished names from the world of art, music, and literature was beyond anything I had imagined. I immediately understood why Jim wanted to be buried there.

I've been to Jim's grave maybe half a dozen times. It was easy to visit back in the seventies and eighties, when I'd run into only a handful of fans, if any. It has since become one of the most visited tourist attractions in Paris and one of the most visited grave sites in the entire world. These days it's nearly impossible to stop by without encountering a crowd. And the cemetery authorities have secured his plot with video cameras, guards, and a barricade, which inhibits intimacy as much as vandalism.

On the rare occasions when I was able to find a quiet moment alone with Jim at Père Lachaise, I didn't make any speeches or perform any rituals. I just took some time to think and reminisce. If I want to speak to his soul, I figure I can do that from anywhere. If he's really gone, then it doesn't matter anyway, and if there is another plane of existence after this life, I'll talk to him when I get there myself. In the meantime, I'm thankful he chose such a serene and breathtaking location where we can all take a moment to reflect on what he meant to us.

On the tenth anniversary of Jim's death, Ray, John, and I mingled with a crowd of well over a hundred fans at the cemetery. It was a happy occasion, not a morose one. People sang Doors songs and passed joints, and Ray said a few words in celebration of Jim's life and poetry. Ray and I visited Père Lachaise together several times while touring after our 2002 reunion, and we celebrated the fortieth anniversary of Jim's death with another group of a few hundred fans there before playing a set at the Bataclan theatre that night. I wasn't there for the twentieth anniversary, but apparently a huge riot broke out, fans set cars on fire, and the police tear-gassed everyone. More proof that, even from beyond, Jim will always have the power to stir people up.

THE GREATEST PAR THREE HOLE IN AMERICA

I have a theory about why so many rock musicians end up loving golf. When you're onstage playing your best and you're in sync with your band and the energy of the crowd is just right, you step outside yourself. You switch to autopilot and let the moment carry you. It's a similar sensation when you're on the golf course and you get out of your own head just enough to allow all those hours of practice to translate into a perfect connection between your club and the ball. As you watch that little white sphere sail silently through the air, you get lost in the moment the same way you do when you hear yourself nailing a guitar solo in front of a screaming crowd. It's addictive, and it's fleeting, but it's the closest I've come to what the Maharishi might describe as "bliss."

Golf was a gift my dad gave my brother and me. He taught us to play when we were little, and by the time I was twelve I could beat him. When he joined the Riviera Country Club, the initiation fee was about six hundred bucks. It has since ballooned up to well over a quarter of a million dollars. Its golf course is considered one of the best in the world. I even met a young Tiger Woods there in 1997, just a few months after his professional debut. I knew his caddie, Fluff, so he made the introduction.

"Hey Tiger, this is Robby Krieger. You know the Doors?"

"What's the Doors?"

"It's a musical group," I interjected helpfully.

"Sorry, I don't know from music."

Oh well.

When I was a kid I would hitchhike to Riviera to make extra money as a caddie for the rich and famous members, like James Garner (who was talented enough to go pro, and a good tipper) and Peter Lawford (who used to play barefoot, and was also a good tipper). And in the eighties my dad was often paired up for games with a guy who was then mostly known for being one of America's favorite football stars: O. J. Simpson. I got to play against O. J. a couple of times myself, and once my dad and I played in a foursome against him and Marcus Allen. O. J.'s knees were shot from his football years, so his swing was never that good and I was able to beat his score pretty easily. Although I'm sure he could still break a tackle better than me. I couldn't believe it when I saw him on the news, fleeing the police in that white Ford Bronco. Everybody loved O. J., but he was kicked out of Riviera soon after his arrest. One of my golf buddies, Leonard, would spot him on public courses after his acquittal and cough out the word "Murderer!" under his breath. I ran into him only one time after his arrest, at Balboa Golf Course up in Encino. I asked him how it was going. He replied with a massive understatement:

"I've been going through some weird shit lately..."

Growing up with unlimited access to a course like Riviera was an exceptional privilege, but when I joined the Doors it no longer seemed cool to spend so much time at a posh country club. But when the band ended I got back into the sport and started golfing with my dad again. It was just the two of us, out in the fresh air, enjoying each other's company with no one else around. I didn't realize how much I would appreciate all that uninterrupted time with my dad until he wasn't around to golf with anymore.

My dad developed dementia as he got older, and his doctor eventually forbade him to drive, but I still took him over to Riviera in his wheelchair. He could still walk, but he was lazy: "Let's take the chair." I'd set him up at the driving range or get him out on the course for a round if he was up to it. He gradually forgot all the names of his golf buddies, but he still said hi and pretended to know who they were.

Dementia shortens your temper, but my dad's temper was the stuff of legend around Riviera already. His caddie, Martin, joked, "Whenever you caddie for Mr. Krieger, you have to know where to stand" unless you want to get taken out by a thrown club. Once, after a bad shot, my dad whacked his ball in anger, attempting to send it into the bushes, but it bounced off a curb and smashed through the window of a refreshment stand, sending everyone inside ducking. He earned himself more than a few monthlong suspensions for his misbehavior, but he was such a nice guy off the course that everyone at the club still loved him, and they found his fits of rage entertaining. His friends at Riviera loved to retell the story of the time he was so frustrated that he threw his wedge up into a tree. His buddy Archie Altounian (affectionately known around Riviera as the Armenian Hustler) threw his own club up into the tree to try and get my dad's club down, but Archie's club got stuck, too. Archie's club eventually fell back to earth, but my dad's stayed up there. One day, almost a full year later, my dad hit a shot from under the same tree, and in an unbelievable coincidence, that was the moment his club decided to free itself and return to him.

In his declining years, my dad was on the driving range next to Archie when he hit a weak twenty-yard shot, and Archie patronized him with a "Great shot, Stu!"

My dad icily extended his middle finger and growled, "Go fuck yourself." I couldn't stop laughing.

During the last game I ever played with my dad, he got turned around on the eighth hole and was about to play his ball backward into the previous fairway until I yelled at him to stop. I would've shrugged it off, but on the next hole he hit a bad drive, walked over to the golf cart I was sitting in, and bashed his driver on the roof of the cart until the club broke. Denting a golf cart wasn't exactly new territory for my dad: when people saw a battered cart around Riviera, they would say it had been "Kriegerized." But this time he almost took my head off. He had become a danger to himself and others. We finished our round, but I knew I could never take him back to Riviera after that.

As his condition got worse, my dad hired a couple of rotating helpers, Joel and Debbie, to take care of him at home. He refused to move into any sort of assisted-living facility, but he was constantly in and out of the hospital into his nineties. During one of his hospital stays I dropped by for a visit. Joel was there in tears.

"Your dad's gone."

He had died only minutes before I arrived.

The fourth hole at Riviera was dubbed "the greatest par three hole in America" by Hall of Fame golfer Ben Hogan. It also happens to be the spot where my dad drove a golf ball into my skull when I was a kid. You can attack the hole straight on and risk your ball falling into a massive sand trap, or you can play conservatively around the trap, lose a stroke, and still go for par. My dad always hit the ball straight. And he always ended up in the sand.

My dad didn't want any sort of funeral, but after he died we held a small get-together at Riviera, where all his buddies reminisced and laughed about his infamous temper. Later on, I played a round of golf in his honor with my friend Leonard. When we got to the fourth hole, I pulled a container of my dad's ashes out of my golf bag and spread them discreetly in the sand trap where he had spent so much of his time.

+   +   +

My mom passed away almost twenty years before my dad. Her funeral was more traditional and well attended, with lots of friends and relatives turning out to see her buried in a mausoleum at Hillside Memorial Park. It's a cemetery in Culver City that's full of old Jewish entertainers, among them Al Jolson, whose grave is marked by a 120-foot cascading waterfall. She's in a mausoleum right next to her own mother. And considering that my mom was one of the first people to encourage me to play music, I find it fitting that she happens to be buried in the same mausoleum as one of my biggest musical influences: Mike Bloomfield from the Paul Butterfield Blues Band.

I was on tour when she died. She had skin cancer that was spreading dangerously, so she went in for an operation. She came through it okay and was in relatively good health for a woman in her early seventies, so I didn't think there was too much to worry about. I chatted with her on the phone after she got home from the hospital. They usually don't discharge you if there's still something wrong, so I had no reason to think it would be our last conversation.

It wasn't the cancer that got her: it was a case of pneumonia she caught at the hospital. Within a week my dad called to tell me my mom was on an IV at home, surrounded by nurses, and more or less in a coma. She couldn't speak. According to my dad she could barely breathe. He didn't know what to do: she seemed to be in agony even with a steady morphine drip. My dad wondered aloud if he should just tell the nurses to give her a big enough dose of morphine to let her go in peace.

I said, "Do it."

She was only getting worse, and the doctors had given my dad no reassurance that things would turn around. It was only a matter of time. There are probably people out there who object to hurrying along the process of dying, but if I were in the same situation as my mom, I would hope she'd do the same for me.

It was my mom who taught me my first instrument by showing me how to play "Chopsticks" on the piano. It was my dad who introduced me to *Peter and the Wolf* and boogie-woogie music. It was my mom who brought Elvis and rock 'n' roll into my life. It was my dad who dragged several handmade acoustic guitars back from a luthier in Spain. It was my mom who got the Doors one of our first gigs at a friend's backyard party. It was my dad who put up the money for us to buy Ray's piano bass. It was both of my parents who allowed the Doors to practice in their living room, celebrated with me when "Light My Fire" hit number one, flew out to Stockholm to see us play, and were by my side when our band was inducted into the Rock & Roll Hall of Fame.

While Jim's grave in Paris is the traditional destination for Doors fans wishing to pay their respects to our music, a true Doors pilgrimage would also include a stop at a Culver City mausoleum filled with old Jewish entertainers and the sand trap on the fourth hole of the Riviera Country Club golf course.

AN AMERICAN PRAYER

In the late seventies, I was going through some old boxes and happened to unearth my copy of the self-published poetry book Jim had given me before he left for Paris. It was small and thin and bound in red leather, with the title embossed in gold letters on the cover: *An American Prayer.* I leafed through it sentimentally, marveling at Jim's supernatural talent with words. I found myself wishing we could still write together. And then wondering if maybe there was a way we still could...

On his birthday in 1970, Jim had gone into a studio to record himself reciting some of the poems I held in my hand. It was something he had wanted to do separately from the Doors, so we weren't a part of the sessions, and we never heard any of the tapes. Out of curiosity I called up John Haeny, the engineer Jim had worked with, and asked him if he still had the recordings. In the aftermath of Jim's death, he had fiercely guarded the tapes from the Morrison and Courson families, who were embroiled in a legal battle over Jim's estate. Haeny refused to turn over the tapes to anyone, but he invited Ray, John, and me over to his house to listen to them.

When Jim's voice came out of the speakers, I instantly heard lifts and falls. Rhythms and hints of melodies. Jim had a naturally musical way of speaking, and it immediately sparked ideas in my head for guitar licks and chord structures. The same way he had inspired me in the old days.

Jim didn't tell us much about what he wanted to do with his poetry recordings. I have a vague memory of him saying he wanted to work with Fred Myrow, a film composer who had worked with him on *HWY*. But yet again, Jim had started something and left it unfinished. Ray, John, and I officially partnered with John Haeny, who knew Jim's wishes best, and set to work on a poetry album that would be named *An American Prayer* after that humble little book I had dug up.

Haeny was the one who suggested that Ray, John, and I score the album as the Doors. We were reluctant at first, but the more we dug through the recordings, the more intriguing the idea became. We knew it wouldn't be easy to try to build music around already recorded spoken words. Some of the performances were lively; others were clearly recorded after one too many belts of whiskey. It wasn't like we could get Jim to do another take if something didn't fit. But the challenge of it was appealing. We found cadences in Jim's speech that informed the beat, and we edited his pauses to smooth out the timing. We wrote a basic blues riff inspired by Jim's reading of an untitled poem we would later dub "Black Polished Chrome." After recording the track, we laid Jim's reading over it. It worked. We were onto something.

One minor inconvenience was our new creative collaborator: Pam's dad, Corky Courson. Since the Courson family had ended up with partial control over Jim's estate, Corky had an official say over the contents of the album. He was a friendly guy who looked like a junior high school principal, which was fitting since he worked as a junior high school principal. Other than vetoing our idea to include a live version of "Gloria" because he thought it was too dirty, he didn't really interfere creatively. But still, have you ever tried recording an album with your junior high school principal looking over your shoulder?

Blues was an easy enough starting point for the soundtrack due to Jim's affinity for it. I once even accompanied him with some acoustic blues guitar at one of his poetry readings. The album was just a better-produced version of that same concept. We brought in some amazing session musicians to add synths, percussion, and bass. Bob Glaub, one of the top session bassists of all time, wrote the bass line to "Ghost Song," which is maybe my favorite bass line on any Doors album. Frank Lisciandro had signed on as a coproducer and he gave us access to some audio recordings of Jim telling stories while they were filming *HWY*. Some of Jim's spoken poems had become songs on Doors albums, so we layered the songs faintly in the background to show how his poetry evolved into lyrics. And for the epic closing track we created a modern arrangement of Albinoni's "Adagio in G Minor" to pair with Jim's reading of a poem we titled "A Feast of Friends." We had already recorded a version of "Adagio" during the *Soft Parade* sessions, when we had access to a full orchestra, but we had never released it. Jim had always loved the recording, so we thought it would be fitting to revive the song for him.

We've taken some criticism from people who claim Jim would've been upset by our involvement since he wanted his poetry to exist separate from the Doors, but the whole album was truly a labor of love. It was put together with painstaking effort over the course of almost two years, and we continually asked ourselves along the way, "What would Jim have wanted?" John Haeny, Frank Lisciandro, and the individual members of the Doors all had completely different relationships with Jim, and all came into the project with completely different perspectives. But we all stand proudly behind the end result. It's actually one of my favorite Doors records, even if it's not the most popular. We'll never know for sure if Jim would've enjoyed the album, but I'm confident he wouldn't have wanted those tapes to just sit in a closet and disintegrate. We did our best to honor his words.

My original copy of Jim's *American Prayer* book has since gone missing. I'm fairly sure it's tucked away in an old box that's sitting among dozens of other old boxes in a rented storage space where I keep the things that belong in old boxes. But it's just as likely that it has vanished over the past few decades. It's one of only a handful that were ever printed, personally signed by Jim Morrison to his bandmate Robby Krieger. It would probably be worth a pretty penny on eBay. If I still have it I could never sell it, of course. But if it's already gone that's okay, too. I haven't bothered to go frantically digging through my storage space to find it for the same reason I don't lie awake at night pining for my lost Gibson SG. To other people, an object itself may be valuable. To me, its value lies in what it inspired.

OCCUPATION: MUSICIAN, ORGANIST

The message on my voicemail said dryly, "Hello. This is Raymond Daniel Manzarek. And I'm dying. Thank you. Goodbye."

That's Ray: a sense of humor 'til the very end. I called him back, of course. After our final tour together in 2012, he was struggling with health problems, and I knew it might be serious. It turned out to be cholangiocarcinoma—a very rare and usually fatal form of bile duct cancer. He had undergone a course of chemotherapy but the cancer wasn't budging, so he was heading to a clinic in Germany to receive a specialized experimental treatment. He wanted to say goodbye before he left.

Ray never wanted us to worry about him. When we first started as a band he came in one day and told us one of his balls had swollen up to twice its normal size. He was out of commission for a few days, maybe a week, but he never looked sick and never whined about the radiation therapy he had gone through. A few years before his bile duct diagnosis, Ray had some sort of major stomach surgery. Again, he avoided sharing details to avoid worrying us, but I was worried. When I visited him in the hospital, he looked frail, having lost a bunch of weight. He was able to make a full recovery, but it left him with severe acid reflux, and he had to stick to a strict diet. That really pissed him off because he was always the gourmet. He loved trying new foods when we traveled. At one of our early reunion shows in Europe, we were given a delicious chocolate cake backstage. It was made of that rich, smooth chocolate that Europe is known for. From then on, Ray decided we should have chocolate cake on our rider every night, and he insisted that everyone in the band and crew celebrate with a slice after we played. After his stomach issue, he couldn't eat chocolate anymore. But he kept the cake on our rider, and he asked us to eat it for him so he could enjoy it vicariously.

I was concerned about the toll our tours were taking on him. Travel, let alone international travel, gets tougher as you get older. Those long-haul flights were really taking it out of me, and Ray was seven years older than I was. And for the last two years of his life I wasn't even the only person Ray toured with. He paired up with a blues guitarist named Roy Rogers and added even more travel to his calendar. Manzarek-Krieger did three weeks in Europe in 2011, and then a week after Ray got home he flew to Fargo to do a show with Roy. In 2012, Ray and Roy flew all the way to Poland for one show, and then a month later Ray and I did a three-week tour of Europe... including Poland. He played a string of shows in Hawaii with Roy just six weeks before he died, and in between all of it he and Roy were even recording an album. It would've been an ambitious schedule for anyone, but for a guy in his seventies with a history of health problems, it had to have worn him down.

But Ray had no choice. He loved playing music. He couldn't just stop. That kind of drive is a hard thing to explain to people who don't share it. But I've always understood. There were plenty of tours I did with my solo band or my jazz combo that lost money. I've put out a bunch of solo albums over the years that I never for a minute expected to come close to matching the impact of the Doors. And these days I'm happy when the Robby Krieger Band breaks even so I can keep my bandmates and crew employed and keep the tours going. I just can't stop myself. The same way Ray couldn't stop himself from boarding all those transatlantic flights.

When we toured through Russia, Ray and some of our crew visited a church built on the spot where the Bolsheviks killed the Romanov family. Part of the church served as a museum, and Ray spotted an antique, upright piano in one of the rooms. He walked over to it and played some soft music in a minor key until someone ran in and yelled at him. When Ray was on the road he would often breathe life into unattended pianos in hotel lobbies, and in between tours he was always sitting in with local bands at small venues near his home in Napa Valley. Even at the very end, his brother Rick sent me a picture of Ray at the hospital in Germany, serenading all the doctors, nurses, and other patients on an electric keyboard. He was put on this earth to play music. It was everything to him.

Our final U.S. tour in the fall of 2012 was a slog. It was only a short run of dates on the East Coast, but Ray was visibly drained. He made us adhere strictly to the set list, he kept the improvisations to a minimum, and he ended the shows as early as possible every night. I assumed it was old age setting in. I don't think he had even been diagnosed at that point.

When he called to tell me about his Germany plan, he sounded good on the phone. He did a convincing job of covering up his illness—he still didn't want anyone to worry. He was disillusioned with chemotherapy since he had gone through all that misery and still ended up with cancer, but he seemed hopeful about his chances overseas. Ray always looked on the bright side.

I was surprised by Ray's death, as silly as that sounds. His survival odds were low, the chemo hadn't worked, and he was desperate for last-ditch treatments. I should've been prepared, but his optimism was infectious. He had conquered testicular cancer; why couldn't he conquer this? He worked out and played basketball and lived a relatively healthy lifestyle, and his mom had lived into her nineties so he must've had decent genes. I figured the same stubborn, determined spirit that often got him into trouble would be the thing that would save him. But cancer doesn't play fair.

John heard the news of Ray's condition and called him up before the end. Since John also took Jim's last phone call from Paris, that gives him the bragging rights to being the last member of the Doors to speak to both of the deceased members. (If I end up feeling ill in Europe in the future, remind me not to take any calls from John.) John and Ray patched things up as best they could. I'm sure some things were left lingering beneath the surface, but they were both grown-ups about it. I'm glad that's how Ray's story ended: with at least some level of reconciliation.

A few years after Ray died, we put together a memorial concert on his birthday to benefit Stand Up to Cancer. The logistics of putting on the show had us all procrastinating for a while, but when I saw Ray's birthday creeping up on the calendar for the third time since his death, I called everyone on the Doors team and demanded we make it happen before another year went by. In a matter of weeks, we secured the Fonda Theatre in Hollywood and recruited a stellar musical lineup. Ray's son, Pablo, opened the evening with a speech, which was cool to see since he's normally so shy. Members of Foo Fighters, Jane's Addiction, X, the Allman Brothers Band, Stone Temple Pilots, the Robby Krieger Band, and others joined John and me onstage to run through some of the Doors' greatest hits. We held a silent auction, we displayed some of Henry Diltz's photos of us at the Morrison Hotel, and at the end of the night everyone spontaneously broke into a rousing round of "Happy Birthday" for Ray. We filmed everything for a documentary called *Break On Thru: A Celebration of Ray Manzarek*. John was deeply involved with the production and said some very sweet things about Ray in his on-camera interview. When those two meet in the next life, I think they'll get along fine.

Taylor Hawkins, John, and me at Ray's tribute concert

I was so exhausted from planning the concert and rehearsing the songs and organizing things and running through soundcheck that I didn't think too deeply about Ray that night. But after it was all over and life settled back into its usual rhythm, I missed him. I still miss him. Especially when I hear someone try to play one of his keyboard parts. His feel was otherworldly, and no matter how hard anyone else tries, they just don't come close. Whenever I rewatch the video of him playing "When the Music's Over" at the beginning of our Hollywood Bowl show, I'm still awestruck by the intensity of his furious keyboard intro. His timing was impeccable and his bass lines were the pulse of our music, giving John and me the freedom to float around on top of his rock-solid foundation. Meanwhile, his operatic, grandiose intros and melodies dazzled the audience like an aural fireworks display. His technique reflected who he was inside: steady, driven, and unshakable while also being bombastic, expressive, and dramatic. There's nobody out there quite like Ray, which is why there's nobody out there who can play quite like Ray.

The memorial concert was the first time John and I shared a stage in over a decade. While Jim's death had given John a bit of a hard edge, Ray's death seemed to soften it. We went out to lunch together. We played an acoustic set at a documentary screening at LACMA. We've done a few other benefit performances since then. I don't know if we'll ever be like we once were. But we're better.

Ray gave John and me some absolutely invaluable gifts. He found Jim Morrison. He came up with the whole crazy idea of starting a band with him. He conjured the intros to "Light My Fire" and "Riders on the Storm" and so many others. And at the end of it all he gave us perspective—a reminder that even if we end up living three times as long as Jim, life's still short, and there's still a bigger picture.

Raymond Daniel Manzarek, this is Robert Alan Krieger. Thank you for everything. And I do mean everything. Goodbye.

NIRVANA

I was still using heroin when I was first hospitalized for cancer in the eighties. Lynn smuggled some dope into my room while I was recovering from lymph node surgery. It's crazy to think I was in the hospital to save my life while stupidly risking an overdose by piling heroin on top of whatever painkillers the doctors had already given me. I shot up in the bathroom, but in my hazy junkie state I left the needle sitting on the edge of the sink. One of the nurses found it and freaked out.

"What's this?!"

"Well . . . your stuff wasn't working very well . . ."

"You can't do that!"

They sent in some orderlies to search my room and found the dirty cotton I had used to prep the shot. They told me they were calling the cops. I didn't know what was going to happen. As I sweated it out, a doctor I had never met before snuck into my room and told me he was a big Doors fan.

"Quick, get your stuff together. We're getting you out of here right now."

I threw on my clothes and he guided me through the hallways and out of the hospital. I'd love to thank him but I was too heavily medicated to remember his name. I don't even remember how I got home. But at least it wasn't in the back of a squad car.

+   +   +

My uncle Sonny, the Arizona dermatologist, warned me when I was sixteen, "Never go out in the sun!" Our family's bloodlines go back to Eastern Europe. We weren't biologically adapted for Southern California. Both my uncle and my mom developed skin cancer, and I followed their lead in my thirties. On one hand, my fair skin was a blessing because, like my faulty eyesight, it kept me from taking baseball or golf or surfing too seriously as a kid, and caused me to dedicate my time to making music instead. On the other hand, well, you know...cancer.

Most of my cancers were common carcinomas, which aren't too dangerous as long as you catch them early. But the reason I was in the hospital was because a basal cell carcinoma made its way into my lymph node and a big lump formed under my armpit. The doctor suggested removing the node and, as a precaution, all the other nodes on that side of my body. Thankfully everything tested clear after the surgery, but removing the nodes left me vulnerable to any future cancers that might wiggle their way inside me. Which is exactly what happened.

In 2017, my elbow and knee joints became swollen, and I noticed that walking my dog up the hill near my house left me completely exhausted. I thought I was just getting old. It took several appointments for the doctors to figure it out. Blood work: fine. Chest X-ray: fine. CT scan: uh-oh.

They found something the size of a lemon on my lung. Lemon isn't a good size for anything they find inside you, so they performed laparoscopic surgery to poke around and see what it was. I had to stay in the hospital for a few days afterward, with nurses coming in regularly to wake me up, make sure I was still alive, and check my vitals. At one point my blood pressure soared over 200. With all the red tape of the medical system, it took a couple of hours to get me the pills to bring it back under control. I'm lucky I didn't die just from the wait.

The lemon turned out to be a melanoma. Usually melanomas start on your skin and work their way into your other organs. Since they spotted it on the inside before the outside, it was immediately classified as stage four cancer. At that stage, the five-year survival rate is only between 15 and 20 percent. With my previous blood pressure scare, I had barely survived the easy, exploratory surgery. Now they wanted to take out half of my lung and put me through chemo. It sounded scary, but if I did nothing I probably had only about six months to live. They gave Ray the same timeline. And they were right. I thought about what poor old Ray had gone through, and how he had suffered through the nasty side effects of chemotherapy only to die soon after anyway. Was I about to share his fate?

Normally I wouldn't condone taking medical advice from one's gardener, but my guy, Jose, may have saved my life. I was moaning to him one day about my condition and he mentioned another client of his named Rob who had the same diagnosis and tried immunotherapy instead of chemotherapy. I wasn't looking for a quack cure. But he wasn't talking about rubbing crystals together or drinking kale smoothies. It was a legitimate medical procedure. I asked my doctor more about it and he put me in touch with Dr. Sean Fischer at Providence Saint John's Health Center in Santa Monica. Dr. Fischer agreed that a skinny old guy like me wouldn't handle chemo too well, so he ran some tests to see if I might be suited for immunotherapy instead. The test classifies you on a scale from 0 (totally incompatible) to 100 (the perfect candidate). I was a 6. But we still decided to give it a try.

I went into an office once every few weeks. They stuck a needle in my arm. A bag of fluid drained into me for about half an hour. I went home slightly tired, and with my mouth feeling a little dry. Otherwise I felt fine. No hair loss, no weight loss, no nausea, no pain.

Three months later my lemon had shrunk by two-thirds. Three months after that my scan was clear. I was in remission.

The drug I took was called Keytruda. It was approved by the FDA in 2014, only a couple of years before my diagnosis. If my cancer had appeared in 2012, like Ray's did, who knows how my case would've turned out? All I know for sure is that even though most of the stuff he plants ends up dying, I will never, ever fire my gardener.

+ + +

A friend sent me an article saying that I had died. It wasn't related to my cancer diagnosis or anything; it was just another internet death hoax. It didn't spread too far, so I didn't get the fun of being Tom Sawyer and watching my own funeral and seeing how much everyone missed me. It was just unsettling. I've watched my friends pass away, I've had my own near miss with cancer, and I've had a headline about my own demise staring back at me. It's only natural to look back and wonder if I've done things right.

Maybe I'm just a guy who attended one too many lectures by the Maharishi, but I can't shake the feeling that we've all been here before and we'll all be here again. Different cultures have different takes on the idea of reincarnation, but the basic concept is a cycle of self-improvement. You're born. You live and learn. You die. You're reborn in a new form. And you repeat the process until you've accumulated enough karma from wisdom and good deeds to move on to a more peaceful spiritual plane.

I wonder if I was once a person from India or Spain. Maybe that's why I've always been drawn to music from those regions. Maybe I was a king, which is why I saw visions of my friends as loyal subjects while smoking boo at Menlo. Maybe I was British, which is why I suddenly adopted an English accent when I first tried morning glory seeds. Taken altogether, maybe I was a British king who once warred with Spain and oppressed the people of India, and maybe my current life is the one that trained me to be a peacemaker instead.

I'm no scientist, and I'm certainly no religious scholar. I just look around and wonder. When I see a video of some little kid with inexplicable natural talent, it reinforces my belief that we carry our best traits into our next form of existence. When I see a young girl painting lifelike images in oils with uncanny skill: that's my mom. When I see a young boy sink a putt that most pros would miss: that's my dad. When I see an even younger boy sink an even tougher putt: that's my brother. When I see a child prodigy playing a spellbinding piece of classical music on piano: that's Ray. When I see... well, to tell you the truth, I've still never seen anyone quite like Jim. But I keep looking.

I can't say I've lived a perfect life, but I've certainly lived one of the luckiest ones, and in the face of that I've tried to stay humble. I've tried to be honest and kind. I've tried to find stillness and calm through meditation. I've tried to be generous and charitable. I've played benefits for youth arts programs and the homeless and public radio and pretty much any organization that has ever asked me. Since 2008 my golf buddy Scott Medlock and I have hosted an annual charity golf tournament and all-star benefit concert for St. Jude Children's Research Hospital to help fund the kind of research that will save kids' lives the same way a new breakthrough saved mine. But of course no matter how much you give, it never feels like enough. And no matter how much you do, cancer still doesn't play fair. After helping to raise millions to help others, Scott Medlock was diagnosed with stage four colon cancer in 2019. Good karma, unfortunately, isn't everything.

Other than a trip to India, a collaboration with Bob Dylan, and a round at Augusta, I'm not left wanting much more from this life. I guess I'll find out in the next cycle how I could've done things better. Maybe I'll come back as an imprisoned exotic cat, to pay for my sins with Poppy. Maybe I'll be a psychiatrist to make up for my inability to help my brother, or an oncologist to cure people like my mom and Ray, or an addiction specialist with the ability to reach people like Jim, or a spinal surgeon who figures out a way to make people like Donna walk again.

Maybe I'll come back as a leaf on the tree that snagged my dad's golf club, or a seedpod on the jacaranda that my brother planted in my backyard, or a red hyacinth on a hillside that will inspire someone to write a new song.

Or maybe I'll come back as a quiet child with an uncanny knack for flamenco and slide guitar who ends up in a Doors tribute band and doesn't even have to wear a wig to replicate the worst hair in rock 'n' roll. But wherever I end up, I hope my family, friends, and fans will keep their eyes open.

You'll see me around here somewhere.

ACKNOWLEDGMENTS

My first thanks will always go to Lynn and Waylon for their endless love and support.

A huge thanks to Jeff Jampol from Jampol Artist Management and Jennifer Gates from Aevitas Creative for setting this project up with such a great publisher. And thanks to Liz Gassman, Michael Noon, Vivian Lee, Nell Beram, Fanta Diallo, Liz Garriga, Elece Green, Anthony Goff, Craig Young, and everyone else at Little, Brown and Company for working so hard and rallying behind this book (and for always being flexible with deadlines).

Thanks to Kenny Nemes at Jampol Artist Management for the endless logistical support, thanks to Dave Dutkowski for dealing with our endless archive requests, thanks to John Logan for staying on top of our endless emails, thanks to Jaime Hale for setting up an endless string of meetings, and thanks to Jesse Nicita for the endless behind-the-scenes help.

Thanks to Arthur Barrow, Bruce Botnick, Michael C. Ford, Jac Holzman, Linda Kyriazi, Rich Linnell, Marco Moir, Julia Negron, Hank Olguin, Forrest Penner, Happy Price, Jess Roden, Bill Siddons,

Cheri Siddons, Neil Storey, Vince Treanor III, Tom Vitorino, Wardie Ward, Nathan Wilmarth, Paul Winters, and Bill Wolff for taking the time to help me untangle my memories.

Thanks to Logan Janzen and Chris Simondet at MildEquator .com for exhaustively documenting Doors history and for their intense detective work. And thanks to Sarah Diamond, Michael Dolgushkin, Jason Kisvarday, Ida Miller, and Erik Sandin for helping us with additional fact checks along the way.

Thanks to Dorothy Manzarek, Pablo Manzarek, Marc Cappello, James Hutchinson, Kuang Lee, Geneva Willis, and everyone else who read the first draft of the manuscript and gave us insightful notes. And thanks to Ty Deran, Myra Gallarza, Toni Tabieros, and Jaime Schwarz for transcribing hours of interviews.

Thanks to Theodore Antoniadis, Aaron Barbero, Michelle Boatman, Ellie Brown, Paige Califano, Michele Crowe, Jonathan Hyams, Carrie Kania, Katherine Kelly, Danny Kosa, and Sue Krieger for help in gathering all of our images and thanks to all the photographers who were so generous with their time and their work.

Thanks to the Alulis family (Lisa, Paul, Gena, Eric, Chrissy, Elle, Teddy, and Dug) and the Howe family (Paul, Sue, Ryan, Angela, Lindsey, and Sabrina) for all the love and support. Thanks to Ryan Harlin for copiloting Jeff's Doors projects since the ninth grade. And thanks to George Paige, Philippa Donovan, and Phil Marino for helping to put this journey in motion at the beginning.

Thanks to Jeff Albright, Carol Berman, John Berman, John Branca, David Byrns, Christine Griffiths, Rob Seltzer, Abe Somer, Gary Stiffelman, Jerry Swartz, Kelly Vallon, and Randall Wixen for always keeping my best interests at heart.

Thanks to the friends I shared time with along the way: John Adams, Denny Alberg, Kemp Alberg, Steve Alberg, Kevin Anderson, Tom Anderson, Peter Axelrod, Donnie Branker, Bob Brunner, Katherine Brunner, Sam Cockins, Steve Davidson, Scotty Dujon,

ACKNOWLEDGMENTS

Laurence Fishman, Ana Flores, Ceferino Flores, Michelle Fox, Amanda Greene, Gregory Greene, Jeff Greene, Don Hoag, Joe Idle, Michael Jeffries, Amy Kendis, Maggie Kendis, Hial King, Keoki King, Clark Kuhl, John Kuhn, Pete Leance, Doug Lee, Jon León, the Leonard twins, Amy Maglieri, Mike McNamara, Phil Nerdrum, Johnny Nuger, Jeff O'Neal, Ryan O'Neal, Sally Patterson, Cappy Robertson, Jack Shumacher, Harleigh Stevenson, Pug Swartz, Barkie Thue, Bobby Thue, Margie Thue, Roy Thompson, Gene Vano, Keith Wallace, Peter Wallace, Bob Wire, Tom Wire, and Tom Zallen.

Thanks to my in-laws: Debbie, Cyndy, Butchie, Bobby, and Ronny.

Thanks to Jim Ladd and Maggie LePique for keeping the Doors on the airwaves.

Thanks to all my golf teachers and partners: Bobby Hinds, Larry Atlas, Matt Baird, Bobby Cavanaugh, Craig Currier, Eddie Galvan, Josh Glotzer, Joe Gugliamo, Betty Hicks, Mike Hunt, Johnny Mathis, Johnny O'Brien, Mel Posner, Sal Rodriguez, Nick Walthery, and Tod Yoshitaka.

Thanks to Rob Dean, Odette Gutierrez, Paul Lester, Edie Ruge, Scott Ruge, Rick Shadyac, and everyone else at Medlock-Krieger and St. Jude's.

Thanks to all the musicians who have played by my side over the years: Dale Alexander, Bill Allen, Tony Alva, Carl Arnold, Ian Astbury, Brian Auger, Karma Auger, Berton Averre, Doug Avery, John Avila, Sebastian Bach, Steve Bach, Angelo Barbera, Paul Barrere, Gary Barone, Angelo Barbera, Arthur Barrow, Dave Belzer, Mike Berkowitz, Jack Black, Bonnie Bramlett, Kevin "Brandino" Brandon, Tom Brechtlein, Dave Brock, Jackson Browne, Eric Burdon, Adrian Byrns, David Paul Campbell, Jerry Cantrell, Bob Carsten, Bill Champlin, Phil Chen, Billy Cobham, Vinnie Colaiuta, Andrew Cole, Alice Cooper, Cheryl Cooper, Sean Cooper, Andy Crosby, Cherie Currie,

ACKNOWLEDGMENTS

Miley Cyrus, Roy Davies, Ty Dennis, Tommy Dietrich, Willie Dixon, Snoop Dogg, Geoff Downes, Michael Dumas, Shayna Dumas, Mark Eddy, Jock Ellis, Perry Farrell, Pat Foley, Lita Ford, Bruce Fowler, Tom Fowler, Ezra Gabay, Val Garay, Bruce Gary, Bob Glaub, Stu Goldberg, Owen Goldman, Scott Gordon, Ray Goren, Kenny Gradney, Joey Gugliamo, Richie Hayward, Ira Heiden, John Hernandez, Catherine Hug, Harper Hug, Billy Idol, Paul Ille, Mike Inez, Marty Jabara, Pam Kath, Terry Kath, Tony Kaye, Lee Kiefer, Waylon Krieger, Jonny Lang, Chris Layton, Darren LeGroe, Peter Leinhuser, Alex Lifeson, Joe Lopez, Doug Lubahn, Sal Marquez, Tommy Mars, Harvey Mason, Greg Mathison, Miljenko "Milli" Matijevic, Reggie McBride, Duff McKagan, Mack McKenzie, Ray Melbaum, Mark Michellini, Marco Moir, Ben Moffit, Steve Molitz, Rick Moors, Gary Mule Deer, Charlie Musselwhite, Dave Navarro, Ray Neapolitan, Craig T. Nelson, Lucas Nelson, Micah Nelson, Prescott Niles, Tech N9ne, Berry Oakley Jr., Orianthi, James Pankow, Joel Patterson, Forrest Penner, Stephen Perkins, Joel Peskin, Tim Petrovic, Don Poncher, Steve Porcaro, Kit Potemkin, Don Preston, Dennis Quaid, Dizzy Reed, Haley Reinhart, Bob Rice, Alex Richman, Rich Robinson, Jess Roden, Cesar Rosas, Ed Roth, Dan Rothchild, Karl Rucker, Chris Samardich, Scott Saunders, Brett Scallions, Jerry Scheff, Jason Scheff, Bernie Schwartz, John Sebastian, Danny Seraphine, William Shatner, Tommy Shaw, Billy Sherwood, Gene Simmons, Skrillex, Matt Sorum, Danny "Splats" Spanos, Paul Stanley, Mike Stull, Joel Taylor, Amber Thayer, Tommy Thayer, Brooks Thomas, Greg Thomas, Linda Thomas, George Thorogood, Paula Trickey, Nik Turner, Shannon Tweed, Barbara Wallace, Patrick Warburton, Wah Wah Watson, Mick Weaver, Leslie West, John Wetton, Michael Wientraub, Skip Van Winkle, Norton Wisdom, Franklin Vanderbilt, Carlos Vega, Tom Vitorino, Edgar Winter, Adrian Young, Dweezil Zappa, and Mitch Zelanzy.

Thanks and apologies to anyone I've forgotten to mention above: it's been a long road...

ACKNOWLEDGMENTS

A sincere thanks to all the Doors fans out there, from those of you who were with us back in the sixties to those of you who are just discovering us for the first time.

And last but never least, my eternal thanks to John Densmore, Ray Manzarek, and Jim Morrison. What you've given me and what we've shared is beyond anything I could list here. But I think it's safe to say that without all three of you this book would've been much shorter.

PHOTO CREDITS

INDEX

(Page references in *italics* refer to illustrations.)

ABOUT THE AUTHORS

ROBBY KRIEGER is the guitarist for the legendary rock band the Doors and the songwriter behind some of the band's biggest hits, including "Love Me Two Times," "Touch Me," "Love Her Madly," and their #1 smash, "Light My Fire." The Doors have sold over a hundred million albums worldwide, inspired a major feature film, been awarded a Lifetime Achievement Grammy, and been inducted into the Rock & Roll Hall of Fame. Robby, meanwhile, has also become a Grammy-nominated solo artist, and was listed among the "100 Greatest Guitarists of All Time" by *Rolling Stone*. He is also an accomplished painter and the co-founder of the annual Medlock-Krieger Rock & Roll Golf Classic & All-Star Concert.

JEFF ALULIS is the coauthor of the *New York Times* best-seller *NOFX: The Hepatitis Bathtub and Other Stories*. He holds an MFA from USC's Graduate Screenwriting Program, he has directed several award-winning music-based documentaries, and he has toured as the vocalist for seminal punk bands Dead Kennedys and Reagan Youth. Aside from writing, film, and music he is an avid traveler, and he documents his journeys at TrueAdventureStories.com.